21

D1080896

13.45

Es

# McNae's
# Essential Law for Journalists

Fourteenth edition

**Tom Welsh**

**Walter Greenwood**

**Butterworths**
London, Edinburgh, Dublin
1997

| United Kingdom | Butterworths a Division of Reed Elsevier (UK) Ltd, Halsbury House, 35 Chancery Lane, LONDON WC2A 1EL and 4 Hill Street, EDINBURGH EH2 3JZ |
| --- | --- |
| Australia | Butterworths, SYDNEY, MELBOURNE, BRISBANE, ADELAIDE, PERTH, CANBERRA and HOBART |
| Canada | Butterworths Canada Ltd, TORONTO and VANCOUVER |
| Ireland | Butterworth (Ireland) Ltd, DUBLIN |
| Malaysia | Malayan Law Journal Sdn Bhd, KUALA LUMPUR |
| New Zealand | Butterworths of New Zealand Ltd, WELLINGTON and AUCKLAND |
| Singapore | Reed Elsevier (Singapore) Pte Ltd, SINGAPORE |
| South Africa | Butterworths Publishers (Pty) Ltd, DURBAN |
| USA | Michie, CHARLOTTESVILLE, Virginia |

A CIP Catalogue record for this book is available from the British Library.

ISBN 0 406 89544 9

Printed and bound in Great Britain by Clays Ltd, St Ives PLC

# Preface

A new edition of *McNae* becomes necessary after only two years largely because of the passage of:
- the Defamation Act 1996, the first major measure in this area of the law since 1952;
- a bundle of laws restricting still further the reporting of courts;
- two Acts, the Police Act 1997 and the Protection from Harassment Act 1997, which were not directed at media issues but which journalists feared would have the incidental effect of inhibiting investigative reporting.

This preface notes these measures and other developments in the order in which they appear in the book.

As always, this edition aims to state the law at 1 May in the year of publication. This time the date could be a significant one because it marked the beginning of a new Government committed to the introduction of a Freedom of Information Bill. The need for such a Bill is discussed in chapter 28, and the inadequacies of the existing Code of Practice on Access to Government Information is explained there and below (Information from government). It is disappointing that the Bill is to be delayed until after publication of a white paper, and cannot therefore be brought forward before 1998.

The Government has said it will also introduce a Bill to incorporate into UK law the main provisions of the European Convention on Human Rights, a change which could be equally beneficial to journalists in searching for and publishing information. The decisions of the European Court of Human Rights, implementing the Convention, have been among the few encouraging events in recent years (see below, European Court of Human Rights, and chapter 1, Sources of law). Journalists may have less cause for pleasure over the Government's intention to strengthen data protection controls – an unavoidable decision in the light of the adoption by the UK in 1995 of the European Community Directive (see chapter 32).

## Free press

The editors have reluctantly qualified the ringing declaration that served as an introduction for 11 editions since 1967, 'We in Britain are proud of our tradition of a free press,' and have acknowledged that in many ways the phrase is illusory (chapter 1). The boldness of the claim must have seemed increasingly naive to readers as each new edition of *McNae* in recent years has recorded a new batch of restrictions on reporting imposed by Parliament or brought about by developments in the courts; the continuing failure of efforts to establish rights of access to basic government information now commonplace among western nations; and the extent to which Britain's restrictive libel laws have inhibited and punished journalists in their role as community watchdogs.

*McNae* has regularly drawn attention to the apathy of the British media when confronted with such problems, and that has continued to be a characteristic of the period under review. Bill Goodwin's victory in the European Court of Human Rights, referred to below, was no quixotic adventure; as the European Commission pointed out, the continuing injunction on his story prevented newspapers and journalists from publishing information which was of a type commonly found in the business press; while it may have derived from a breach of confidence, so did much of the information provided by the press. In other words, Goodwin's fight was the media's fight. Yet his challenge was made possible only by the financial support of the National Union of Journalists, and the only publication giving support was the Wall Street Journal.

The media are constantly complaining, with justification, that the law of libel prevents them from exposing wrongdoing. This branch of the law is reformed by statute about once every half-century, so it might have been thought the media would have been working hard during the last decade to ensure that the Defamation Act 1996 brought about much needed reforms. The media did in fact take the unprecedented action of combining to employ a lobbyist to press for extended privilege, but they waited until the Bill was going through Parliament, and hardly surprisingly achieved little.

The reporting restrictions introduced  by the Criminal Justice and Public Order Act 1994 to cover the new transfer-for-trial procedure due to be implemented early in 1995 presented considerable problems to journalists, but it was the opposition of the lawyers not the journalists that led to the abandonment of this ill-considered legislation in 1996.

A rare bright spot in this story was the action of the Newspaper Society and the Guild of Editors in successfully opposing the more outrageous aspects of the Police Bill, as originally introduced. It showed what the media might achieve in this field if they set their collective mind to it.

## European Court of Human Rights

The European Court has again passed down important judgments in British cases (chapters 1, 23, and 24). Earlier editions of *McNae* reported the progress through the English courts of the case of Bill Goodwin, the young reporter fined £5,000 after defying a ruling that he must identify the source of a news story. Distinguished judges expressed indignation at the reporter's conduct on what seemed to most journalists an entirely justifiable news story, written in the public interest. Section 10 of the Contempt of Court Act 1981 gives journalists the right to refuse to name their source unless disclosure is necessary, among other things, 'in the interests of justice'; but in the Goodwin case Lord Bridge, in the House of Lords, said this phrase could simply refer to the wish of a private company to discipline a disloyal employee 'notwithstanding that no legal proceedings might be necessary to achieve this end'. The finding against Goodwin appeared to threaten the ability of journalists to protect their sources in even the most mundane of situations. The European Court, however, ruled that the order breached his rights to freedom of expression under the Convention. The court said protection of journalistic sources was one of the basic conditions for press freedom, and an order of source disclosure must be justified by an overriding requirement in the public interest.

The court found also in favour of Count Tolstoy, against whom an English jury had awarded £1.5m in libel damages. Tolstoy had also been ordered to pay £1m in costs. The court held that the award violated his rights to freedom of expression.

The court's rulings were increasingly exercising a benign effect on British courts. In 1996, for example, two chief constables failed to have a journalist, Daniella Garavelli, jailed over her refusal to reveal the sources of a story to a police disciplinary tribunal. A High Court judge said Garavelli had 'put before the public, fully and fairly, a question which had been raised of considerable public importance'. The police had failed to show that the 'interest of justice' outweighed her right not to disclose her source. It seems inconceivable the court would have reached the same conclusion without the example of the European Court in the Goodwin case.

## Committal proceedings reprieved

It might be argued that for many journalists, particularly those on local newspapers, the main media law event of the past two years has been a non-event, the fiasco of the Government's abandonment of its elaborate legislation, contained in the Criminal Justice and Public Order Act 1994, which abolished committal proceedings and replaced them with a transfer-for-trial procedure. The measure was introduced as an amendment halfway through the progress of the Bill through Parliament, and had all the marks of inadequate consideration that have characterised so much legislation affecting the media in recent years. The 13th edition of *McNae* was in fact published principally to record the changes, due to be implemented early in 1995, and the associated reporting restrictions, of great importance to journalists. These restrictions, as *McNae* pointed out, had a number of bizarre characteristics, but it later became clear from ministerial pronouncements that these resulted not from a desire to make life as difficult as possible for journalists but from a failure on the part of the legislators to understand the implications. Fortunately for the media, lawyers were as badly inconvenienced as the journalists, and their response was so effective that the measure, after a number of postponements, was abandoned in April 1996.

The Government then used the Criminal Procedure and Investigations Act 1996 to reprieve the existing committal procedure and introduce changes (chapter 5). Magistrates will consider only documentary evidence and exhibits tendered by the prosecution, together with oral representations made by prosecution and defence. Neither prosecution nor defence will call witnesses. The effect will be to abolish the old-style committal where the prosecution calls its witnesses and the defence also does so when submitting there is no prima facie case to answer.

## Power to name juveniles

Under the Crime (Sentences) Act 1997, a youth court is given power to waive the restrictions on identifying a juvenile if magistrates believe it would be in the public interest (chapter 6). Previously, the court could lift the restrictions only if it was in the interests of the accused juvenile to do so, or (under the Criminal Justice and Public Order Act 1994), if the juvenile was on the run and wanted for a violent or sexual offence, or for an offence for which an adult could be jailed for 14 years or more.

## Restrictions on reporting pre-trial hearings

The Criminal Procedure and Investigations Act 1996 provides for preparatory hearings before long and complex crown court trials, and, unless the judge lifts the restrictions, limits reports to seven items (chapter 7). The Act also gives judges power to rule on the admissibility of evidence or other points of law before the start of a trial, to cater for cases where a full preparatory hearing is not needed. The aim is to shorten trials. Reporting of such a ruling or its variation or discharge is banned until after the trial of all the accused, unless a judge makes an order lifting the ban.

## Ban on reporting pleas in mitigation

Under the Criminal Procedure and Investigations Act 1996 a court has the power to restrict reporting of assertions made in a speech of mitigation which are derogatory of a person's character, such as where it is suggested that his conduct has been criminal, immoral, or improper (chapter 4). An order lasts 12 months, and could affect subsequent investigative stories.

## Disability Discrimination Act 1995

The Act enables industrial tribunals to make temporary anonymity orders known as restricted reporting orders when considering complaints in respect of unlawful discrimination in employment on disability grounds (see chapter 16); the orders are similar to those involving allegations of sexual misconduct under the Trade Union Reform and Employment Rights Act 1993.

## Contempt of court

The preface of our last edition drew attention to the more liberal attitude of the courts in deciding what conduct amounts to a 'substantial risk of serious prejudice', leading to conviction for contempt of court, and that tendency has continued (chapter 17). In 1996 the Queen's Bench Divisional Court refused to hold five national newspapers in contempt for reports they had carried after the arrest of Geoff Knights, boyfriend of the television actress Gillian Taylforth, on a charge of wounding a cab driver. The papers quoted witnesses saying Knights had committed the offence and describing how he did it ('Knights beat me to a pulp', 'Knights went berserk with an iron bar') and referred to his previous convictions. There were no precedents for newspapers escaping liability for contempt after publishing such material after an arrest, but in this case the court said it had to take account of the 'saturation publicity given over previous months, indeed years, to the relationship between Miss Taylforth and Mr Knights and in particular to the disclosures which had been made previously of Mr Knights' violent behaviour on previous occasions and his previous convictions'.

## Defamation Act 1996

Some changes brought about by the Act came into effect on 4 September 1996. Others were expected to be implemented in 1997, but the date had not been announced when *McNae* went to press in May, so the book has to give the provisions both of the 1996 Act and its predecessor, the Defamation Act 1952 (chapters 18 to 20).

Significant changes are made in the law of qualified privilege. Statutory qualified privilege for reports now applies for the first time to free newspapers and magazines. *McNae* includes the Schedules to both Acts, which list the privileged occasions. Matters to which the Act extends privilege include:

- reports of proceedings in foreign courts, foreign legislatures, or public inquiries appointed by governments and held in public anywhere in the world;
- copies of documents circulated among shareholders of a UK public company with the authority of the board or the auditors or by any shareholder 'in pursuance of a right conferred by any statutory provision';
- reports of findings and decisions of associations in the UK formed to promote charitable objects 'or other objects beneficial to the community'.

Paragraph 12 of the Schedule to the 1952 Act used clear language to give vital protection for a copy or a fair and accurate summary of any notice or other matter issued for the information of the public by or on behalf of any government department, officer of state, local authority, or chief officer of police. *McNae* recommended students to learn the paragraph by heart. These protections are repeated and extended by para 9 of the new Act (given in full on p 170), but in terms so obscure the paragraph will no doubt give problems to students and probably to lawyers too – even though the Government reluctantly amended the Act during its passage through Parliament to explain that 'any authority performing governmental functions' includes those performing 'police functions'.

The Act followed a report on 'Practice and procedure in defamation' by the Supreme Court Procedure Committee, presided over by Lord Justice Neill, and was indeed concerned mostly with procedural matters, the most important of which are noted in the following pages.

It made no attempt to bring about the sweeping reform in the libel law for which succeeding editions of *McNae* have argued. In 1993 Lord Keith of Kinkel, giving judgment in a House of Lords case, acknowledged the media's problems when he said the 'chilling effect' induced by the threat of civil actions for libel was very important. Quite often, the facts that would justify a defamatory publication were known to be true, but admissible evidence capable of proving those facts was not available. That might prevent the publication of matters which it was very desirable to make public.

But the Neill committee showed itself indifferent to the hazard to which Lord Keith drew attention when it reported: 'In our view, the media are adequately protected by the defences of justification and fair comment at the moment, and it is salutary that these defences are available to them only if they have got their facts substantially correct.'

The new Act does give a government the power to extend privilege to the reports of statements by bodies, officers or other people designated by it, a power that would, for example, enable it to extend privilege to the reports of quangos and other such non-governmental bodies that now spend so much taxpayers' money and provide so many of the services they rely on. The active use of this power by the Government elected as this edition of *McNae* went to press would go a little way, at least, to make up for the lost opportunities for reform represented by the Defamation Act 1996.

## Police Act 1997

The Act gave the police the power to authorise entry upon property and the placing of surveillance devices ('bugging and burgling') (chapter 24). As originally drafted, this power would not have been subject to any kind of prior judicial consent, a fundamental breach of the principle famously established in 1765 in *Entick v Carrington*. This was one of a series of civil actions for damages against state officers who, using general warrants and without prior judicial consent, raided homes and other places in search of material connected with the attacks by John Wilkes, editor of the North Briton, in his newspaper against the government of King George III.

The Newspaper Society and the Guild of Editors worked with other organisations to ensure the provision of some safeguards, and the Act now provides that in 'sensitive cases' – which include journalistic material – police authorisation is subject to prior approval by a government-appointed commissioner. But this is not the judicial consent known previously; commissioners must not 'second-guess' police officers; they must approve police decisions if they are satisfied there are reasonable grounds for believing the action is 'likely to be of substantial value in the prevention or detection of serious crime and that what the action seeks to achieve cannot reasonably be achieved by other means'. And approval may be obtained after the event, rather than before, where the matter is urgent.

## Gambling

The chapter on Gambling (chapter 27) does its best, as in previous years, to cover the complex, restrictive, and paternalistic law relating to the advertising and reporting of bingo that prevailed as the chapter was written, but reports that the Deregulation (Betting and Gaming) Order

1997, expected to come into effect 'later that year', removes all restrictions on bingo advertising, including advertising on radio and television. In fact, as noted at the end of the chapter, the order was made on 22 March 1997 and came into force on 19 April. The order also allows the advertising in print media – but not in broadcast media – of betting shops.

## Information from government

The 13th edition of *McNae* took a sceptical look at the Code of Practice on Access to Government Information introduced in 1994 after the White Paper on Open Government published in 1993. This edition (chapter 28) reports the view that the parliamentary ombudsman charged with adjudicating on complaints about the way the Code is being implemented, or not implemented, is taking a robust attitude to government departments that withhold information without good reason. Journalists, however, were reluctant to make complaints, partly because they had to do so through a member of Parliament, and were reluctant to be 'in hock' to a politician, and partly because the process is so slow. In the only media complaint the editors have managed to trace, it took five months for the ombudsman to 'prise the information out of Whitehall'.

## Protection from Harassment Act 1997

The Act had the laudable aim of protecting the victims of stalking and others suffering from disruptive neighbours and racial abusers (chapter 31). Journalists, however, feared that wrongdoers would be able to use the Act to avoid their attentions. A wealthy and litigious villain who is telephoned twice by an investigative journalist could argue he was harassed because he had been 'alarmed or distressed' by the calls which, as they had been made on 'more than one occasion', could amount to a 'course of action' under the Act. The villain might be able to get an injunction banning the reporter from phoning him. A breach of the injunction would be a criminal offence, carrying the power of arrest, with a maximum penalty of five years in prison or an unlimited fine, or both.

## Language of the law

In the glossary, the editors have made a greater effort at alerting readers to some of the more confusing nonsenses of legal terminology. Lords justices are not, in fact, lords. Lords of Appeal do not sit, as one might expect, in the Court of Appeal. Circuit judges do not go on circuit, though High Court judges do. The Supreme Court is not supreme – the House of Lords is. Does any of this matter to young journalists? Probably not. Much more important is the misleading terminology of much of the substantive law. In libel, for example, the defence of fair comment has nothing to do with fairness, nor justification with what laymen understand by the word. It is now 22 years since the Faulks Committee recommended the defences should be renamed 'comment' and 'truth'. Why could this not have been done in the 1996 Act?

## Leonard McNae

Leonard Cyril McNae, first editor of the book that now bears his name, died on New Year's Day 1996 aged 93.

The book had its origins in 1938 in a volume *The Pressman and the Law* produced by GFL Bridgman of the Middle Temple for the National Union of Journalists (NUJ). Towards the end of the 1939-45 war Bridgman revised the material for a correspondence course produced for journalists in the Forces about to return to civilian life.

By 1953, however, the course needed drastic revision and amplification as a result of changes in the administration of criminal justice and the structure of local government. It was taken over by the recently formed National Council for the Training of Journalists (NCTJ), and the task of revision was shouldered by McNae, then an executive in the sub-editors' department of the Press Association and later news editor, then editor, of the special reporting service. The legal material in the course was published as a book in 1954 by Staples Press Limited under the title *Essential Law for Journalists*.

McNae ceased to edit new editions of the book when he retired from the Press Association in 1967, but continued to take a keen interest, attending as an honoured guest of Butterworths, the current publishers, and the NCTJ all launches of successive editions until 1995, when he was kept by Alzheimer's disease from the 13th.

The Times obituary repeats the apocryphal story, recounted at the delegate meeting of the NUJ in 1962 which bestowed honorary membership on McNae for his work on the book, that a judge to whom LCJ McNae's work was referred said he did not recall a lord chief justice of that name. McNae had no legal training but he was ideally placed in his work for the special reporting service to study the legal problems faced by journalists, in particular in their work of reporting a great variety of courts, tribunals and authorities.

McNae had the help of a team of journalists and others who attached great importance to the training of journalists. Among them was the youthful lawyer Peter Carter-Ruck, who contributed the chapters on defamation (and has continued to help with each successive edition).

McNae's work in building up the Press Association's special reporting service is recorded in 'Reporters Anonymous' by George Scott and his work as a pioneer of the national training scheme in Clement J Bundock's history of the NUJ.

## Acknowledgments

As mentioned above, we continue to be indebted to Peter Carter-Ruck, author of *Libel and Slander* (Butterworths), and also to Andrew Stephenson of Peter Carter-Ruck and Partners for reading the chapters on defamation, and for their valued advice.

District Judge Dick Greenslade of Gloucester has read our chapter on the civil courts for the eighth time, somehow managing to do so while he was president of the Association of District Judges and an assessor to the Woolf Inquiry. He retired as district judge in April 1997.

Our thanks also to: Professor Gerald Dworkin, Herbert Smith Professor of European Law, King's College, London; Maurice Frankel, Director, Campaign for Freedom of Information; Professor Nigel Lowe, Professor of Law at Cardiff Law School, University of Wales; Stuart Patrick, legal adviser to media organisations; Roger Pearson, UK Law News Ltd; David Raderecht, Home Office; Santha Rasaiah, head of legal affairs, Newspaper Society, and her colleagues; John Robertson, legal correspondent, the Scotsman; Nicola Shroeder, Olswang; Antony Whitaker, legal manager of Times Newspapers Ltd; Graham White, chief inspector of the Gaming Board and John Buckle, also of the Gaming Board, responsible for lotteries and gaming machines; Bob Whitehouse, justices chief executive for County Durham. They have read new passages of the book and given valuable advice.

The National Council for the Training of Journalists, and particularly its law examinations board, has given valuable support, as have Butterworths editorial and library staff.

Any errors or omissions, however, are those of the editors.

The law stated in the book is the law at 1 May 1997.

**Tom Welsh**
**Walter Greenwood**
*May 1997*

# Contents

## 33 The broadcast journalist 298

# 1 General introduction

## Journalists and the law

Britain has a tradition of a 'free press'. In many ways, as this book will show, the phrase is illusory, but even when journalists were less restricted in their work than they are today the words did not mean that they had rights distinct from those of the ordinary citizen – except in a few cases, all of which are explained in the pages that follow. The journalist has no legal right to go anywhere, do anything, say anything, or publish anything beyond what is the legal right of any private citizen in these matters.

The journalist's position in relation to the law was summed up by Sir John Donaldson (later Lord Donaldson) when he gave judgment in the *Spycatcher* case in the Court of Appeal in 1988. Sir John, Master of the Rolls (head of the Court of Appeal), said:

> ... a free press ... is an essential element in maintaining parliamen-
> tary democracy and the British way of life as we know it. But it is
> important to remember why the press occupies this crucial position.
> It is not because of any special wisdom, interest, or status enjoyed
> by proprietors, editors, or journalists. It is because the media are the
> eyes and ears of the general public. They act on behalf of the general
> public. Their right to know and their right to publish is neither more
> nor less than that of the general public. Indeed it is that of the general
> public for whom they are trustees.

The journalist may find he enjoys a number of privileges and facilities which private citizens do not enjoy, extended to him by people or organisations to make it easier for him to do his job. If these are withdrawn, he can and should protest, but these privileges are not rights and unless their withdrawal infringes the law he has no legal redress.

For example, reporting the courts is accepted as an important part of a journalist's work, and a press bench is provided for his use, but the journalist is in court, in nearly every case, merely as a member of the public. Normally he has no right to enter, or to remain, when the public has been legally excluded.

The other side of the coin is that the journalist, like any other citizen, may legally go anywhere and report anything provided that in so doing he does not transgress the laws of the land, such laws as those concerning theft, trespass, and defamation.

## Freedom of speech

The rights of citizens in the United Kingdom are not guaranteed by statements of general principle as they are in some countries that have written constitutions. In Britain the rights are said to be 'residual' – that is, the citizen may do anything that is not specifically forbidden by law.

As a result of this situation, rights and freedoms can be whittled away by legislation. Let us consider that statement in relation to freedom of speech, the important right that journalists share with other citizens, and which includes not only the right to comment but the right to communicate information.

Without this freedom, democratic life as it is known in Britain would be impossible, because there would be no public discussion of the issues affecting the citizen, and he could have no access to the facts upon which to base his opinions and decisions. Like other freedoms, however, this one is restricted by law, and this book is largely concerned with these restrictions.

Most citizens, including journalists, believe it is reasonable that certain restrictions on their freedom of speech exist. For example, the law must strike a balance between the public interest in exposing wrongdoing and the individual's right to have his reputation defended from malicious and baseless attacks. The law of libel and slander tries to strike that balance.

Freedom of speech has been so highly valued in this country, and the tradition of freedom has been so strong, that for many years legal restrictions were kept to a minimum. In the past generation, however, Parliament has made many inroads into that freedom, passing a number of Acts that restrict the journalist's ability to report, particularly in the area of the courts of law.

For example, before the Contempt of Court Act 1981, it was extremely rare for a judge to use his power, derived from the common law, to order journalists to postpone the reporting of a criminal trial. Once that power had been expressed in the Act, and given for the first time to magistrates, it became a commonplace. The constitutional principle of open justice was thus eroded.

Many people believe such legislation restricts freedom of speech too severely. Journalists, even more than other citizens, should be alive to the danger that freedoms that have long been enjoyed may be lost if they are not defended with sufficient vigour.

For the individual journalist a practical problem is that too often he is prevented from reporting matters of public interest by courts that make decisions while paying little regard to the judicial principle that justice must not only be done but must be seen to be done.

Some of the actions resulting from these decisions are invalid, and the journalist should be alert to challenge such actions when he can. Chapter 12 of this book, 'Challenging the courts', should help him in doing so.

In the absence of a written constitution, freedom of speech in Britain has depended traditionally on two constitutional bulwarks, jury trial and the rule against prior restraint.

The history of the development of freedom of speech in Britain has several instances of journalists and others being brought before the courts and charged with publishing material which provoked the anger of the government of the day, and then being found not guilty by independently minded juries, sometimes in flagrant disregard of the strict legal position. An example of such a jury decision was seen in the trial of Clive Ponting (see chapter 28, Central government, and chapter 30, Effects of the Act).

The jurist Albert Dicey said: 'Freedom of discussion is, then, in England little else than the right to write or say anything which a jury, consisting of 12 shopkeepers, think it expedient should be said or written.'

But if jury trial is to defend the journalist, there must first be a published story upon which the jury can adjudicate. That cannot happen when there is censorship, because a censor prevents the story going into the paper. Official censorship died out in England in the 1690s, and in the next century the jurist Sir William Blackstone said: 'The liberty of the press ... consists in laying no previous restraints on publication, and not in freedom from censure for criminal matter when published.'

This 'rule against prior restraint', as it is known, has an important place in the English legal system, but it appeared to be losing its validity in cases affecting the media in the 1980s and 1990s. For example, in the network of cases relating to the book *Spycatcher* the Government used the law of breach of confidence to prevent publication of stories it disapproved of by means of injunctions granted by judges sitting without juries, and the injunctions were enforced by the use of the law of contempt of court, again dispensed by judges sitting without juries (see chapter 23).

In 1987 the Court of Appeal declared that an injunction against one newspaper restraining it from publishing confidential information caught all the media, even though they had not been named in the injunction and it had not been served upon them. The ruling was confirmed by the House of Lords in 1991. The development gave the Government a very effective means of silencing the entire press, which it used first to ban publication of *Spycatcher* material and then references to a highly controversial report by the Department of Trade and Industry on the takeover of the House of Fraser.

Such a power had not been available to a British government in time of peace since the end of censorship in the 1690s.

In 1991 the European Court of Human Rights at Strasbourg considered the use of injunctions in the *Spycatcher* saga and said that although the European Convention on Human Rights (see next section) did not prohibit the imposition of prior restraints on publication the dangers inherent were such that they called for the most careful scrutiny on the part of the court.

That was especially so with regard to the press, for news was a perishable commodity and to delay its publication even for a short period might well deprive it of all its value and interest.

A number of influential voices have been urging that Britain needs its own Bill of Rights to preserve such basic rights as freedom of speech against encroachment by government. Meanwhile, the European Convention is the nearest we have to a written constitution.

## Sources of law

The law is the set of rules by which the sovereign authority in a society regulates the conduct of citizens in relation to other citizens and the state.

In the United Kingdom there is no single written set of rules. We say the law in this country is not 'codified'. Whether an action is recognised as being in conformity with the law is determined by a consideration of various authorities. These authorities may be, for example, regulations of the European Community, Acts of Parliament and statutory instruments, byelaws of a local authority, or reports of decided cases. If none of these fits the circumstances, the judge makes his decision by analogy with past decisions made in somewhat similar circumstances and increasingly, if the domestic law is uncertain, by reference to the European Convention.

The main sources of the law are custom, precedent, and statute.

When the English legal system began to take shape in the Middle Ages, royal judges were appointed to administer the 'law and custom of the realm'. This part of the law was called 'common'– that is, common to the whole kingdom – in contrast to that which was particular or special, such as ecclesiastical law or local law.

As judges applied the common law to the cases before them, their decisions were recorded by lawyers. Reports of leading cases give the facts found by the court, sometimes the arguments put forward, and the reasons given by the judge for coming to his decision. The principles on which these decisions are based are binding on all lower courts. The decisions are known as 'precedents', and the system as 'case law'.

A judgment of the House of Lords, the highest court in the land, is binding on all other United Kingdom courts. The Lords can refuse to follow their earlier decisions in later cases, if circumstances make this desirable. However, if their interpretation of a point of law is contrary to the intentions, policies, or wishes of the government, it can be reversed only by new legislation.

Below the Lords, decisions of the Court of Appeal bind the High Court and the lower courts. Decisions of High Court judges, though binding on all lesser courts, can be disregarded by other High Court judges – although they do so reluctantly because the tradition of unanimity is strong.

The common law is supplemented by the rules of equity. In common speech, equity means fairness and impartiality. In the law, the word refers to a system of doctrines and procedures that developed through the centuries side by side with the common law; historically, the rules of equity were based on considerations of conscience.

Certain 'maxims of equity' are sometimes quoted in courtrooms and express important principles behind equitable doctrines, They include: 'Equitable remedies are discretionary', 'He who comes into equity must do so with clean hands', 'Equity acts on the conscience', and 'Equity regards the balance of convenience'.

Common law, supplemented by equity, remains the basic law of the land, but increasingly it is being modified or changed by statute, that is, by Acts of Parliament. Their interpretation by the courts gives rise to a great number of new precedents.

Governments are also making increasing use of delegated legislation known as 'statutory instruments'. Parliament frequently legislates on principles, leaving the detailed application of the new measure to be ordained by the Government or the departmental minister concerned, in detailed regulations made under powers given in the main statute. Statutory instruments are also used to bring legislation into force on dates different from those on which it becomes law, for administrative reasons. This process often causes uncertainty as to the current law.

Under the European Communities Act 1972, Community treaties and legislation are part of United Kingdom law. In 1981, for example, the British Government banned importation of a German magazine carrying accounts of what the magazine claimed were tapes of telephone conversations between Prince Charles and Lady Diana Spencer (later the Princess of Wales), under Article 36 of the Treaty of Rome, which allows prohibition of goods 'justified on grounds of public morality, public policy, or public security'.

As stated above, Britain has no legally binding written constitution guaranteeing rights. But it is a party to the European Convention on Human Rights.

For journalists, the most important part of the Convention is Article 10, which says in part: 'Everyone has the right to freedom of expression. This right shall include freedom to hold opinions and to receive and impart

information and ideas without interference by public authority ...'
Restrictions on this right have to be justified. They must be 'necessary in
a democratic society'. They must also be 'prescribed by law'.

But this Convention, unlike European Community legislation, has not
been incorporated into domestic law. The House of Lords said in 1991 the
courts had to enforce domestic law even when it conflicted with the
Convention.

The court said the Home Secretary had not exceeded his powers by
acting in breach of Article 10 in prohibiting the television and radio
authorities from broadcasting interviews with various organisations in
Northern Ireland, including those proscribed under the Prevention of
Terrorism Act. (The ban was lifted in 1994.)

The Lords added that courts could apply the Convention only when
domestic law was ambiguous. In that case, they would presume Parliament
had intended the law to conform with the Convention.

There was an application of this principle in 1992 when the Court of
Appeal considered the question whether a local authority could sue for
libel. Derbyshire County Council wished to sue the *Sunday Times* for
criticising its pension fund dealings. English law was unclear on this point.

The court, applying Article 10, said a local authority had adequate
remedies for protecting its reputation without having the right to sue in
defamation and thereby be able to stifle legitimate public criticism of its
activities. For this and other reasons the court found for the newspaper (see
chapter 18).

(In 1994 the Law Lords upheld the decision without needing to rely
upon the Convention, ruling that the common law matched Article 10.)

Nationals who believe they have been wronged because their own law
operates in contravention of the Convention can challenge a decision
before the European Commission, and ultimately the European Court of
Human Rights at Strasbourg (which is not part of the European Community
and must be distinguished from the European Court of Justice in
Luxembourg, which is). If The European Court of Human Rights finds
against the national court, the country involved is required by its treaty
obligation to change its law to conform with the Convention.

There have been important cases where the British Government initiated
changes in the law to meet the requirements of the Convention. For
example, it introduced a new defence for those accused of contempt of
court after the European Court held that the House of Lords' decision
preventing the *Sunday Times* from publishing an article about the drug
thalidomide was an interference with the paper's freedom of expression
(see chapter 17, 'Discussion of public affairs').

In this case the European Court said a restriction was 'necessary in a
democratic society' only if it answered a 'pressing social need', and in a
later case the court added that interference with freedom of expression,
even if lawful, must be 'proportionate to the legitimate aim pursued'.

Important British cases involving freedom of speech that have come before the European Court include those of Bill Goodwin and Count Tolstoy.

In 1990 Bill Goodwin, a reporter on *The Engineer* magazine, was fined £5,000 by a British court after defying a ruling by the House of Lords that he must identify the source of a news story (see chapter 23, The *Bill Goodwin* case).

Backed by the National Union of Journalists, he took his case to the European Court which in 1996 ruled that the order breached his rights to freedom of expression under the Convention.

The court, answering the question 'Was the interference "necessary in a democratic society"?' said protection of journalistic sources was one of the basic conditions for press freedom. An order of source disclosure could not be compatible with Article 10 unless it was justified by an overriding requirement in the public interest and the order in this case did not meet that criterion.

In 1995 the Court found in favour of the author Count Tolstoy, against whom and a co-defendant an English jury had awarded £1.5 million, the largest libel award ever, for allegations against the Conservative politician Lord Aldington, contained in a pamphlet.

The pamphlet said Lord Aldington, when a brigadier in Austria at the end of the 1939-45 war, handed over 70,000 Cossacks and anti-Tito Yugoslavs to Communist forces knowing they faced imprisonment or death. Count Tolstoy was also ordered to pay nearly £1 million in costs.

The Court held that the award violated Count Tolstoy's rights to freedom of expression. It said that in 1987, when the words were published, the UK Court of Appeal did not have the power it acquired later (see chapter 18) to vary excessive jury awards, and the European Court said its decision had regard to the size of the award in conjunction with the state of national law at the time.

The European Court's criteria were increasingly being referred to by judges in British courts in the 1990s, even where there was no obvious ambiguity. The judges regarded them as 'persuasive' if not binding.


## Divisions of the law

There are two main divisions of the law: criminal law and civil law.

Criminal law deals with offences that are deemed to harm the whole community and thus to be an offence against the sovereign.

A lawyer writing about a crown court case in which John Smith is accused of an offence will name it R v Smith. 'R' stands for Regina (the Queen) or Rex (the King), depending on who is reigning at the time.

When speaking about this case, however, he will generally refer to it as 'The Queen (or the King) *against* Smith'.

Civil law concerns the maintenance of private claims and the redress of private wrongs.

A case in which John Smith is sued by Mary Brown will be known in writing as *Brown v Smith*. Lawyers will *speak* of the case as 'Brown *and* Smith' (our italics).

In practice, it will be found that the two divisions overlap to some degree. Many acts or omissions are not only 'wrongs' for which the injured party may recover compensation, but also 'offences' for which the offender may be prosecuted and punished. A road accident may lead to a claim for damages and also to a prosecution for dangerous driving. Similarly, defamation and breach of copyright, usually dealt with in the civil courts, may in certain circumstances be regarded as criminal matters, and dealt with in the criminal courts.

In spite of this overlap, the issues will generally be considered in different courts, depending upon whether the action is a criminal or a civil one. Young reporters must be careful to remember the basic differences in the nature of the actions.

It would be quite wrong, for example, to say that a defendant in a county court action is being 'prosecuted'. That is the language of the criminal courts.

In civil courts the person taking legal action, normally known as the *plaintiff*, is said to *sue* the other. The person sued is known as the *defendant* – the same term as in the criminal courts – but if he loses the case it is wrong to say that he has been 'found guilty': he is 'held liable'.

You should not describe the civil court's order in terms of punishment, as is generally the case with the *sentence* in a criminal court.

## The legal profession

Lawyers adopt one of two branches of the profession: they become either solicitors or barristers.

By tradition and practice, the solicitor is the lawyer who deals directly with a lay client. He advises him. He prepares his case, taking advice, when necessary, from a barrister specialising in a particular branch of the law – although solicitors themselves increasingly specialise.

The solicitor may represent his client in court, but in the past has generally been allowed to do so only in the lower courts – that is, the magistrates courts and the county courts. From 1993, however, a solicitor in private practice who has been granted a higher courts qualification by the Law Society has been allowed to appear in the higher courts, where he competes with barristers in representing clients. Anyone applying for a higher courts qualification must have practised as a lawyer for at least three years.

Any solicitor can represent an accused person in the crown court in an appeal from a magistrates court or in a committal for sentence when he has represented the person in the lower court. He can also appear in the High Court in formal or unopposed proceedings, and in proceedings when judgment is delivered in open court following a hearing in chambers (in the judge's private room) at which the solicitor conducted the case for his client. In court, he wears a gown but no wig.

In other cases, the solicitor 'briefs' (instructs) a barrister to conduct the case. His title derives from this procedure: on behalf of his client he 'solicits' the services of a barrister.

Solicitors are officers of the Supreme Court and for misconduct may be struck off the roll or suspended for a period. In that case, they are unable to practise.

The barrister is so called because he practises at the 'bar' of the court. Originally, the bar was a partition or barrier separating the judges from laymen attending court. Nowadays, there is no physical barrier in most courts.

Barristers are known, singly or collectively, as 'counsel'. In court reporting, it is a common error to apply the word to solicitors, but it refers to barristers only.

Except for certain conveyancing matters counsel have hitherto not been allowed to accept instructions directly from lay clients. They had to be instructed by solicitors. Now, however, there is limited direct access for other professions such as surveyors, accountants, and town planners seeking advice on the legal aspects of the disciplines.

A barrister wears a wig and gown in the higher courts and in the county courts.

A successful barrister who has been practising for at least ten years may apply to the Lord Chancellor for appointment as a Queen's Counsel. If this application is successful, he is said to 'take silk' because henceforth he will wear a gown of silk instead of cotton.

The terms Queen's Counsel and King's Counsel are interchangeable: which is used depends on whether the reigning monarch is a queen or king.

For unprofessional conduct, a barrister may be censured, suspended, or disbarred – that is, deprived of his standing as a barrister and therefore unable to practise.

Eminent lawyers who have also pursued a political career may aspire to the offices of Lord Chancellor, Attorney-General, or Solicitor-General. The Lord Chancellor is head of the judiciary. He is a member of the Cabinet, Speaker of the House of Lords, and the senior judge in the House of Lords sitting as the Supreme Court of Appeal.

The main duty of the Attorney-General and the Solicitor-General, the two law officers, is to advise the government of the day on legal matters. Some holders of the post are ministers of cabinet rank. The Attorney-General or, in his absence, the Solicitor-General, conducts the prosecution in certain important types of cases. The Attorney-General is the leader of the bar. The Lord Chancellor and the law officers change with a change of government.

## Questions

1   What is meant by the expression 'a free press'?
2   Is freedom of speech guaranteed in any way in the United Kingdom?
3   What is the importance of 'precedents' in the law?
4   How do the criminal law and the civil law differ?
5   What is the relationship of the barrister to the solicitor?

# 2    Reporting the courts

Every journalist reporting or sub-editing court stories should be familiar with both criminal and civil procedure.

Many unlawful acts can result in both criminal and civil cases, as we have seen.

## Types of offences

Magistrates courts deal with three types of criminal offences:
(a)   those triable only on indictment at crown court, eg murder, rape;
(b)   those triable either way — at crown court or at magistrates court — eg theft, indecent assault;
(c)   those usually triable only at a magistrates court (summary offences), eg minor motoring offences, drunkenness.

The Magistrates Courts Act 1980 sets out a list of those offences triable either way, where the defendant can, if he wishes, choose to be tried by a jury at crown court rather than by magistrates. Even if he wishes to be tried by magistrates, they may, after hearing representations by the prosecution, still decide that he should go for jury trial.

When sending a case for trial at crown court on an offence triable either way, they may also send the defendant for trial on any summary offence punishable by imprisonment or by a driving disqualification.

An indictable offence is defined as one that may be tried by a jury.

Trials at crown court are listed as issues between the Queen and the accused (see chapter 1).

Most prosecutions, both at magistrates court and crown court, are the responsibility of the Crown Prosecution Service in each of the 43 police areas in England and Wales. It is the task of this state service to decide on prosecutions, and conduct prosecutions in court except where the police prosecute in the most minor offences. Prosecutions can, however, be brought by private individuals, local authorities, and government departments.

Private prosecutions rarely go beyond the magistrates court. No one can be tried for certain serious offences without the Director of Public Prosecutions being informed, and the law allows the DPP to take over the prosecution. The Attorney-General has the power to stop such a case.

Normally a criminal prosecution starts in one of two ways — either by the defendant being arrested without the need for a warrant in the case of an arrestable offence, or by the police or some other person laying an information (usually a signed, sworn statement giving particulars of the alleged offence) before a magistrate.

The magistrate can, if he is satisfied that there are reasonable grounds, issue a warrant for arrest, or a summons to attend court at a stated time and date.

Sometimes when a warrant is issued by a magistrate, it is 'backed for bail', thus allowing the defendant his freedom for the time being, once he has been to the police station to complete certain formalities.

Magistrates may hear these applications for warrants or summonses either privately or in open court.

A clerk to the justices may also issue a summons.

## Arrestable offences

An arrestable offence is one for which the penalty on first conviction can be at least five years' imprisonment, or for which the penalty is fixed by statute (eg life imprisonment for murder). In addition, some offences, eg taking a car without authority or driving with excess alcohol, have been declared arrestable by Parliament, even though the maximum penalty is less than five years in jail.

A police officer may arrest a person without a warrant where he suspects that person of an arrestable offence.

Alternatively a police officer may seek a warrant from a magistrate for the arrest of any person suspected of having committed any indictable offence, whether arrestable or not.

A police officer may also arrest for any offence when a summons would be impractical or inappropriate, eg drunkenness, failing to stop after an accident.

## 'Helping the police with their inquiries'

This phrase, and 'detained for questioning', are often used to describe interrogation of suspects, but the latter is a legal fiction.

Under the Police and Criminal Evidence Act 1984, the police have no right to keep a person at a police station to help them with their inquiries unless he has been arrested. They are however entitled to question anyone. A person who attends a police station voluntarily is under no obligation to stay unless arrested.

The Act lays down that a person arrested must be told the grounds for the arrest. The information need not be given if it is not practicable to do so because of the person's escape from arrest before it can be given.

Under the code of practice adopted under the Police and Criminal Evidence Act, once a person has been charged, police questioning must stop.

Defendants are often detained for many hours without a charge being laid while they and witnesses are questioned and evidence is sifted. No person can be detained for more than 24 hours without being charged. If not charged within that time, further detention can be authorised only by a police superintendent for a further 12 hours and after that by a magistrates court. The Police and Criminal Evidence Act stipulates that the magistrates must not sit in open court when hearing applications for extended detention. A person can be detained longer under the Prevention of Terrorism Act 1976.

If a person is subsequently released without being charged, his claim for damages for false arrest or wrongful imprisonment or both will depend on whether he was actually deprived of his liberty and, if so, whether the grounds were reasonable. If he is subsequently charged and convicted, such an action will fail.

While a person is in custody, his friends or solicitor can apply to the High Court for a writ of habeas corpus to secure his release, if no charge is brought against him within a reasonable time.

The phrase 'a man is helping the police with their inquiries' is a convenient one for a newspaper even though it has no legal force. But even at this stage proceedings may have become active and liability for contempt of court may have started under the Contempt of Court Act 1981 (see chapter 17).

Apart from this, if you name the man and he is later released without being charged, he may sue for libel, claiming the phrase imputes guilt. The point has never been settled. But the Defamation Acts of 1952 and 1996 (see chapter 20) give qualified privilege to reports of information issued by or on behalf of the police, as these statements often are.

The Queen's Bench Divisional Court ruled in 1991 that the press has no automatic right to be told by the police the name of a person being investigated or who has been charged with a criminal offence.

Once charged, a man must either be granted bail by the police or be brought before a magistrates court no later than the next day, unless that day is Sunday, Christmas Day, or Good Friday.

Under the Bail Act 1976, the court is required to remand the accused on bail unless it is satisfied there are substantial grounds for believing he will abscond, commit other offences, or interfere with the course of justice; or he should be kept in custody for his own protection; or he is already serving a prison sentence; or there is not yet sufficient information available to make a decision. Bail cannot however be granted to a defendant charged with homicide or rape if he has been previously convicted of such an offence. It need not be granted if he is charged with an offence committed on bail.

The court must give reasons for refusing bail and must state the reasons for granting bail if the charge is murder, manslaughter, or rape.

If bail is refused by magistrates the defendant may apply to a judge in chambers. The prosecution can similarly appeal if its objection to bail is overruled where a defendant is accused of a serious offence. The prosecution must give immediate oral notice and the defendant may then be held in custody pending the appeal to the judge.

A surety is a person who guarantees the accused will surrender to his bail. He agrees to forfeit a sum of money fixed by the court if the accused jumps bail. A surety cannot be compelled to deposit the money in advance, but he can be jailed if subsequently he cannot find the money.

## Privilege

This book sets out in detail (see chapter 8) the many restrictions imposed by law on court reports in newspapers and broadcasting.

The court reporter should be aware of the restrictions which apply to the particular case or court which he is attending.

He also needs to be aware of the conditions which must be met if his report is to be protected against an action for libel.

The law recognises that the proceedings of the courts should be reported in the Press and it has given such reports a special protection.

This protection, known as absolute privilege, requires the report to be a fair and accurate report of court proceedings, published contemporaneously (see chapter 20).

To be fair and accurate a report need not be verbatim. It can be a paragraph. But it must be balanced, giving proper weight to both sides, stating for example that the accused denied the charge, and giving an outline of his defence if the report sets out the prosecution's case.

The reporter must be careful not to single out allegations made in court and present them as facts. He must attribute such remarks to the person who made them in court. A reporter can never be absolutely sure that opening statements made by barristers, solicitors, or police officers, when they outline the case they hope to prove, will actually be borne out by the evidence. Such statements should never be reported as fact without attribution to the speaker.

Care is also needed when the reporter, in writing his story, sets out to abbreviate and paraphrase complex charges. The danger is that in simplifying the legal jargon he commits inaccuracies or makes the charge seem more serious than it is. It is usually safer in the introduction to use a phrase like 'charges connected with' certain happenings, but the young reporter in doubt should consult his news editor.

Any inaccurate statement in a court report does not have the protection of privilege, should the inaccuracy be defamatory.

Headlines and introductions to court stories are privileged only if they are fairly and accurately based on statements made in court.

As a working rule, a contemporaneous report means one that is published in the first available issue. All protection is not lost if a report is not contemporaneous, but the privilege is only qualified.

Absolute privilege does not protect anything added to a court report that has not actually been said in court — for example, information given to a reporter after the hearing by a lawyer or a police officer. Nothing which is not part of the proceedings is protected.

Outbursts made in court by people who are not directly involved in the case need care in reporting, because they may be held not to be part of the proceedings. Many interruptions made by people in the public gallery are not defamatory and may be freely reported. Other remarks, however, may represent an attack on someone's character or truthfulness. In this case, it is wiser to report merely that the interruption was made, without using the actual words.

Written reports handed to the bench but not read out could also be ruled to be outside privilege.

They are not strictly evidence, but they become privileged if read out in the course of the case.

## Contempt of court

Besides many statutory restrictions on court reports, the journalist also needs to recognise the limitations sometimes imposed by the law of contempt, as already indicated.

The courts have power under section 4 of the Contempt of Court Act 1981 to order the postponement of publication of a report of any part of court proceedings to avoid the substantial risk of prejudice to the administration of justice in those proceedings or any other proceedings. But this section also says that provided no such order has been made there is no strict liability for contempt for fair and accurate reports of proceedings held in public when published contemporaneously and in good faith. It is possible there could be liability for contempt at common law if intent to prejudice is established. Common law contempt is explored in chapter 17.

Newspapers should in any case be careful to exclude references made in court to previous convictions and any extraneous material that could be prejudicial where a case is to be tried by a jury (see also chapter 5, restrictions under the Magistrates' Courts Act 1980).

The courts also have power under section 11 of the Contempt of Court Act to protect the identity of a witness or accused, but sympathy with a witness or accused is not a reason for making such an order. Section 11 orders are dealt with in greater detail in chapters 12 and 17.

## Questions

1   In what circumstances can magistrates refuse bail?
2   Detail the protection against an action for defamation that a newspaper has in reporting court proceedings. What are the requirements of this defence?
3   How should interruptions from the public gallery of a court be reported?
4   A criminal prosecution starts with an arrest without warrant or with the laying of an information. Explain what may happen in each case.

# 3   Crimes

Misdeeds triable in the criminal courts are numerous and varied. Their names, together with the legal jargon associated with them, sometimes present problems to young journalists and their newspapers. For example, the crime of theft is sometimes referred to in introductions and headlines as 'robbery'; this not only makes the paper look foolish to those many readers who know the difference, but also puts the paper at risk of a solicitor's letter, because robbery is a much more serious offence.

There are two elements in most crimes, a criminal act and a guilty mind. Lawyers refer to these two elements as the *actus reus* (which they pronounce, in lawyers' Latin, actus reeus) and *mens rea* (menz reeah). Without a guilty intent, no crime is committed.

But for some crimes, no guilty intent is necessary. These crimes are said to be subject to *strict liability* and called 'absolute offences'.

The crime for which a journalist is most likely to appear, as a journalist, before a court is contempt of court. Under the common law, contempt is a crime of strict liability — the prosecution does not have to prove that the journalist intended to impede the course of justice. But the Contempt of Court Act 1981 limited the circumstances in which journalists could be guilty of contempt of court in the absence of intent (see chapter 17).

This chapter mentions some of the main crimes and indicates pitfalls in referring to them. Simple explanations are given that in many cases would not satisfy a lawyer. The journalist seeking further information is advised to consult *Stone's Justices' Manual*, a three-volume reference book for magistrates that some newspapers and many public libraries have.

## Crimes against people

*Murder* The unlawful killing of another human being 'with malice aforethought' — that is, with the intention to kill or cause grievous bodily harm to that person. A person found guilty of murder must be sentenced to imprisonment for life.

*Manslaughter* The unlawful killing of another person, but in the absence of malice aforethought.

*Suicide* The killing of oneself. This is not a crime — though it was until 1961 and at one time resulted in the forfeiture of the dead person's property — but it is a crime to help another person to commit suicide or to attempt suicide.

*Infanticide* The killing of an infant under 12 months old by its mother, whose mind is disturbed as a result of the birth.

*Assault and battery* In these offences legal language differs from ordinary speech. Assault is technically a hostile act that causes another person to fear an attack. Battery is the actual application of force. It is normal newspaper practice to use the word 'assault' in court stories to indicate a physical attack.

*ABH* An assault (in the usual sense of the word) that causes actual bodily harm. The offence is frequently referred to as ABH, but in court lawyers sometimes refer to 'a section 47 offence', a reference to section 47 of the Offences Against the Person Act 1861.

*Malicious wounding and GBH* An assault (in the usual sense of the word) that causes a wound or grievous bodily harm. The offences are variously referred to as malicious wounding or GBH, or as 'a section 20 offence' (from the 1861 Act).

*Wounding with intent and GBH with intent* An assault (in the usual sense of the word) which causes a wound or grievous bodily harm, with the intention to do grievous bodily harm; the offences carry a maximum penalty of life imprisonment. They are often referred to in court as 'a section 18 offence' (from the 1861 Act).

*Rape* Having unlawful sexual intercourse with a person without his or her consent. The Criminal Justice and Public Order Act 1994 extended the law to cover male victims as well as women and anal as well as vaginal rape.

*Unlawful sex* Having unlawful sexual intercourse with a girl under 16.

*Indecent assault* An assault (in either sense) in circumstances of indecency. The offence can be committed by a male or female, upon a male or female.

## Crimes against property

*Theft* The dishonest appropriation of property belonging to another with the intention of permanently depriving the other of it. The act of theft is stealing. Do not refer to the offence as robbery.

*Robbery* Theft by force, or by threat of force.

*Burglary* Entering a building as a trespasser and stealing or attempting to steal; or inflicting or attempting to inflict grievous bodily harm. It is also burglary to enter a building as a trespasser *with intent* to steal, inflict grievous bodily harm, commit rape, or do unlawful damage. Before the Theft Act 1968, burglary was an offence which could be committed only at night.

*Aggravated burglary* The act of burglary while armed.

*Obtaining property by deception* The name defines the offence. The crime is often referred to in court as 'a section 15 offence' (from section 15 of the 1968 Act). It can safely be referred to as 'fraud'.

*Obtaining a pecuniary advantage by deception* Again, the name defines the offence. An example is staying at a hotel and leaving without paying. The crime is often known as 'a section 16 offence' (section 16 of the 1968 Act). It can safely be referred to as 'fraud'.

*Blackmail* Making an unwarranted demand with menaces with a view to gain.

*Handling* Dishonestly receiving goods, knowing or believing them to be stolen; or dishonestly helping in their retention, removal, disposal, or sale by or for someone else.

*Taking a vehicle without authority* This offence does not imply an intention to deprive the owner permanently and must not be confused, either in text or headline, with theft. You can say the defendant took a car, but not that he stole the car. The offence is sometimes referred to on court lists as TWOC (taking without owner's consent).

*Aggravated vehicle taking* The offence was introduced in 1992 in response to increasing public disquiet over joy-riding. It occurs when a vehicle has been taken (as above) and, before it is recovered, injury or damage is caused.

## Motoring crimes

*Dangerous driving* A person drives a motor vehicle dangerously if the way he drives falls far below what would be expected of a competent and careful driver.

*Causing death by dangerous driving* This and the previous offence were substituted for reckless driving and causing death by reckless driving by the Road Traffic Act 1991. The offences require only that bad driving be demonstrated through its consequences rather than by establishing a driver's intentions.

*Careless or inconsiderate driving* Driving a motor vehicle on a road without due care and attention or without reasonable consideration for others. The level of bad driving that must be proved is considerably less than that required in cases of dangerous driving.

*Driving while unfit* Driving a motor vehicle on a road while unfit to drive, through drink or drugs. The case will normally include evidence of the accused person's driving before he was stopped.

*Driving with excess alcohol* Driving a motor vehicle on a road at a time when the proportion of alcohol in the driver's body exceeds the prescribed limit; that is, 80 milligrammes of alcohol in 100 millilitres of blood, 35 microgrammes of alcohol in 100 millilitres of breath, or 107 milligrammes of alcohol in 100 millilitres of urine.

*Causing death by careless driving when under the influence of drink or drugs* The driver must be unfit to drive through drink or drugs; or must have consumed excess alcohol (as above); or must have failed to provide a specimen. The offence was introduced in the Road Traffic Act 1991.

## Questions

1   Define murder, manslaughter, suicide, and infanticide.
2   What is the difference between wounding with intent and GBH?
3   A man is found guilty of stealing money which has been left to pay for newspapers at an unattended stand. The headline of a newspaper report reads 'Paper seller robbed'. What is wrong with this headline?

4    You have reported a case in which a man has been found guilty of entering premises as a trespasser with intent to do unlawful damage there. How can this offence be named in one word?

5    A tramp gets money from a householder by promising to mow his lawn, but he has no intention of doing the work. What crime has he committed?

# 4    Magistrates courts: summary proceedings

All criminal cases in England and Wales start in the magistrates courts, except when, very rarely, a voluntary bill of indictment is granted. (See also chapter 5.)

## Magistrates

Magistrates (or justices of the peace) are appointed to serve in a county, and allocated to a petty sessional division, except that in a metropolitan district they are appointed for that district. At the age of 70 magistrates go on to a supplemental list, and can no longer sit in their courts.

Magistrates are non-salaried laymen and women who may, however, draw expenses and an allowance for financial loss. They are appointed by the Crown on the recommendation of the Lord Chancellor who acts on the suggestion of a local advisory committee.

At least two magistrates must sit for most summary trials; one is sufficient when the case against the defendant is being committed to crown court (see chapter 5).

Magistrates also carry out some other duties in civil and administrative law. They are also needed to sit with a judge in the crown court when it is hearing appeals and committals for sentence.

Some large cities have one or more stipendiary magistrates. These stipendiary magistrates (known as metropolitan magistrates in London) are salaried full-time magistrates, are legally qualified, and may sit alone and decide both on the law and on the facts of the case. There are also provincial stipendiary magistrates who can be asked to take cases (usually lengthy or complex) at any magistrates court in the area.

The Queen's Bench Divisional Court ruled in 1986 that a magistrates' bench and their clerk who had withheld names of magistrates hearing cases from press and public were acting contrary to law. Lord Justice Watkins said there was no such person known to law as the anonymous JP (see chapter 11, 'Magistrates court information').

Most cases are dealt with in their entirety by the magistrates, and are called summary proceedings. However, as already stated, the most serious charges must be committed for trial at crown court, while in some other cases the defendant has a choice.

The magistrates of each division appoint a chairman for the year. Because he cannot be present in every court, another magistrate, from a list of chairmen who have been trained for the work, presides in his absence.

Sitting in front of the magistrates in court is the magistrates clerk (clerk to the justices is his formal title). He is a solicitor or barrister who is appointed by the magistrates themselves, subject to the approval of the Lord Chancellor's Department. He advises the magistrates on the law.

When they are in session he or his clerks sit in court to record the proceedings and advise the magistrates on law. In many large towns and cities where a number of courts are sitting simultaneously, some members of the clerk's staff act practically full-time as court clerks.

Responsibility for the day-to-day administration of the courts and the head of the service in each area is the justices' chief executive, a newly-created post. He is responsible for the management of all staff including magistrates clerks but cannot interfere in advice given in individual cases by court clerks.

## Prosecutions

Most prosecutions are started by the police and taken over immediately by the Crown Prosecution Service. The case is presented in court by a solicitor or barrister employed by the service. Some prosecutions are also brought by public bodies such as British Rail or a local authority. Minor offences, mainly road traffic cases, are still prosecuted by the police.

An individual bringing a private prosecution may either engage a solicitor or present the case himself but the prosecution may be taken over by the Crown Prosecution Service and even discontinued by them if, for example, they consider the prosecution frivolous.

The person prosecuting outlines the case to the magistrates, whether or not the defendant has pleaded guilty. If the defendant has pleaded not guilty, witnesses for the prosecution are called.

The defendant, whether represented by a solicitor or conducting his own case, may himself testify and call witnesses. He cannot be compelled to give evidence.

If he goes into the witness-box himself, like any witness he is liable to be cross-examined by the other side. Adverse comment is allowed where a defendant over 14 who has pleaded not guilty chooses without good cause not to give evidence, or, when giving evidence, not to answer a question. Failure to give evidence or to account for incriminating circumstances cannot itself lead to a conviction however.

A witness can be compelled to give evidence if a court issues a witness summons or warrant. But a person cannot be compelled to give evidence against his or her spouse or co-habitee, except where the spouse or co-habitee is charged with an offence against him or her or their children, and in a few other cases.

If a witness appears to be refusing to testify or to go back on the statement he made to the investigators, application may be made for the court to allow the advocate to treat him as a hostile witness. The effect of this is that he may be challenged and asked leading questions by the side who called him, suggesting to him what answer is expected. Questions put by the side which calls the witness are called examination or evidence-in-chief. Questions put by the opposing side are known as cross-examination.

When the court has heard all the witnesses, the defence may address the court, arguing how the facts and the law should be interpreted. (Either side may, with permission, address the court twice.)

If the magistrates find the defendant guilty, the court will be told of any relevant previous convictions. Often sentence is postponed to await a pre-sentence report. Except in cases where there are special circumstances, previous convictions cannot be introduced by the prosecution until this stage. Among these special cases are those where the defendant 'puts his character at issue' or attacks the character of prosecution witnesses, or where the facts in the case are so strikingly similar to the facts in previous incidents as virtually to rule out coincidence.

Sometimes the defendant may ask for other offences to be 'taken into consideration'. This should not be confused with previous convictions. It means that the defendant is also admitting other offences which are not on the charge sheet, so that he can be sentenced for these at the same time.

## Tainted acquittals

If a person has been acquitted and the procedure has been tainted by intimidation of a witness (or a juror at crown court), the High Court can, under the Criminal Procedure and Investigations Act 1996, quash the acquittal, allowing the person to be tried again, thus departing from the general principle of British law that a person cannot be tried twice for the same offence. Before the High Court can exercise this power a person must have been convicted of interference with, or intimidation of, a witness or a juror and the court convicting him must have certified there is a real possibility that but for the interference or intimidation the person would not have been acquitted. If the court believes there is a possibility of a new trial of the person who was acquitted, it can order the postponement of reporting of the proceedings, or part of the proceedings, against the person accused of the interference with, or intimidation of a witness, until after the new trial of the acquitted person. It can do this under section 4 of the Contempt of Court Act 1981 where it believes that otherwise there would be a substantial risk of prejudice to the new trial of the acquitted person.

Liability for contempt of court under the strict liability rule of the 1981 Act starts in relation to the new trial once the certificate is granted as a first step towards allowing the High Court to quash the original acquittal, thus restricting publicity generally about the acquitted defendant's role in the crime. (See chapters 2, 12 and 17: substantial risk.)

## Mitigation

Where magistrates find a person guilty, or he has pleaded guilty, the defence will be given an opportunity to make a plea in mitigation of punishment, citing extenuating circumstances.

Under the Criminal Procedure and Investigations Act, a court has power to restrict reporting of assertions made in a speech of mitigation which are derogatory to a person's character, such as where it is suggested that his conduct has been criminal, immoral, or improper. The Act allows the court to order that the assertion made in mitigation shall not be reported for 12 months if there are substantial grounds for believing that the assertion is false or that it is irrelevant to the sentence. An order cannot be made if it appears that the assertion was previously made at a trial at which the person was convicted of the offence alleged in the assertion. The order can be made at any time before sentence is decided or as soon as reasonably practicable afterwards and may be revoked at any time.

The order makes it an offence to publish the assertion during the 12 months even if the person whose character is attacked is not named, if the report contains enough information to make it likely that the public will identify him.

The order may also be made where a magistrates court has been hearing a plea of mitigation before considering sending the defendant to crown court for sentence.

## Sentences

Generally, sentences may run from the moment they are announced. For summary offences, magistrates have wide powers in the way they deal with the defendant. They may not, however, impose a jail sentence of more than six months for one offence, or over twelve months for more than one offence. Prison sentences can be imposed for the first time only when the defendant is legally represented, or has been given the chance to apply for legal aid.

Consecutive sentences — that is, sentences running one after the other — may be imposed within the twelve months maximum, where the defendant is guilty of more than one offence.

Sentences may, however, be ordered to run concurrently. This means that the defendant remains in prison effectively only for the length of the longest sentence imposed.

Some prison sentences are suspended, with the effect that the defendant does not have to go to jail unless he commits a further offence, for which a jail sentence could be imposed, during the period the sentence is suspended. It should always be made clear in a court story that the sentence is suspended, and it is incorrect to refer to the defendant as being jailed.

Maximum fines for most offences are fixed by statute. The normal maximum is £5,000 but higher penalties may be imposed for such offences as customs duty and tax evasion.

A defendant over 16 can, under a community service order, be directed to work for a specified number of hours, unpaid, for the good of the community, such as in a hospital or old people's home, under the direction of a probation officer. These orders can be made only where the defendant agrees.

A defendant under 21 may be ordered to put in a stated number of hours at an attendance centre.

The court can, if it does not wish to impose a penalty, grant the defendant an absolute discharge. This means that he is discharged without any conditions. Alternatively, he may be conditionally discharged for a given period. Again, no penalty is imposed, but if the defendant commits another offence within the period laid down he is liable to be dealt with for the first offence as well as subsequent offences.

A defendant over 16 can be placed on probation if the court feels he is in need of guidance. The court makes a probation order for a given period, placing him under the supervision of a probation officer. The probation order can be combined with an order to do community service (a combination order). If the defendant proves unco-operative, or breaks any condition imposed in the order, he can be brought back to court.

Magistrates have power to bind over to be of good behaviour any person such as a defendant, witness, or complainant, in cases of violence or the threat of violence. Sometimes the prosecution will drop such a charge if the defendant agrees to be bound over in this way. No conviction has been recorded if this happens because such an order is regarded as a civil matter. In common assault cases, often the complainant as well as the defendant is bound over instead of the case being tried to a conclusion.

Sometimes when a man has admitted, or has been convicted of, an offence the magistrates may feel the sentence they can pass is insufficient.

In this case they can send him to crown court for sentence. It is important not to confuse this with his being sent for trial (see chapter 5).

Magistrates have powers to order a defendant to make restitution, and can order a motor vehicle used in the furtherance of theft, even shoplifting, to be confiscated. They can order an offender to pay compensation for personal injury, or for loss or damage to goods.

A magistrates court can vary or rescind a sentence within 28 days and, where it would be in the interests of justice, can re-open a case, to be heard by a different bench of magistrates, if a person has pleaded not guilty or has been tried in his absence.

## Court lists

In 1989 the Home Office wrote to justices' clerks commending the practice of making available to the press court lists and, where they are prepared, provisional lists on the day of the hearings. The court may charge the economic rate for providing court papers and newspapers and news agencies may co-operate to share any such cost (Circular 80/1989).

The Home Office circular said that, as a minimum, the list should contain each defendant's name, age, address, and, where known, his occupation, and the charge he faced. The circular also approved the practice of some courts of supplying copies of the court register of the day's proceedings.

In 1967 and 1969, the Home Office recommended that addresses of defendants should be stated orally in magistrates courts. The 1967 Circular (No 78/1967) stated: 'A person's address is as much part of his description as his name. There is, therefore, a strong public interest in facilitating press reports that correctly describe persons involved.'

Lord Justice Watkins said in the Queen's Bench Divisional Court in 1988 that while no statutory provision laid down that a defendant's address had publicly to be given in court it was well established practice that, save for a justifiable reason, it must be (*R v Evesham Justices, ex p McDonagh* 1988) (see also chapter 12, Obstructive courts).

Under section 15 of the Defamation Act 1996, due to come into operation during 1997, qualified privilege (subject to explanation or contradiction) is given to publication of a fair and accurate copy of, or extract from, a document made available by a court or by a judge or officer of a court.

## Appeals

If a person pleads guilty, he or she cannot usually appeal against conviction, but may appeal to crown court against sentence. A person who pleads not guilty can appeal to crown court against conviction and/or sentence (see chapter 7).

Either defence or prosecution may appeal to the Queen's Bench Divisional Court on a point of law. The procedure is described in chapter 7.

## Questions

1   What is the procedure when a defendant pleads not guilty at a magistrates court?
2   Explain the difference between previous convictions and cases taken into consideration.
3   What is meant when the prosecution asks the bench to declare someone a hostile witness?
4   What length of prison sentences may magistrates impose?
5   State what has already happened when magistrates:
    (a)  commit a case for trial at crown court
    (b)  commit for sentence
6   What is a stipendiary magistrate?

# 5   Magistrates courts: preliminary hearings

The most serious offences cannot be tried by magistrates but must be committed by them for trial at crown court if there is evidence of a case to answer.

Both at this committal stage and at earlier hearings where the accused charged with an indictable offence is remanded for, say, a week, either on bail or in custody, reporting restrictions are imposed by section 8 of the Magistrates' Courts Act 1980. These restrictions apply even in the case of an 'either way' offence where the accused may have the choice of a summary trial before the magistrates or trial before a jury at crown court (see chapter 2: types of offences). When a person is brought before magistrates and charged with an 'either way' offence, the accused must, under the Criminal Procedure and Investigations Act 1996, be asked to indicate whether he will plead guilty or not guilty. Unless reporting restictions are lifted, as explained later, the Act does not permit the reporting of the accused's indication as to how he will plead, although a report which mentions the accused's intention to plead not guilty is unlikely to lead to a prosecution.

If, at any time, a decision is taken to try the 'either way' offence case summarily by magistrates, however, reporting restrictions under section 8 cease.

Magistrates when acting at the committal proceedings or earlier hearings leading up to them are said to be *examining justices*. Their task is to decide whether there is a prima facie case to go before a jury. Under the 1996 Act, however, they may commit the defendant for trial on the basis of written statements, sometimes known as depositions, without consideration of the contents of these documents, unless there is a submission that there is insufficient evidence to put the accused on trial, or one of the accused is not legally represented. Under the 1996 Act, witnesses, whether for prosecution or defence, are not called to give oral evidence and any submission of insufficient evidence must be decided merely on contentions put forward by prosecution and defence. If magistrates decide there is insufficient evidence, they must discharge the accused.

Examining justices may sit singly because they are not a court of trial, but are merely making a preliminary examination.

Even if the accused has elected for the reporting restrictions to be lifted, there is no provision for the written statements or depositions to be made available to the Press. However, if the magistrates accept a submission of insufficient evidence to go before a jury and none of the accused is committed for trial, reporting restrictions on the whole hearing are lifted. Additionally, the Magistrates' Courts Act 1980, as amended by the 1996 Act, provides that when the accused is not committed for trial, as much of the written statements or depositions as has been accepted as evidence shall be read aloud unless the court otherwise directs. Where a direction is given against reading the evidence aloud, an account must be given of such evidence.

If the accused is not committed for trial because of insufficient evidence, this should not be described as an acquittal because there has been no trial. It is possible, though rare, for the accused to be brought to court again if further evidence comes to light, since this would not infringe the general principle that a person cannot be tried twice for the same offence.

If the accused is sent for trial and is refused bail pending appearance at crown court, he can apply to a judge in chambers (ie sitting in private) to allow him bail.

The prosecution may object to bail, eg on grounds that the accused might abscond, interfere with witnesses or commit another offence.

As stated in chapter 2, newspapers should in no circumstances mention previous convictions or other information which carries a substantial risk of serious prejudice. Section 8 of the Magistrates' Courts Act further restricts what may be reported of bail applications to 'arrangements as to bail on committal or adjournment'. This has been widely interpreted as meaning that any conditions as to bail may be reported, eg the amount of the surety, that the accused reports regularly to the police, that he surrenders his passport, or that he does not interfere with witnesses. But arguments as to whether bail should be granted are ruled out. So are the reasons for refusing bail, which magistrates must give under the Bail Act 1976.

The law obliges the clerk of the court to display at the court house a notice giving the accused's name, age, address, the charge(s), and whether he is committed (and to which court) or discharged. Exceptions are made in cases involving juveniles.

A newspaper report of such a notice is protected by qualified privilege under the Defamation Act 1996, expected to come into force in 1997.

If magistrates rule there is insufficient evidence to go before a jury, the prosecution can turn to the rare procedure of applying to a High Court judge for a voluntary bill of indictment. The effect of this is that although magistrates have discharged the accused, he will still be brought to trial at crown court. The application for a bill of indictment wll be heard by a judge in chambers. Under the Administration of Justice Act 1960, it would not be a contempt of court to report the judge's decision (see chapter 17, 'Report of hearing in private').

## Notice of transfer

A new procedure was introduced in 1992 for cases involving violence or cruelty against a child .

The Crown Prosecution Service may serve a notice of transfer on magistrates and the case is then transferred to crown court without the usual committal proceedings. The only function of the magistrates is then to make orders requiring witnesses to attend crown court or for bail or legal aid.

A similar notice of transfer procedure for cases of serious complex fraud was introduced in 1989.

In both cases, of offences against children and of serious fraud, the accused can apply to crown court for the charge to be dismissed on grounds of insufficient evidence.

Reporting restrictions on preliminary hearings, under section 8 of the Magistrates' Courts Act 1980, described below, apply to hearings before magistrates where notice of transfer is served by the prosecution, although usually there will be little to report other than basic details. (See also chapters 6 and 7).

## The reporting restrictions

The restrictions on newspaper or broadcast reports of committals for trial by the magistrates, or of adjournments on charges *triable* at crown court, were introduced to avoid a potential juror being influenced by what he might read or hear of the prosecution case. There are occasions when it seems difficult to present a report of preliminary proceedings that is fair to the accused if all the restrictions are strictly observed – such as where in an 'either way' charge the accused has himself chosen jury trial and is being formally committed for trial for this reason only, and not because of the seriousness of the offence or of his record. The same is true where an accused or his solicitor protests his innocence or complains of police treatment during questioning.

Yet some reports which infringe the restrictions cannot be said to be in the interests of the accused. Almost daily, newspapers and broadcasting add to a court story background material either about the defendant or the alleged crime, even though reporting restrictions have not been lifted. It is arguable that such background material is not itself a report of the court proceedings and is not therefore a contravention of the Act (even though the general law of contempt still applies).

In 1975, however, the editor of a weekly newspaper was fined for a story which combined an account of a fire with a report of a man's first appearance before a magistrates court on an arson charge. The prosecuting solicitor contended that reports must be resticted to matters permitted by the Act. He said it did not matter where other information came from, whether it was said in court or was known to the reporter – it was a breach of the Act. This conclusion has not been contested in the High Court.

One legal view is that in this situation the newspaper ought to run separate stories, each with its own headline – a story on the incident, conforming to the law of contempt (see chapter 17) and a court story conforming to section 8 of the 1980 Act.

Apart from the exceptions, which follow, reports of preliminary hearings on offences triable by jury are limited by the 1980 Act to ten points:
(a) the name of the court, and the names of the magistrates;
(b) names, addresses, and occupations of the parties and witnesses, ages of the accused and witnesses;
(c) the offence(s), or a summary of them, with which the accused is or are charged;
(d) names of counsel and solicitors in the proceedings;
(e) any decision of the court to commit the accused, or any of the accused for trial, and any decision on the disposal of the case of any accused not committed;
(f) where the court commits the accused for trial, the charge or charges, or a summary of them, on which he is committed and the court to which he is committed;
(g) where proceedings are adjourned, the date and place to which they are adjourned;
(h) any arrangements as to bail (which is taken to include any conditions as to bail, but not any reason for opposing or refusing it);
(i) whether legal aid was granted;
(j) any decision of the court to lift or not to lift these reporting restrictions.
These restrictions are not in force when:
(a) the accused applies to have them lifted. Magistrates are then required to formally make an order lifting restrictions. If there is more than one accused all of them must be given the opportunity to make representations before a decision on lifting the restrictions is taken. If any of the accused objects, restrictions may be lifted only on the grounds that it is in the interests of justice to do so. Even if reporting restrictions are lifted, newspapers should not refer to previous

convictions or report other information that carries a substantial risk of serious prejudice to a fair trial at crown court;

(b) the court decides to commit none of the accused for trial;

(c) the court decides to try one or more of the accused summarily. In this case, a report of the summary trial may be published even if it impinges on the case of other defendants not tried summarily. If the accused is committed for *sentence* to crown court, there are no restrictions on the report because he has been tried summarily.

(d) all the defendants have eventually been tried at crown court. This means that submissions made at the committal weeks or months earlier can now be reported, if thought newsworthy, without waiting for any appeal. This belated report of the committal proceedings, provided it is fair and accurate, will be treated as a contemporaneous report, and will be privileged under the Defamation Act 1996.

Some important interpretations of the Magistrates' Courts Act 1980 have been given by the High Court.

In one case it was ruled that where there is a multiplicity of charges which have properly been made the subject of one committal proceeding, any lifting of the restrictions must apply to the whole of the committal.

In 1972, it was held in the Queen's Bench Divisional Court that once lifted, the restrictions cannot be reimposed. It is however possible to impose other restrictions under section 4 of the Contempt of Court Act 1981 (see chapter 17).

There have been a number of prosecutions for reports of preliminary hearings in magistrates courts that were infringements of the restrictions under the 1980 Act even though it later transpired that the reports could not have influenced the subsequent crown court trial.

In 1996, the former editor of *The Citizen*, Gloucester, and the paper's owners were each fined £4,500 for a report of the first appearance in magistrates court of Fred West. The report was an accurate report of what was said in court but included a statement that West had admitted killing his daughter.

Every court reporter should understand the basis of the Act but not allow it to inhibit him more than necessary. For instance, point three of the ten permitted points allows the reporter to give detail *in the charge*. The reporter's difficulty is that the charge as set out on the information available to the reporter is often only a summary. If the case merits it on its news value, he should approach the clerk of the court or the prosecution to obtain particulars of the charge, such as where and when the offence is alleged to have been committed and against whom, information which the 1980 Act allows him to publish.

## Questions

1  Under the Magistrates Courts Act 1980, what details can a newspaper report of committals for trial?

2  Do these restrictions apply when the magistrates (a) commit the defendant for sentence at crown court; (b) remand him for a week to await committal proceedings? State your reasons.

3  List the circumstances in which the restrictions of the Act do not apply.

4  Discuss the difficulties of newspapers reporting committals for trial, and proceedings leading up to committals, under the 1980 Act.

5  What happens when four accused are jointly charged with burglary, only one of them asks for the reporting restrictions to be lifted, and the others oppose lifting of the restrictions?

# 6 Juveniles in the news

The law on what may be reported about children involved in legal proceedings has become increasingly complex, with the implementation of the Children Act 1989 and fresh interpretations in the High Court of parts of the Children and Young Persons Act 1933 and of the common law governing publicity for children in civil cases. Some journalists have been known to assume that there is an automatic prohibition on identifying a juvenile and his or her family in cases where no such ban existed.

In 1991, the Lord Chancellor announced a review to cover the inconsistencies in access to, and reporting of, family proceedings, to be followed by consultations with representatives of the judiciary and of the media. A consultation paper was issued in 1993, setting out the present law but, as this book went to press, the review body had yet to produce any recommendations.

The law on reporting these matters varies substantially according to the type of court at which such family proceedings involving children take place.

This chapter sets out to cover the restrictions in reporting cases involving children before the various courts and deals with the effects on such reports of the Criminal Justice Act 1991.

## Youth courts

Juvenile courts, established in England and Wales under the Children and Young Persons Act 1933, were renamed youth courts in 1992, and now deal with young people who were under 18 at the time they committed an offence. In law a child is defined as being under 14 years and a young person as being over 14 but under 18. A child under 10 cannot be charged with a criminal offence.

The general public are barred from youth courts but reporters are entitled to attend (see chapter 11).

Youth courts do not deal with applications for a child to be put into the care of the local authority (care orders). The fact that a child has committed an offence may however be evidence on which a local authority may rely in applying for a care order at a magistrates court, sitting in family proceedings (see later, this chapter). The youth court has power to remand the offender to local authority accommodation as a temporary measure. The court may also put the offender under the supervision of the local authority and such a criminal supervision order can include a residence requirement, compelling the offender in serious cases to live for up to six months in accommodation provided by the local authority. Orders of this kind are intended to deal with persistent offenders who have committed a serious offence.

The youth court may also order a juvenile to put in a stated number of hours at an attendance centre.

When the youth court deals with a juvenile acused of a grave crime, it may send him for trial at crown court. Reports of such a committal for trial are restricted by the Magistrates' Courts Act 1980 (see previous chapter) in addition to the restrictions on reports of youth court proceedings which now follow.

## Restrictions on reports

Under section 49 of the 1933 Act, reports of proceedings at a youth court must not contain:
(a) the name, address, or school, or any particulars leading to the identification of any child or young person involved in the proceedings as a defendant or witness;
(b) any photograph of, or including, any such juvenile.

Reporters need to be careful not to include in a youth court story anything that could identify a juvenile. To say 'a 14-year-old Bristol boy' would not identify him but to use the name of a small village might, as would a statement that the boy was the 12-year-old twin son of a village policeman. The test must always be whether any member of the public could put a name to the child as a result of information given in the report.

There is nothing to stop the naming of adults concerned in youth court proceedings, provided this does not identify a juvenile.

It should be noted that there is a complete ban on naming the juvenile's school, however large.

These restrictions also apply to reports of appeals from the youth court to a crown court or on a point of law to the Queen's Bench Divisional

Court. They also apply to any proceedings in any court (for example, a crown court) for varying or revoking a supervision order against a juvenile.

However, in appeal proceedings or proceedings for varying or revoking supervision orders, the restriction on identifying the child does not apply unless it is announced in court.

A youth court or the Home Secretary has the power to lift the restrictions on identifying any juvenile concerned in the proceedings to avoid injustice to him. Under the Crime (Sentences) Act 1997 a youth court is given power to waive the restrictions on identifying a juvenile if magistrates believe it would be in the public interest. Before it can waive the restrictions, the court must allow parties to the proceedings to make representations.

Under the Criminal Justice and Public Order Act 1994, a youth court, on the application of the Director of Public Prosecutions, may dispense with the restrictions in order to trace a juvenile who is wanted for a violent or sexual offence or an offence where an adult could be jailed for 14 years or more. The Act provides that the court may specify to what extent the restrictions are being lifted which appears to allow it to stipulate how long the dispensation lasts.

## Juveniles in adult courts

When a juvenile appears as defendant or witness in any court other than a youth court, or other than in an appeal from a youth court, there is no automatic ban on identifying him.

Section 39 of the 1933 Act however gives the court the power to direct that:

(a)  no report of the proceedings shall reveal the name, address, or school, or include any particulars likely to lead to the identification of any child or young person concerned in the proceedings;

(b)  no picture shall be published of any child or young person so concerned.

It has now become the practice in many magistrates courts to make a section 39 order in almost every case where a juvenile is involved.

Sometimes the making of the order borders on the absurd. After a woman had given a newspaper a story about her 14-year-old son being wrongly served with a summons to appear in court for not paying council tax, Birmingham magistrates in 1994 made a section 39 order forbidding his further identification in a report of the summons being withdrawn in court.

In 1990, Lord Justice Watkins said in the divisional court that the mere fact that the person before the court was a child or young person would normally be good reason for restricting, under section 39, reports of proceedings. Several judges did not accept this view. When two boys aged 15 and 16 were accused at the Old Bailey of taking part in a gang rape,

Judge Nina Lowry said : 'I do not think it right or in the public interest that the identity of the two perpetrators of this crime should be cloaked in anonymity. The matter should be out in the open in the community where they live'.

Lord Justice Watkins' view was rejected by the Court of Appeal in 1992 when Lord Justice Lloyd said: 'For our part we would not wish to see the court's discretion fettered so strictly. There is nothing in section 39 about rare or exceptional cases. There must be a good reason for making an order under section 39 (see chapter 12, Section 39 orders).

In its judgment, the Court of Appeal gave its approval to the refusal of Judge Michael Coombe at the Old Bailey the previous month to continue a section 39 order in relation to a 14-year-old boy who took part in a robbery while on bail on a rape charge. Judge Coombe had said he could see no harm to the boy, and a powerful deterrent effect on his contemporaries, if his name and photograph were published. The public interest in knowing the identity of the boy outweighed any harm to the boy.

Courts sometimes make section 39 orders attempting to ban the identification of dead children — even though the name of the dead child has usually been published already in a report of the death or of an inquest. Several High Court judges have said the courts do not have this power and such an order appears to be a nullity (see chapter 12).

Marylebone magistrates in 1991 made a section 39 order to prevent the identification of an alleged victim of a sexual offence who although 11 at the time had reached the age of 31 before the defendant was prosecuted. The order was withdrawn after Malcolm Starbrook, group editor of the Croydon Advertiser series, wrote pointing out that it appeared to be invalid.

Courts have also attempted to use section 39 in cases involving child battery or sexual abuse within families to order that the name of the adult defendant should not be published.

In 1991, however, the Court of Appeal held that the courts could not use section 39 to order that the names of defendants should not be published, unless such defendants were themselves young persons (see chapter 12).

Newspapers have frequently persuaded courts against imposing or renewing section 39 orders to prevent identification of young babies who have been victims of violence. It is difficult to see that a child of such tender years would suffer any ill-effects from being named. For an example of a successful challenge on these grounds, see chapter 12.

In 1992, Lord Justice Lloyd giving judgment in the Court of Appeal said of section 39 orders: 'The section enables any court to make an order in relation to "any proceedings". But "any proceedings" does not mean "any proceedings anywhere": it must mean any proceedings in the court making the order'. From this, it would appear that if a section 39 order is made by magistrates in respect of a juvenile whose case they send for trial to crown court, that order is no longer in force when the juvenile reaches crown court. For him to remain anonymous, a fresh order must be made by the crown court judge.

There is no power prohibiting the identification of a person who has reached his 18th birthday.

See also chapter 12, Section 39 orders.

## Jigsaw identification

Although the Court of Appeal decision means that while a section 39 order cannot stipulate that newspapers suppress the name of an adult defendant in order to prevent the identification of a child, there remains the danger of jigsaw identification of a child or young person who is the subject of a section 39 order — through one newspaper giving the name of the defendant and suppressing details of the relationship, and another paper, or radio or television programme, withholding the name but giving the full story.

The code of practice, ratified by the Press Complaints Commission in 1996, for newspapers to follow to avoid jigsaw identification, says:

> In any press report of a case involving a sexual offence against a child—
> (1) The adult should be identified.
> (2) The term incest, where applicable, should not be used.
> (3) The offence should be described as 'serious offences against young children' or similar appropriate wording.
> (4) The child should not be identified.
> (5) Care should be taken that nothing in the report implies the relationship between the accused and the child.

The code of practice also says that even where the law does not prohibit it, the press should not identify children under the age of 16 who are involved in cases of sexual offences, whether as victims or witnesses or defendants.

Although most newspapers have agreed to follow the recommendation of naming the defendant and suppressing matter that might suggest a connection with the child, some editors have felt it impossible to adhere to the practice where the details of the story were more important than the name.

When a defendant accused of a sexual offence against a child first appears before a court and newspapers decide to give details of the relationship while omitting names, it will be difficult to have a change of mind and name the defendant where a section 39 order is in force.

In 1995 the Independent Television Commission, which has statutory powers to impose penalties on commercial television companies, amended its programme code to provide that an accused adult should be identified, if the law allows, and the child should not be identified.

## Offences against children

Procedure was introduced under the Criminal Justice Act 1991 to speed up proceedings against people charged with a serious sexual offence or offence of violence or cruelty against a child (see chapter 5, Notice of transfer).

The prosecution can serve on the magistrates' court a notice of transfer and the magistrates are compelled, without consideration of the evidence, to commit the accused for trial at crown court. Their only function is then to decide on bail and legal aid.

A person who is committed for trial under this procedure may at any time before he is charged at crown court apply at crown court for the charge, or any of the charges, against him to be dismissed on the grounds of insufficient evidence.

The Criminal Justice Act 1991 clearly envisages such an application at crown court being heard in public for it lays down restrictions on what may be reported in these proceedings.

Reports of the application must be confined to eight points:
(a) the identity of the court and of the judge;
(b) names, ages, home addresses, and occupations of accused and witnesses;
(c) the offences, or a summary of them, with which the accused is charged;
(d) names of counsel and solicitors;
(e) where proceedings are adjourned, date and place to which they are adjourned;
(f) arrangements as to bail;
(g) whether legal aid is granted;
(h) whether reporting restrictions are lifted.

The restrictions on reporting the application do not apply if the judge decides to lift them (but if an accused objects the judge may lift the restrictions only if he considers it in the interests of justice).

The restrictions also do not apply if the case against all the accused is dismissed on grounds of insufficient evidence. The Act does not allow for the reporting of the fact that the application was unsuccessful, thus creating the odd situation that it is lawful to report that an application for the case to be dismissed was made, but not to report the outcome if any accused is unsuccessful in his application.

## Children Act 1989

The purpose of the Act is to rationalise the law on caring for, bringing up, and protecting children.

Cases under the Act are heard in the magistrates court, the county court, or the Family Division of the High Court and may be transferred within these three tiers. Care proceedings (for the child to be put into or removed from the care of the local authority) no longer come before the juvenile court but are heard or started before magistrates courts sitting in family proceedings.

Reporting of family proceedings in the magistrates court is controlled by complex restrictions. It is governed by two overlapping Acts — the Children Act 1989 and that part of the Magistrates' Courts Act 1980 originally dealing with the old domestic courts, but now relating to family proceedings, which besides handling children's cases also hear domestic issues between husband and wife.

Section 69 of the Magistrates' Courts Act 1980, as now amended by the Children Act, denies admission to the general public but says that representatives of newspapers or news agencies may attend these family proceedings (except when adoption cases are being heard). Nevertheless, magistrates in family proceedings do have power under magistrates courts rules, to sit in private when exercising powers under the Act in relation to a child under 18.

Even where reporters are allowed to remain when children are involved, there are two sets of restrictions on what may be published. The combined effect of the two Acts is that few details can be published and the child cannot be identified in any way, making it difficult for a meaningful story to be compiled.

Although section 71 of the Magistrates' Courts Act permits names to be published, this permission is removed in respect of children by section 97 of the Children Act, which makes it an offence to publish any material which is intended or likely to identify any child under 18 as being involved in proceedings in a magistrates court in which any power is being exercised under the Children Act, or to publish an address or school as being that of a child involved in any such proceedings.

Section 71 of the Magistrates' Courts Act says no report of family proceedings in a magistrates' court shall be published containing matter other than the following:
(a) the names, addresses, and occupations of parties and witnesses;
(b) the grounds of the application and a concise statement of the charges, defences, and counter-charges in support of which evidence has been given;
(c) submissions on any point of law arising in the proceedings and the decision of the court on the submissions;
(d) the decision of the court, and any observations made by the court in giving it.

The effect of the Magistrates' Courts Act restrictions is to prevent the reporting of evidence and the newsline in the case, unless the chairman of the magistrates refers to it in announcing the decision of the court (see item (d) above). Under the Children Act, magistrates are bound to give reasons for their decision.

By the use of the words 'as being involved in proceedings', this ban on identification appears to extend not merely to reports of the proceedings but to any story, such as an interview with parents in dispute with social workers, which identifies the children as having been involved in the proceedings. The ban may be lifted or relaxed by the court or by the Home Secretary, if satisfied that the welfare of the child requires it. It is a defence for a publisher to prove that he did not know, and had no reason to suspect, that the material was likely to identify the child.

For further details on family proceedings see chapter 9.

## Children's cases heard before judges sitting in chambers

There is no provision in the Children Act governing the reporting of ward of court applications and of other matters relating to children which are heard by a judge at county court or by a judge of the Family Division of the High Court, who usually sit in chambers.

Section 12 of the Administration of Justice Act 1960 deals with the question of reporting such cases. It says that it is not a contempt of court (see chapter 17) to publish a report of *proceedings* in private, with certain exceptions, notably proceedings concerning children. The section also states however that the publication of the whole or part of any order made by the court sitting in private shall not of itself be a contempt except where the court has prohibited publication.

Thus, there is no automatic ban on publishing the *decision* in children's cases heard in chambers in the higher courts but there is normally a ban on publication of other details of what took place when the court was sitting in private. The prohibition is on reporting the proceedings but a judge has powers at common law to extend the ban to the child's identity.

It was established in the Court of Appeal in 1977 that for there to be a contempt in reporting child cases in chambers, it has to be shown (a) that the publication was of information relating to proceedings before a court sitting in private; the words 'information relating to proceedings' cover confidential reports submitted to the court by, for example, the Official Solicitor or social workers, once wardship proceedings have been commenced and are not limited to information given to the judge at the actual hearing; and (b) that the publisher knew that he was publishing information relating to private wardship proceedings, or published the information recklessly not caring whether or not publication was prohibited. It followed, the court held, that it was a defence to a charge of contempt under section 12 that the publisher did not have guilty knowledge or intent in publishing the information.

Lord Justice Lane (later Lord Chief Justice) said in this case: 'Proceedings includes such matters as statements of evidence, reports, accounts of interviews, and so on prepared for use in court once the wardship proceedings have been properly set on foot.'

Lord Justice Scarman said: 'What is protected from publication is the proceedings of the court; in all other respects the ward enjoys no greater protection against unwelcome publicity than other children. If the information published relates to the ward but not to the proceedings there is no contempt.'

Mr Justice Waite said in the High Court Family Division in 1991 that the mere status of being a ward of court did not confer on a child any right as such to have its affairs cloaked in secrecy. The privilege of confidentiality was that of the court, not of the child, and the primary purpose was to protect the court in the exercise of its paternal functions.

In 1994, the *Sun* newspaper was fined £5,000 and its editor £1,000 for contempt of court arising from the publication of extracts from a doctor's report which had been presented at proceedings before a judge in chambers about a child.

There also remains a danger for newspapers in publishing what is seen as a story of a parent's struggle to retain control of a child, should the story contain matters from the proceedings in chambers.

On the other hand, judges in the Court of Appeal and in the Family Division have said on numerous occasions that it is not a contempt to publish the name and address of the ward or to identify him or the fact that wardship proceedings were taking place, or had taken place, in the absence of an express prohibition.

The law governing publication of matter about wardship proceedings can also apply to other proceedings in chambers concerning children. In 1992, Lord Justice Balcombe said in the Court of Appeal:'The court's inherent jurisdiction can be exercised whether or not the child is a ward.'

Exercising this inherent jurisdiction, the High Court can issue an injunction forbidding identification or other information even if the child is not a ward of court. After two schoolboys had been found guilty at Preston Crown Court in 1993 of the murder of a young boy, James Bulger, Mr Justice Morland issued an injunction forbidding the seeking or publishing of information about the addresses of the schools or the care or treatment of the two accused boys, or the taking of further photographs or film of them.

## Injunctions

In addition to the reporting restrictions on family proceedings in the magistrates courts and on children's cases before judges in chambers, it is possible for a local authority or individual to seek an injunction from a judge banning *all* reporting of the matter, even if the report does not identify the children.

In the past, local authorities, faced with allegations of widespread child abuse, have frequently sought injunctions in the interests of the children, or, possibly, to prevent the actions of their social workers from being open to public criticism.

The Court of Appeal in 1991 gave guidance to judges on how far these injunctions should go in banning publicity for children. Lord Justice Neill said a distinction could be drawn between cases of mere curiosity and cases where the Press was giving information or commenting about matters of genuine public interest.

In almost every case, he said, the public interest in favour of publication could be satisfied without any identification of the child to persons other than those who already knew the facts. The injunction had to be in clear terms and had to be no wider than was necessary to achieve the purpose for which it was imposed.

In a case in 1989, the Master of the Rolls, Lord Donaldson, said if a temporary injunction had been granted in the absence of the other side (the newspaper), a judge should be ready and willing at short notice to consider any application by those affected to withdraw or modify it.

See also chapter 12, Wards of court.

## Questions

1  What age group of juvenile offenders is dealt with in the youth courts?
2  Define what is meant in law by (a) a child (b) a young person?
3  What are the restrictions imposed on reports of youth proceedings?
4  Under what circumstances may a juvenile appearing at a youth court be named in a newspaper?
5  What ruling has the Court of Appeal given as to the use by the courts of orders under section 39 of the Children and Young Persons Act 1933 to suppress the names of defendants?
6  What does the Children Act 1989 stipulate about the naming of children involved in family proceedings in the magistrates court?
7  What are the rights of reporters to attend applications for care orders before magistrates courts sitting in family proceedings?
8  If the reporter is allowed to attend family proceedings where a child is involved, what difficulties does he face in filing his report?
9  What dangers exist in publishing interviews with parents who complain that their children have been removed from them without just cause?

# 7 The crown court and the appeal courts

Crown courts try both criminal and civil cases, but the criminal business is greater.

Crown courts were set up in England and Wales in 1972 to replace the old assizes and quarter sessions. All serious crime is eventually tried there. Even the Central Criminal Court (the Old Bailey) in London is, in effect, a crown court.

When dealing with civil business, the crown court acts as a provincial branch of the High Court.

Crown courts have three main functions in criminal cases:

(a) to try indictable offences sent for trial by magistrates courts (some serious offences, for example murder and rape, must be tried at crown court);

(b) to deal with cases sent for sentence from magistrates courts; and

(c) to hear appeals from magistrates courts.

There are six crown court areas (known as circuits). Each has a circuit administrator, a senior civil servant who, with the assistance of courts administrators, runs all the crown courts in the circuit. There are in each circuit, however, two High Court judges, known as presiding judges, who guide circuit administrators on legal matters, on the allocation of cases, and on other administrative matters.

Four types of judges sit in crown courts — High Court judges, circuit judges, recorders and assistant recorders.

Any of the four types of judges has power to deal with civil cases.

High Court judges, for instance, while on circuit frequently hear Queen's Bench Division or Family Division cases, which would otherwise be tried in London.

Similarly, circuit judges, recorders and assistant recorders may try civil cases in the county court (see chapter 10). The Lord Chancellor has power to remove a circuit judge on the grounds of inability or misbehaviour.

## High Court judges

They are referred to in reports as Mr Justice Smith, or Mrs Justice Smith, never Judge Smith. They sit only in the more important centres and only they can try the most serious offences, like murder. Other serious offences such as unlawful killing and rape are also tried by them, unless referred to a circuit judge.

## Circuit judges

Circuit judges are referred to in reports as Judge John Smith or Judge Mary Smith. They must be barristers of at least ten years' standing or be solicitors who have been recorders. There are about 550 circuit judges.

## Recorders and assistant recorders

They are part-time judges. Both must be barristers, or solicitors who have held right of audience at crown court for at least 10 years. Assistant recorders are appointed for short periods, to sit at least 20 days a year. Recorders are appointed for three years, to sit at least 20 days a year, and have usually been assistant recorders. Recorders are usually referred to as the recorder (or assistant recorder) Mr John Smith or Mrs Mary Smith.

An exception to the status of recorder is that the historic title of the Recorder of London has been preserved for one of the full-time judges who sit at the Central Criminal Court.

## Rights of audience

Prosecutions at criminal trials are conducted by barristers, and barristers usually appear for the defence. Experienced solicitors with a record of experience as advocates and who have passed a test may also appear for the defence however.

Additionally, a solicitor may appear for the defence at appeals or committals for sentence at crown court if he or his firm has represented the accused at the lower court (see chapter 1, The legal profession).

## Juries

A jury consists of 12 people aged between 18 and 70 taken from the electoral list. Certain people, including peers, lawyers, MPs, and clergymen, are barred from jury service. There are also disqualifications on those who have been jailed or who are on bail after being charged with a criminal offence. Others like doctors are automatically excused.

Those over 65 are not compelled to serve. A judge may sit in chambers to hear a challenge against any person being on a jury.

Majority verdicts of 11-1 or 10-2 are allowed, but only if the jury has been out at least two hours and ten minutes and has failed to reach a verdict.

If a jury is reduced for any reason, a majority of 10-1 or 9-1 is possible.

A newspaper may report that a defendant has been convicted by a majority of the jury. It is regarded as undesirable, however, to report that a defendant is acquitted by a majority, as this suggests that some members of the jury did think him guilty and leaves a stain on his character even though he has been cleared.

Under section 8 of the Contempt of Court Act 1981, it is contempt of court to seek or disclose information about statements made, opinions expressed, arguments advanced, or votes cast by members of a jury in the course of its deliberations. The Royal Commission on Criminal Justice pointed out in 1993 that even it was barred by section 8 from conducting research into juries' reasons for their verdicts.

The House of Lords held in 1994 that the prohibition applies not just to the jurors themselves but to anyone who publishes the information they reveal. The Lords dismissed an appeal brought by the *Mail on Sunday* against being found guilty of contempt of court after it published interviews with jurors disclosing details of the discussion in the jury retirement room. Lord Lowry said at the Lords hearing that section 8 was aimed at keeping the secrets of the jury room inviolate in the interests of justice. The paper, the editor, and a journalist had been fined a total of £60,000.

Prosecutions under section 8 must be by a crown court or higher court, or be with the consent of the Attorney-General.

It is permissible to publish a juror's views at the end of the case provided they do not refer to statements made, opinions expressed, arguments advanced, or votes cast in the course of the jury's deliberations. This would seem to allow for publication of a juror's account of his general impressions of the case or his ability to follow the evidence. On the other hand some lawyers believe that the naming in a newspaper or broadcast of a juror who has had a part in reaching a verdict could be treated as a contempt of court at common law as this could expose the juror to intimidation or attack. Photographing a juror may also be regarded as a contempt. The danger in identifying jurors would not appear to apply where a juror is discharged in the middle of a case, for example when he is excluded from the jury for failure to attend on time and is then fined.

If the jury returns a not guilty verdict it is final as far as the accused is concerned, although the Court of Appeal can be asked by the Attorney-General to give its opinion on a point of law (see later in this chapter).

Juries are used in civil actions mainly for defamation, false imprisonment, or malicious prosecution. A judge has power, rarely exercised, to allow a jury in other civil actions. Fewer than 12 people may sit on the jury with the consent of the parties in the civil action.

## Preparatory and pre-trial hearings

In advance of a long and complex criminal trial, a judge may order a preparatory hearing to rule on points of law and the admissibility of evidence and to clarify issues to go before the jury. Where a full-scale preparatory hearing is not needed, he may have a pre-trial review to rule on law and the admissibility of evidence.

### Preparatory hearings

Where a preparatory hearing takes place reports must, under the Criminal Procedure and Investigations Act 1996 Act, be restricted to eight points:
(a)  name of the court and the judge;
(b)  names, ages, home addresses, and occupations of accused and witnesses;
(c)  charges or a summary of them;
(d)  names of lawyers;
(e)  date and place to which proceedings are adjourned;
(f)  arrangements as to bail;
(g)  whether legal aid was granted.
    A judge may lift the restrictions but if any accused objects may do so only if he is satisfied that it is in the interests of justice.

### Pre-trial hearings

It is an offence under the 1996 Act to publish a report before the end of the subsequent trial of a ruling, or its variation or discharge, at a pre-trial hearing, unless the judge lifts the restriction. Again, a judge may lift the restriction, but if any of the accused objects may do so only if he is satisfied it is in the interests of justice to do so.
    In both pre-trial hearings and preparatory hearings, the restrictions cease when all the accused have been tried.

## Procedure at trials

A man charged at crown court is said to be arraigned. The counts (charges) on the indictment are read out to him by the clerk of the court and his plea recorded.
    The charges may differ slightly from those on which he was committed by magistrates for trial at crown court, and the reporter should not rely on

cuttings of the earlier report. For instance, the dates between which an offence is alleged to have been committed may be different.

Counsel (a barrister) will appear for the prosecution, and a barrister or a solicitor will conduct the defence.

If the defendant pleads guilty, the prosecution will outline the evidence and his criminal record, and social inquiry reports will be given. The defendant or his lawyer may also be allowed to address the court in mitigation of sentence before it is passed. The court may restrict the reporting of derogatory assertions made during pleas of mitigation (see chapter 4).

The jury take no part, because the guilty plea has dispensed with their function.

If the defendant pleads not guilty, a jury of 12 will be sworn in and the substance of the indictment will be read to them. Counsel for the prosecution will normally 'open the case', outline the evidence, and state the relevant law.

The defence knows beforehand what evidence the prosecution intends to call because it is set out in the documents containing the evidence which were served on the defence at the time the case was committed for trial, or in documents containing any additional evidence. The defence may also be required to disclose information about its case before the trial, to narrow the issues in dispute.

Prosecuting counsel then calls his witnesses, who will be examined by him and cross-examined by the defence.

The defence then begins. Provided the defence lawyer intends calling witnesses on fact (as distinct from character) he has the right to address the jury before his witnesses are called. But if the only witness as to the facts is the accused, the defence may not 'open the defence' before the accused testifies.

After the case for the defence, prosecuting counsel makes his final speech and the defence addresses the jury last.

The judge then sums up the case to the jury. He directs the jury as to the law, but questions of fact are the province of the jury. The judge should, however, if he feels that the evidence is not sufficient to support the charge in law, direct the jury to bring in a verdict of not guilty.

If the jury returns a not guilty verdict, that is usually final as far as the accused is concerned.

However, under the Criminal Procedure and Investigations Act 1996, where a court convicts a person of interference with or intimidation of a juror, witness, or potential witness in a trial at which the accused has been acquitted, application may be made to the High Court for an order quashing the acquittal.

Subject to certain conditions, the accused in this tainted acquittal may then be tried again, thus breaking with the principle that a person acquitted by a jury cannot be tried again for the same offence.

Under the Criminal Justice Act 1972, the Attorney-General can ask the Court of Appeal after an acquittal to give its opinion on a disputed point of law, but under that Act the accused cannot be brought back to court.

The Court of Appeal has power in giving its opinion to ban or restrict disclosure of the identity of the acquitted defendant.

## Defendants' addresses

In 1989 the Lord Chancellor said it was reasonable for a crown court to supply a defendant's address to the press if it was available in the court record. Detailed instructions were sent to crown courts as to how this should be done (see chapter 12).

## Murder charges

The death penalty was abolished in 1965 for murder. Now the only sentence provided by law is one of life imprisonment. In cases where the accused is insane, an order for detention is not technically a sentence.

The judge may recommend a minimum term of the life sentence which the defendant should actually serve. Sometimes he may recommend that it should actually be for life. In practice, each case may be reviewed by the Parole Board, and it is the Home Secretary who has the ultimate power to order release. The Home Secretary must, however, consult the trial judge, if available, and the Lord Chief Justice before releasing a convicted murderer.

In law, death remains the ultimate penalty for treason, although it has not been imposed for many years. The gallows have been retained at one prison, Wandsworth in London, to provide for any contingency.

Sentences of life imprisonment may still be imposed for other offences (eg arson, robbery, rape, buggery with a boy under 16) where there is no statutory penalty limit, and the judge considers life proper.

## Offences against children

A new procedure was introduced under the Criminal Justice Act 1991, for these cases to be transferred to crown court from the magistrates court, by-passing the normal procedure.

Where a person's case is transferred to crown court in this way, he may apply at crown court for the case to be struck out on the grounds of insufficient evidence.

Reports of such applications at crown court are restricted under the 1991 Act. The restrictions are set out in chapter 6.

## Serious fraud charges

Similarly, where a serious complex fraud case has been transferred from magistrates court to crown court without the usual normal procedure, the defendant may apply to crown court for the case to be struck out on the grounds of insufficient evidence.

Where a trial does go ahead at crown court, a judge may, as soon as a plea of not guilty is entered, order a preparatory hearing before the jury is sworn in to clarify the issues to go before them.

There are reporting restrictions on both applications for the case to be struck out and on the preparatory hearings. The crown court may order that these reporting restrictions do not apply if one or more of the accused requests. But if any accused objects to the request by his co-accused, the judge can grant the request only if he feels it is in the interests of justice.

The Criminal Justice Act 1987 says reports of such applications or of preparatory hearings before a judge must be confined to:

(a)  the identity of the court and the name of the judge;
(b)  the names, ages, home addresses, and occupations of the accused and witnesses;
(c)  any relevant business information;
(d)  the offence or offences, or a summary of them, with which the accused is or are charged;
(e)  The names of counsel and solicitors engaged in the proceedings;
(f)  where the proceedings are adjourned, the date and place to which they are adjourned;
(g)  any arrangements as to bail;
(h)  whether legal aid was granted to the accused or any of the accused;
(i)  whether reporting restrictions are lifted.

'Any relevant business information' includes names and addresses of businesses concerned.

All the restrictions cease to apply if all applications for a case to be struck out are granted, or at the end of a trial of all the accused.

These restrictions, like those applying to applications under the Criminal Justice Act 1991 (see chapter 6, Offences against children), do not allow the journalist to report a crown court judge's decision not to allow a case to be struck out.

## Appeals

*To the crown court*

When the crown court is hearing appeals from conviction or sentence (or both) imposed by the magistrates, or is hearing cases sent for sentence by the magistrates, the judge of whatever status must sit with at least two and not more than four magistrates. (Up to four magistrates may sit with judges at trials, but this is not obligatory and here the magistrates' real contribution is in discussing sentence with the judge.)

At appeals and committals for sentence, magistrates are equal members of the court with the professional judges on matters of fact and on deciding sentence, and the judge can be outvoted by his lay colleagues. In matters of law, however, the magistrates must defer to the judge.

An appeal against conviction will take the form of a complete rehearing but there will be no jury. It is for the prosecution to prove afresh the defendant's guilt. The court may confirm, reverse, or vary the magistrates' decision or send the case back to them for a re-trial.

In an appeal against sentence, the crown court may confirm the sentence or substitute a lesser penalty. The crown court may increase the sentence, but not to more than that which the magistrates could have imposed.

A man sent to crown court for sentence who receives more than six months' imprisonment may appeal to the Court of Appeal against the sentence.

### To Queen's Bench Division

A man who has been dealt with by the magistrates or who has appealed unsuccessfully to the crown court may also appeal on a point of law to the Queen's Bench Divisional Court on the grounds that the decision was wrong in law.

This procedure, which is also open to the prosecution, is known as appeal by way of case stated. The magistrates or the crown court will be asked by the appellant to state their findings on fact and the questions of law which arose.

The divisional court can make an order of certiorari (quashing the lower court's decision), of mandamus (directing the lower court, eg to convict or acquit), or of prohibition, forbidding them to hear a charge not known to the law.

A further appeal is possible to the House of Lords. For this to take place, the divisional court must certify that there is a point of law of public importance. In addition, either the divisional court or the House of Lords must grant leave for the appeal as one that ought to be heard by the House.

### To Court of Appeal

Appeals from crown court are heard by the judges of the Queen's Bench Division (although other High Court judges may also sit at the request of the Lord Chief Justice), who share the work of the Court of Appeal with the Lords Justices of Appeal. The Lord Chancellor may also appoint a circuit judge to sit with a High Court judge for a criminal appeal.

The accused man's right of appeal on a point of law from a crown court trial is automatic.

Other appeals by him from a crown court trial require leave of the trial judge or of the Court of Appeal.

The Court of Appeal may, if it allows the appeal, quash his conviction. It may order a new trial at crown court, and this has resulted in at least one case of a man charged with murder being tried twice, and acquitted at the second trial.

The court also has power to substitute a conviction for a different offence. It does not have power to increase the sentence imposed by the crown court, but can order that the time spent in custody awaiting the hearing should not count towards the sentence.

Under the Criminal Justice Act 1988, the Attorney-General may ask the Court of Appeal to review an unduly lenient crown court sentence in a range of serious offences. The Court of Appeal may change the sentence to any other sentence that was within the crown court's power.

## Questions

1   In newspaper reports of a crown court, how would you refer to the various types of judges who may sit there, assuming the name is John Smith or Mary Smith?
2   Outline the three main criminal functions of a crown court. When is a jury required?
3   In what circumstances may magistrates sit at crown court?
4   When should you report that a jury's verdict was by a majority only?
5   May a reporter question a juror on how a jury reached its verdict?
6   What happens at crown court when a man is appealing against conviction by a magistrates court? Is any further appeal possible by the defendant?
7   In what circumstances may the prosecution appeal against the magistrates finding a defendant not guilty?
8   How does the Court of Appeal deal with appeals from crown court? What are its powers?
9   If the prosecution feels that the crown court has misinterpreted the law in hearing an appeal from a magistrates court, what action may be taken?
10  What right of appeal is there against an unduly lenient sentence imposed at crown court?

# 8    Sexual offences and other statutory restrictions

The law gives anonymity to victims of sexual attacks.

This anonymity is enforced through the Sexual Offences (Amendment) Act 1992, which applies to many sexual offences and to an attempt to commit any of them, and through the Sexual Offences (Amendment) Act 1976 (as altered by the Criminal Justice Act 1988) which applies to six offences in which the word 'rape' appears.

Failure to remember that complainants in sexual offences other than rape must also not be identified, either by name or other particulars, has led to a number of newspapers being prosecuted.

## Rape offences

Subject to a number of exceptions which follow, restrictions on identifying the complainant apply under the 1976 Act if the charge is one of the following six offences: rape; attempted rape; aiding, abetting, counselling, or procuring rape or attempted rape; incitement to rape; conspiracy to rape; burglary with intent to rape.

The restrictions on identifying the complainant apply in two stages.

1    Once an allegation of rape has been made either by the victim or some other person, the victim's name, address, and picture must not be published in his or her lifetime if it is likely to identify him or her as a victim of the offence.

2    After a person has been accused of a rape offence *no matter* likely to lead to the victim being identified as a complainant must be published during the victim's lifetime.

The anonymity for the complainant remains in force even if the allegation is later withdrawn or the accused is eventually tried for a lesser offence than rape. It also applies to victims of male rape — a new offence created by the Criminal Justice and Public Order Act 1994.

The restrictions at stage one provide a limited form of anonymity before anyone has been arrested for the offence. This stage does not prohibit all identifying material and enables newspapers to publish, for example, some particulars which may help the police to trace the rapist.

The prohibition on identifying a rape complainant does not apply to all reports of criminal cases. It does apply where the charge is one of the six listed above. But section 1 (4) of the Act says that it does not restrict publication of matter consisting *only of a report of criminal proceedings* where a person is charged with other offences. This overrides the normal anonymity. This was apparently intended to provide for situations where the complainant makes a false accusation of rape and is later tried for wasting police time or perjury, but the Act makes it clear it applies whatever the charge is other than the six noted above.

The anonymity for life does apply to reports of *civil proceedings*, for example a claim for damages for rape or to allegations made at an industrial tribunal (see also the Trade Union Reform and Employment Rights Act 1993 later in this chapter).

A judge at crown court may remove the anonymity if he is satisfied that it imposes a substantial and unreasonable restriction on the reporting of the trial and it is in the public interest to lift it. The judge may also remove the anonymity, on the application of the defence, to bring witnesses forward, where he is satisfied the defence would otherwise be substantially prejudiced or the accused would suffer substantial injustice. In neither case can the power be exercised by magistrates.

In a number of cases, editors have written to the trial judge applying successfully for the judge to use his power (under section 4(2) of the 1976 Act) to lift the restriction on naming a rape complainant because of the difficulty in reporting the case. The approach might be made informally in a note from the reporter to the judge, via the clerk.

Sometimes a newspaper gives certain particulars of a rape victim but withholds others, and in this way intends to protect the victim's anonymity, but another paper gives other particulars and the two stories read together make the victim's identity obvious. The former Press Council urged newspaper editors and broadcasting organisations to co-operate in following the same policy in the reporting of individual rape cases to avoid this patchwork identification. The Press Complaints Commission code of practice says that newspapers should not publish material likely to contribute to identification of victims of sexual assault, unless there is adequate justification and by law they are free to do so. In cases affecting children the code says that the adult should be identified and that care should be taken that nothing in the report implies the relationship between the accused and the child (see chapter 6, Jigsaw identification).

Since the passing of the Criminal Justice Act 1988 there has been no legal anonymity for rape defendants — but publication of the identity of the defendant, combined with other particulars, could lead to the identification of the complainant, as where a husband is accused of raping his wife.

The 1976 Act contains a provision for the complainant to give consent in writing to being identified, provided that no person interfered unreasonably with his or her peace or comfort to obtain that consent.

It is a defence where a person is accused of a breach of these reporting restrictions to prove that the publisher was not aware and had no reason to suspect the publication was in breach of the Act.

## Other sexual offences

The 1992 Act provides a similar two-stage anonymity for complainants in the following offences: intercourse with a mentally handicapped person; indecent conduct towards young children; incitement to commit incest with a granddaughter, daughter, or sister under 16; procurement of a woman by threats or false pretences; administering drugs to obtain intercourse; intercourse with a girl under 13 or between 13 and 16; procurement of a mentally handicapped person; incest by a man or woman; buggery; indecent assault on either man or woman; assault with intent to commit buggery.

A complainant is defined in the 1992 Act as a person against whom the offence is alleged to have been committed and thus the anonymity covers consenting parties, unless they are prosecuted.

The restrictions may be lifted by a magistrate, either at summary trial or where the mode of trial has not yet been decided, or by a judge at crown court, if he is satisfied they impose a substantial and unreasonable restriction on reporting the proceedings. It will usually be up to the press to apply for lifting in this way. As in the 1976 Act, restrictions may be lifted to assist in tracing witnesses for the defence.

The 1992 Act contains a provision like that in the 1976 Act that the restriction does not affect the reporting of criminal proceedings where the charge is not one of those listed in the Act. There is also a similar defence to show that publication of the identity was with the complainant's written consent, and it is a defence to show that the publisher had no reason to suspect that publication identified the victim.

Other principal statutory reporting restrictions.

**1 Criminal Justice Act 1925**, section 41, prohibits the taking of any photograph, or making any portrait or sketch, in court with a view to publication, and prohibits publication of any such photograph, portrait, or sketch. The same section says that this shall apply also to any photograph, etc, taken of any person entering or leaving the court or its precincts. 'Precincts' is not defined in the Act, and this has caused practical difficulties.

Irrespective of the 1925 Act, a judge at crown court or High Court may treat the taking of photographs as contempt of court at common law. In 1988, a Press Association photographer was bound over by a judge at the Old Bailey for trying to take a picture of a murder trial witness as she left court. Later the same year, in the Court of Appeal, the Lord Chief Justice said a defendant, witness, or anyone else with a duty to perform at a criminal or civil court was entitled to go to and from the court, whether on foot or otherwise, without being molested, which could amount to interference with the administration of justice.

Photographing a juror may also be treated as contempt of court, or as the common law offence of embracery — interfering with a juror (see also chapter 7).

Although the 1925 Act makes it an offence for an artist to make in court any sketch for publication, this does not prevent an artist sitting in court and later in the office sketching the scene from memory. In 1987, an editor was fined £500 by a judge at a crown court in South Wales for aiding and abetting an artist to make a sketch in the court itself.

**2   Judicial Proceedings (Regulation of Reports) Act 1926**, section 1(a), prohibits publication in any court report of any indecent medical, surgical, or physiological details which would be calculated to injure public morals and section 1(b) restricts reports of divorce, nullity, and judicial separation actions to four points (see chapter 13).

Publication of details of actual indecencies or perversions could also result in a prosecution, although the mere reporting of a charge is not likely to have this effect.

The test of what would injure public morals in today's climate has yet to be applied.

See also chapter 21, Obscenity.

**3   Children and Young Persons Act 1933**, section 49, says no report of youth court proceedings shall reveal the name, address, school, or any other particulars identifying any person under 18 involved in any way, and says that no photograph of *or including* any such juvenile shall be published.

Section 39 of the Act empowers any adult court in any circumstances to prohibit publication of any picture or other matter leading to the identification of juveniles under 18 involved in any way in proceedings before it (see chapters 6 and 12).

The restriction on identifying juveniles involved in any way in youth court proceedings may be lifted by the court or by the Home Secretary for the purpose of avoiding injustice to that juvenile. A youth court, on application on behalf of the Director of Public Prosecutions, may also lift the restriction to any specified extent where a juvenile is at large after committing a sexual offence or offence of violence.

The Crime (Sentences) Act 1997 also amends the 1933 Act to permit magistrates to make an order lifting the restriction on naming a convicted juvenile where they believe it is in the public interest to do so. Before making such an order they must allow representations from parties to the proceedings.

**4 Wireless Telegraphy Act 1949** prohibits the use without authority of wireless apparatus with intent to obtain information about the contents of any message, and prohibits the disclosure of any such information (for example, police radio messages)(see also chapter 31).

**5 Administration of Justice Act 1960**, section 12, provides that publication of information relating to proceedings before a court sitting in private shall not of itself be a contempt of court, except in wardship, mental health, national security, or secret process cases, or where a court which has the power to do so expressly prohibits publication. It also provides that the publication of the text or a summary of the whole or part of a court order shall not be contempt, in the absence of express prohibition(see chapter 7).

**6 Theft Act 1968**, section 23, makes it an offence to offer a reward for the return of stolen goods, using any words to the effect that no questions will be asked. A newspaper has been fined for printing a news item referring to such an offer.

**7 Domestic and Appellate Proceedings Act 1968** gives courts hearing appeals power to sit in private if the lower court had that power. It also restricts reports of applications for declarations of legitimacy and the like to the four points permitted in divorce hearings (see chapter 13).

**8 Rehabilitation of Offenders Act 1974**, section 8, says any newspaper, etc, when defending a libel action will not be able to rely on the defence of justification if publication of a spent conviction is shown to have been made with malice.

It also says that a newspaper will not be able to rely on privilege to defend a reference in court reports to a spent conviction where the conviction has been ruled to be inadmissible (see chapter 22).

**9 Magistrates courts Act 1980**, section 71, limits newspaper reports of family proceedings to four brief points (see chapter 9).

It says that only officers of the court and parties involved may attend adoption hearings and says that any newspaper report of the hearing (presumably one that is obtained afterwards) must not give the child's name, address, school, photograph, or any particulars leading to his identification.

**10   Contempt of Court Act 1981** modifies some of the common law on contempt, dealing in particular with the starting point for liability and the circumstances in which strict liability for contempt applies to publications (see chapter 17).

**11   Interception of Communications Act 1985** prohibits unauthorised interception of public, postal, and telecommunications systems (see also chapter 31).

**12   Public Order Act 1986** makes it an offence for a person to publish threatening, abusive, or insulting material if he intends to stir up hatred against any group in Great Britain defined by reference to colour, race, nationality, citizenship, or ethnic or national origins, or if it is likely to stir up hatred having regard to all the circumstances (see chapter 25).

**13   Criminal Justice Act 1987** imposes restrictions on reports of serious fraud cases at crown court pre-trial hearings where (a) the defendant is applying for the case to be struck out or (b) the court is sitting to clarify the issues to go before the jury (see chapter 7).

**14   Official Secrets Act 1989** makes it an offence to make an unauthorised disclosure which is, or is likely to be, damaging, of information on security, intelligence, defence, or international relations, or of information entrusted in confidence by Britain to another country or to an international organisation. It makes it an absolute offence to disclose telephone tapping etc which has been authorised by a warrant under the Interception of Communications Act.

It makes it an offence to disclose without authority information obtained from a crown servant (including police and prison officers) or government contractor where such disclosure would, or would be likely to, result in: an offence being committed; escape from custody being facilitated; or the prevention, detection, or prosecution of crime being impeded (see chapter 30).

**15   Children Act 1989** makes it an offence to publish any material intended or likely to identify a child as being involved in family proceedings before a magistrates court, or his address or school, where the court is exercising powers under the Act. It also allows the court to sit in private when exercising such powers (see chapter 6).

**16   Criminal Justice Act 1991** imposes restrictions on reports of pre-trial proceedings at crown court where the accused is charged with a sexual offence or an offence involving violence or cruelty against a child and is applying for the case to be struck out (see chapter 6).

**17   Trade Union Reform and Employment Rights Act 1993** allows an industrial tribunal to make a restricted reporting order preventing the immediate publication of the identity of a person complaining of sexual misconduct or of a person affected by such a complaint. The identity of a person complaining at an industrial tribunal of a sexual offence against him or her is also protected by the Sexual Offences (Amendment) Act 1992 mentioned earlier (see also chapter 16, industrial tribunals).

**18   Disability Discrimination Act 1995** empowers an industrial tribunal to make an order banning immediate identification of any person complaining to the tribunal under the Act, where evidence of a medical or intimate nature which might cause significant embarrassment is likely to be heard (see chapter 16, industrial tribunals).

**19   Criminal Procedure and Investigations Act 1996** allows a court to restrict reporting of derogatory assertions made in pleas of mitigation. Unless the judge permits it, the Act makes it an offence to publish a report of a ruling made at crown court at a pre-trial hearing or to publish more than seven permitted points in a report of a preparatory hearing.

*Note:* The Rehabilitation of Offenders Act contains no sanctions under the criminal law for offending reports. Newspapers contravening any of the other Acts above, other than the Contempt Act itself, are usually prosecuted under the terms and penalties laid down in the Act concerned, rather than for contempt of court.

However a judge who has made an order restricting reporting may use his inherent powers to treat defiance of the order as a contempt. In January 1997 a judge at Newcastle Crown Court fined Channel 3 Television (formerly Tyne-Tees) £10,000 for contempt after a news broadcast had quoted prosecuting counsel's statement that a man accused of indecently assaulting a boy was a neighbour. Channel 3 had not disclosed the street in which the accused lived, but newspapers had published his address. At the start of the trial the judge had made an order under section 39 of the Children and Young Persons Act 1933 prohibiting publication of anything leading to identification of the boy.

If the matter had been dealt with as a breach of the 1933 Act, the maximum fine would have been £5,000. The company later lodged an appeal against the fine.

A person who believes he has been injured by a contravention of one of these Acts restricting reporting may be able to sue in the civil courts. In 1994 a rape victim won £10,000 damages from a free newspaper that gave sufficient details about her to enable her to be identified. In doing so, the

paper was liable for the tort of breach of statutory duty. The paper had not
been prosecuted under the Sexual Offences (Amendment) Act 1976 (see
also chapter 31, Privacy).

## Questions

1   In what circumstances may the complainant be named in a rape case?
2   To what charges does the Sexual Offences (Amendment) Act 1976
    apply?
3   How does the Sexual Offences (Amendment) Act 1992 protect the
    identity of people concerned in sexual offences other than rape?
4   In what way does the Criminal Justice Act 1925 prohibit photography
    in and around a court?
5   How does the law prevent journalists from listening to police,
    ambulance, and fire brigade radio systems?

# 9   Magistrates courts: civil functions

## Family proceedings

Family proceedings before magistrates courts were constituted in 1991 under the Children Act 1989.

Family proceedings replace the old domestic courts dealing with husband and wife disputes and hear applications for maintenance orders, separation orders, adoption orders, and affiliation orders (for the maintenance of an illegitimate child). They also deal with the custody and upbringing of children (care cases), which formerly came before the juvenile court.

Under section 71 of the Magistrates courts Act 1980 reports must be confined to:
(a)  names, addresses, and occupations of parties and witnesses;
(b)  the grounds of the application and a concise statement of charges;
(c)  submissions on any point of law arising in the proceedings and the decision of the court on the submissions; and
(d)  the decision of the court and any observations made by the court in giving it.

Additionally, under the Children Act, no particulars must be published that would lead to the identification of a child under 18 involved in proceedings under that Act, or his school (see chapter 6). The combined effect of the two Acts is that very little information, and no identification of the child, can be published if proceedings under the Children Act take place.

Family proceedings are not open to the public. Representatives of newspapers and news agencies may attend under section 69 of the 1980 Act but the court can exclude them, under magistrates court rules, when exercising powers under the Children Act in relation to a child. A consultation paper reviewing access to and reporting of family proceedings, prepared for the Lord Chancellor's Department, said in 1993 that it seemed as if magistrates must make a specific decision as to the interests of the particular child and not simply rely on a general policy of excluding the press. Magistrates also have power under section 69 of the Magistrates courts Act 1980 to exclude the press during the taking of indecent evidence. Magistrates must exclude the press when dealing with adoption cases (see chapters 6 and 11).

What is meant in (b) above by 'grounds of the application and a concise statement of the charges' has never been tested in court, so far as is known, but opinion is usually that one may report one sentence stating, for example, that the wife made the application on the grounds of the husband's adultery at a hotel in Majorca in July and that the husband denied this and alleged that his wife had committed adultery with an unknown man in Batley in March.

The broad rule is that evidence and lawyers' speeches may not be reported, and that summaries of the accusations, defences, and counter-accusations must be concise and fair.

Although one can report anything in (d) above said by the chairman of the bench in announcing the court's decision, other remarks made by him in the course of the proceedings are not reportable.

Often during family proceedings, magistrates will take cases of arrears of payment of maintenance by a husband or will deal with the method of payment.

On their own, these cases can be reported without restriction, since a man may be sent to prison for his failure to pay.

But sometimes these cases are heard together with cross-summonses to revoke the original order on the grounds, for example, that the wife is living with another man. If this happens the whole hearing is subject to the reporting restrictions.

Applications for the variation, discharge, or temporary suspension of a maintenance order are also subject to the reporting restrictions, and where the application could be heard in private, any appeal may also be heard in private.

A maintenance order is an order to make payments to a wife and/or family. Such an order can also be made against a wife who, in certain circumstances, can be ordered to make payments to her husband if he is incapable of work, or cannot find work.

A separation order, which may or may not be made at the same time, is merely an order that the people are no longer bound to cohabit.

Consent to marry applications (by young people aged 16 or 17), now rarely heard, are treated as family proceedings and are subject to the same restrictions. They may be taken in private, and usually are.

Permission to marry may also be sought from a High Court judge or a county court district judge, both in chambers.

## Licensing justices

Another function of magistrates is to exercise control over hotels, public houses, off-licences, dance halls, betting shops, etc.

These matters are dealt with by the licensing committee or by the betting licensing committee.

The licensing committee meets annually to review the conduct of licensees and these meetings are known as brewster sessions. The committee may renew, renew for only a short time, or refuse to renew any licence for any person or premises after hearing any objections by the police and other interested parties.

Objections may be made because of the conduct of a licensee or because the police maintain the premises are unsuitable.

At the brewster sessions, an annual licensing report is presented, usually by a senior police officer. This deals with public houses, etc, and with the total number of offences of drunkenness, drinking under age, and driving with excess of alcohol that have occurred during the previous 12 months.

The licensing committee must also approve the granting of new licences before any public house or off-licence is allowed to open and may hear opposition from residents, other licensees, temperance organisations, and others.

## Questions

1 What restrictions apply to reports of magistrates family proceedings?
2 What other restrictions apply when the family proceedings are exercising powers under the Children Act?
3 What are brewster sessions?

# 10  The civil courts

As we have seen, criminal law is concerned with offences that are deemed to harm the whole community, while civil law deals with the resolution of private disputes and the redress of private wrongs.

Most civil litigation is decided in the county courts and the High Court of Justice, although magistrates courts do have some civil functions and a few civil cases are heard at crown courts as branches of the High Court.

The mass of civil litigation is concerned with breaches of contract, including the recovery of debts; torts – that is, civil wrongs for which monetary damages are recoverable, such as negligence, trespass, and defamation; property matters, such as bankruptcy, the winding up of companies, and the administration of estates; and family proceedings, such as separation and divorce and associated disputes over matrimonial assets and over contact with the children of divorced or separated parents, and their place of residence.

## County courts

County courts were originally intended to provide an inexpensive court for the trial of the small, everyday kind of civil disputes in which the ordinary person is likely to get involved. Nowadays they have virtually unlimited common law jurisdiction and can be regarded as the normal civil court, the High Court being used increasingly for more specialised cases.

County courts have nothing specifically to do with counties. There are some 250 of them situated so as to be convenient to the centres of population they are intended to serve.

The courts are organised into groups consisting of one or more courts, depending on the amount of work to be done. In some courts where sessions are virtually continuous there may be two or more senior judges known as circuit judges; in other groups the circuit judges may travel between several towns.

Circuit judges may also sit in the crown court to deal with criminal cases. They are referred to the first time in copy as Judge John Smith or Judge Mary Smith, and later as Judge Smith or the judge.

Each court has one or more district judges, who are appointed from among practising solicitors and barristers. They deal in open court with many of the smaller cases and actions for possession of land. They also deal in chambers (privately in their own rooms) with arbitrations (informal settlement of disputes), many family disputes, insolvency matters, and many routine matters.

They are referred to the first time in copy as District Judge John Smith or District Judge Mary Smith and later as Judge Smith or the judge.

Rules of procedure in county court trials are a little less strict than in the High Court and the cost of litigation is also less.

The jurisdiction of the judge covers almost the whole field of civil affairs, though there are certain excepted matters. Even so, the county court can hear any case remitted to it by the High Court. Circuit judges also hear actions for divorce that have not been previously disposed of by the district judge (see chapter 13).

County courts hear actions concerning contract and tort, whatever the amount claimed, and trust and property cases where the property value does not exceed £30,000. Trust actions in which more is at stake have to be begun in the High Court. Personal injury actions where the amount claimed is less than £50,000 must all be begun and will normally be heard in the county court.

Many county court cases are landlord and tenant matters; many others concern debt. But the courts also deal with complaints of racial or sexual discrimination, dissolution of partnerships, actions for work done, cases of negligence, recovery of land and questions of title, bankruptcies and winding up of companies, and guardianship and adoption proceedings.

Proceedings in the county court are begun by the issue of a summons. This is a document issued by the court and served on the defendant, warning him that unless he files a defence within 14 days, judgment may be entered against him in default.

The summons is usually prepared by the court but is accompanied by, or may incorporate, particulars of the claim, prepared by the plaintiff (the person beginning the action) which sets out the facts on which he relies to recover damages or some other remedy from the defendant.The vast majority of actions, other than those seeking possession of land, go no further because the defendant does not file any defence. Judgment is entered (the plaintiff is declared to have made out his case), though there may need to be further court hearings over how any judgment is to be paid. Occasionally there may need to be a hearing to assess damages.

If a defence is filed, the next steps depend on the nature and amount of the claim. If the claim is for less than £3,000 it will normally be referred automatically to arbitration and the case will be dealt with by the district judge, generally sitting in private. (The exceptions are claims for possession or for damages for personal injury exceeding £1,000.) This procedure is often referred to as 'the small claims court'. The district judge can allow people other than the parties to attend, but this seldom happens.

Cases where the sum claimed exceeds £3,000 may be dealt with by arbitration if the parties agree or the district judge so orders.

Both circuit judges and district judges can hear cases by arbitration, but the district judge conducts most such cases.

In most county courts, procedure at arbitration is informal and the circuit judge or district judge has greater freedom than in a trial to try to discover the truth by calling for additional evidence.

Some cases, including, in particular, claims for possession of land, have a hearing date fixed at the time the summons is issued and the case is generally dealt with on that day, but more complex cases may have to be adjourned.

In some actions the district judge holds a pre-trial review at which he gives directions telling the parties the main steps to be taken before the case is set down for hearing. In certain circumstances he may be able to give judgment at the pre-trial review. In any case not exceeding £3,000 a plaintiff can make an application for summary judgment; this application will be heard by the district judge in chambers and judgment can be given if the judge is satisfied there is no genuine defence to the action.

In most cases where more than £3,000 is claimed the court issues automatic directions, so avoiding the need for a pre-trial review.

Most cases are not heard in court because there is no defence, as stated above, or because they are disposed of at an early stage. Many more are settled by agreement between the parties.

Where a hearing is to take place, a date is generally fixed on the application of one or other party. However, courts are tending to take a more active role to prevent delays. Actions are struck out if a date is not sought within 15 months and 14 days (15 months and 28 days if there is a counter-claim by the defendant) of a defence being filed.

Generally speaking, arbitrations are heard within about three months of proceedings being begun but trials can be delayed for much longer, primarily because one or both parties are not ready.

If a party wishes to be legally represented he may engage a lawyer; or, by leave of the court, some other person can assist a litigant who is conducting his own case in person. The detailed procedure at the trial is the same as in the High Court (see next section).

At the end of the evidence and after the advocates' speeches, the judge sets out the facts of the case as he finds them, deals with the law, and gives judgment.

Although there is machinery for trial by jury, such an event is extremely rare. A party has a right to trial by jury where there is an allegation of fraud, of false imprisonment, or of malicious prosecution, or where the High Court has sent a defamation case to the county court.

The judge, however, replaces the jury in a very real sense, for in many actions his findings of fact are final. Appeal is possible in certain circumstances.

In all cases, there is a right of appeal from the circuit judge on questions of law. Such appeals go to the Court of Appeal. The appellant must state in his notice of appeal the grounds on which he seeks a review of the judge's decision, and his arguments must be confined to points raised in the county court. Appeals from the district judge go to the circuit judge.

Generally, trials in the county court are in public and the press has a right to be present. However, the judge may direct that a case, or part of a case, shall be heard privately if publicity would prevent justice being done (see next chapter).

By statute, certain matters must or should normally be heard in private: these include applications to adopt children, most family disputes, domestic violence injunctions, and applications for possession of mortgaged houses. The judge is given discretion under the county court rules to hear certain other matters in chambers. He may sit 'in court as chambers', in which case the proceedings are equally private.

Even if the reporter is aware of details of proceedings in chambers, through contact with interested parties, it is unwise to publish without consideration of whether this could constitute contempt (see chapter 17).

The district judge, subject to certain safeguards, hears possession actions and cases in which the amount in dispute does not exceed £5,000. He may deal with actions in which the defendant does not appear or admits the claim; and other actions by leave of the judge and with the consent of the parties.

The district judge deals with the bulk of bankruptcy matters; and he also acts as 'taxing master' for the assessment of the costs that the loser of an action must pay to the winner. 'Taxation of costs' is the examination of costs lawfully chargeable to the unsuccessful party in a legal action to ensure that they are not excessive.

## The High Court

The High Court of Justice sits at the Royal Courts of Justice, in London, and in certain large centres of population throughout England and Wales.

The court has three divisions, the Queen's Bench Division, the Chancery Division, and the Family Division.

The Queen's Bench Division has jurisdiction over most types of civil action, but is especially concerned with cases of contract and tort.

As we have seen, it is the divisional court of the Queen's Bench Division that hears appeals on points of law from magistrates courts and from the appellate jurisdiction of the crown courts (see chapter 7). High Court judges normally sit singly to try cases, but a *divisional* court consists of two or, occasionally, three judges.

The divisional court also has a supervisory jurisdiction over inferior courts and by the process of judicial review can order bodies and individuals to perform their public duties. It hears contempt of court cases brought against newspapers by the Attorney-General.

The division also includes the Commercial Court and the Official Referees' Court. The former, as the name suggests, deals with major commercial disputes. There are also a number of commercial and mercantile courts sitting permanently in the provinces and a Business List at the Central London County Court.

The Official Referees' Court deals primarily with building disputes, cases relating to professional negligence, and similar technical matters. The main court is in London, but circuit judges are appointed to act as official referees in major provincial centres.

The work of the Chancery Division includes the administration of estates, trusts, patents and copyrights, company matters, some tax cases, partnerships, and mortgages. The division also deals with probate business, such as a dispute as to the meaning of a will or the legality of a bequest.

The Family Division hears cases concerning matrimonial business. It is responsible for wardship (that is, declaring a minor a ward of court), guardianship, and adoption cases.

The procedure described below is that followed in a civil claim in the Queen's Bench Division. There are differences in Chancery, and more particularly in Family Division procedures.

A High Court action is started by the issue of a writ (or, when the issues concern law rather than fact, an originating summons) in the High Court setting out the nature of the plaintiff's claim and the relief or remedy sought. The writ or summons is served on the defendant. It may be accompanied by a statement of claim, or this may be delivered later.

The defendant replies by filing an acknowledgment of service, indicating whether or not he wishes to defend. If he intends to dispute the claim he does so by going on to file a defence. These are the main documents that form the pleadings.

The object of pleadings is to set forth the real issues between the parties and to confine them within these limits. Anything not contained in the pleadings will not be adjudicated upon, although the judge will consider applications by counsel to amend or extend pleadings during the trial.

Pleadings are usually made available to the press for the purpose of ascertaining names, ages, addresses, etc. But they are not covered by privilege. Any other information taken from them must be treated with extreme care, especially when the case is settled and no details are announced in court. Settlement of a case – for instance the award of agreed damages in a personal injury claim – does not imply acceptance of liability by the defendant.

The master, or district judge, has power to transfer any action (other than a few chancery proceedings) to a county court.

If the case is set down for trial in the High Court it will in due course appear in the list of cases for trial.

The case on each side is prepared by a solicitor, who eventually briefs counsel to present it in court unless the solicitor has the right of audience (see chapter 1, The legal profession).

A brief consists of a file of documents comprising the solicitor's narrative of the case and copies of all the documents, such as pleadings, the written exhibits material to the case, and the full statements of witnesses.

In most cases, there will be no jury. The only civil cases now heard by juries are libel, slander, wrongful arrest, and malicious prosecution.

The plaintiff's advocate opens the case by giving an account of the facts and of the documents relied on, and his view of the relevant law. He then calls his witnesses and examines them by asking questions. They may then be cross-examined by the defendant's advocate.

If the defendant is going to call witnesses, the case for the defendant may be opened similarly, although it is more common for the defence to call witnesses without formally opening the case. After the witnesses have been called, the defence advocate summarises the evidence and presents his arguments. The plaintiff's advocate then has the last word.

Should the defendant not propose to call witnesses, the plaintiff's advocate will make his final speech after calling his witnesses. The defendant's advocate will then comment on the evidence for the plaintiff. He has the last word except that the plaintiff's advocate has a right of reply on any new legal points raised by the defence.

If there is no jury, the judge then delivers judgment, giving his decision and the grounds on which it is based. In more difficult cases he may reserve judgment so that he can ponder on his notes and consult the law books. He will then write out his judgment, referred to as a 'reserved judgment'. He may then, at his discretion, read it out in court at a later date announced in the High Court's Cause List, or he may have the judgment typed and 'handed down' at a similarly convened court hearing. The latter course has been increasingly adopted – mainly in the Court of Appeal, Civil Division, at the behest of the Master of the Rolls – to speed up justice and help to work off a backlog of cases. Accredited court reporters as well as lawyers are usually provided with a copy of the judgments.

If there is a jury, the judge will sum up after the advocates have made their final addresses. In some cases he may ask them for a general verdict, but in the more complicated cases he will put a series of questions to them. Finally, the judge gives judgment (simply recording the verdict) and makes an appropriate order as to costs.

## Court of Appeal

The Court of Appeal, Civil Division, hears appeals from the county courts, the High Court, and the Employment Appeal Tribunal. The court, together with the High Court and the crown court is known as the Supreme Court.

Appeals are usually heard by three judges, though two will suffice with the consent of the parties, and certain applications are heard by the Registrar of the Court of Appeal or a single judge.

The decision of the court is by a majority of the bench. Each member may express a view. A newspaper can make itself look foolish if it gives great prominence to the outspoken views of one judge without pointing out that these views were overruled by a majority of his colleagues. A 2:1 majority of the court is binding unless overturned by the House of Lords.

## House of Lords

The final court of appeal in the United Kingdom for civil cases is the House of Lords, the official title of which is the House of Lords Appellate Committee.

The court is not a sitting of the full House of Lords. Appeals are heard by five law lords (Lords of Appeal), paid professional judges holding life peerages. The Lord Chancellor presides in some cases. Peers who have held judicial office (including former Lord Chancellors) are entitled to sit in this court. Majority decisions of four to one or even three to two are binding. There is no further appeal in England and Wales.

## European Court of Justice

The European Court of Justice is part of the European Community. It adjudicates upon the law of the Community, and its rulings are binding on British courts. It sits in Luxembourg. See chapter 1, Sources of law.

## European Court of Human Rights

The European Court of Human Rights is part of the Council of Europe. It investigates breaches of the European Convention on Human Rights (see chapter 1). Its judgment is final, but is not binding on United Kingdom courts. It sits in Strasbourg. See chapter 1, Sources of law.

## Questions

1 What work do county courts do?
2 What is the function of the district judge?
3 Describe the procedure for hearing an action in the High Court.
4 What are the divisions of the High Court, and what does each division do?
5 You are an evening paper reporter attending a Court of Appeal case in which judgment is now being given. The first judge to speak gives a very outspoken judgment. What danger should you bear in mind when deciding whether to phone a story through at this stage?

# 11 Admission to the courts and access to court information

Some courts seek improperly to exclude public and press when in fact the law does not permit them to do so.

As long ago as 1913, the House of Lords in *Scott v Scott* affirmed the general principle that courts must administer justice in public.

Only if the administration of justice would be made impracticable by the presence of the public was their exclusion justified, it was ruled.

It was held by the Lords that considerations of public decency or private embarrassment are not sufficient to justify the exclusion of the public.

Today, more than ever, it is important that attempts to negate the open justice principle should be challenged in the public interest (see next chapter).

The reporter who finds himself excluded from court should ascertain under what powers the exclusion is taking place. He should tell his editor if he thinks he is being excluded illegally.

The powers that the courts do have to sit in private in certain circumstances are limited. They can arise in two ways — at common law or by Act of Parliament.

The common law principle of open justice has been reiterated by the courts many times.

In 1983 magistrates in Surrey were persuaded to exclude press and public to hear pleas in mitigation made on behalf of a defendant who had given assistance to the police.

Subsequently, the magistrates were strongly criticised in the Queen's Bench Divisional Court. Lord Justice Ackner said hearing a matter *in camera* was a course of last resort to be adopted only if the proceedings in open court would frustrate the process of justice (*R v Reigate Justices, ex p Argus Newspapers* [1983] 5 Cr App R CS, 101, CA).

In another case, in 1987 Malvern magistrates excluded press and public during pleas in mitigation on behalf of a woman who admitted driving with excess alcohol. The divisional court later held that although magistrates were entitled to use their discretion to sit *in camera*, it was undesirable that magistrates should do so unless there were rare compelling reasons (*R v Malvern Justices, ex p Evans* [1988] 1 All ER 371, QBD).

It is generally held that exclusion of the press and public at common law extends only to (1) where their presence would defeat the ends of justice, for example, where a woman or child cannot be persuaded to give evidence of intimate sexual matters in the presence of many strangers; (2) where a secret process is the subject of evidence and publicity would defeat the purpose of the litigation; (3) matters affecting children, for example, wardship and guardianship cases; (4) where the security of the state demands it; (5) lunacy cases.

In certain cases there is specific provision in an Act of Parliament to sit in private.

If the public are lawfully excluded, does it follow that the press must go too? The question was considered in the Court of Appeal in November 1989 in a case brought by journalist Tim Crook (see next chapter).

Crook's counsel said that even if the public were excluded while a judge received information on a procedural matter the press could have been allowed to remain and publication of reports postponed by an order under section 4 of the Contempt of Court Act 1981 (see chapter 17).

Lord Lane, Lord Chief Justice, said it would not be right generally to distinguish between excluding the press and the public. There might be cases however during which the press should not be excluded with the other members of the public, such as a prosecution for importing an indecent film, where the film was shown to the jury and some members of the public might gasp or giggle and make the jury's task more difficult.

## Magistrates courts

Section 121 of the Magistrates' Courts Act 1980 stipulates that magistrates must sit in open court when trying a case or imposing prison sentences in default of payment of fines etc. The only exceptions to this by statute are mentioned below. Where a juvenile is a witness in a case involving indecency, any court can exclude the public under section 37 of the Children and Young Persons Act 1933. The section goes on to say however: 'Nothing in this section shall authorise the exclusion of bona fide representatives of a newspaper or news agency.'

## Magistrates court information

The Queen's Bench Divisional Court held in 1987 that the names of magistrates dealing with a case must be made known to press and public.

Lord Justice Watkins said any attempt to preserve anonymity was inimical to the proper administration of justice (*R v Felixstowe Justices, ex p Leigh* [1987] QB 582).

The Divisional Court held in the following year that a defendant's address should normally be stated in court. A newspaper company successfully brought an action for judicial review against the magistrates' decision to allow a defendant to conceal his address because he feared harassment from his ex-wife. Lord Justice Watkins said: 'While no statutory provision lays down that a defendant's address has publicly to be given in court, it is well established practice that, save for a justifiable reason, it must be' (*R v Evesham Justices, ex p McDonagh* [1988] 2 WLR 227).

Additionally, two Circulars from the Home Office, which formerly had oversight of magistrates courts, urged in 1967 and 1989 that names, addresses, charges, and occupations should be made available to the press (see chapter 4 and chapter 12,'Section 11 orders').

## Warrant for further detention

Where police wish to continue to detain a suspect before charging him, their application must, under section 45 of the Police and Criminal Evidence Act 1984, be heard by at least two magistrates not sitting in open court (see chapter 2).

## Youth courts

Only certain persons have the right by law to be present. Among them are bona fide representatives of newspapers and news agencies (section 47, Children and Young Persons Act 1933).

## Family proceedings in magistrates courts

Representatives of newspapers and news agencies may attend under section 69 of the Magistrates' Courts Act 1980. However, magistrates courts rules, made under the Children Act 1989, allow magistrates to sit in private when exercising powers under the Children Act in relation to a child under 18. Section 69 of the 1980 Act also allows for the exclusion of the press from family proceedings during the taking of indecent evidence, in the interests of the administration of justice or of public decency.

## County courts

The county court rules provide that evidence should normally be given orally and in open court and the press has a right to be present. By statute, certain matters must usually be heard in private. These include applications to adopt children, consent to marry applications, most family disputes (see High Court, later this chapter), and applications under the Domestic Violence and Matrimonial Proceedings Act 1976, or under the Mental Health Act 1983. Applications for possession of mortgaged houses must also be heard in chambers unless the judge otherwise directs.

The judge is given discretion under county court rules to hear some other matters in chambers. Applications for injunctions (other than a domestic violence injunction) heard where the person against whom the injunction is sought is represented must be heard in open court. Applications which are made ex parte (in the absence of the person against whom the application is sought) are heard in private.

District judges (formerly known as county court registrars) deal in open court with many of the smaller cases and often with actions for possession of land, not involving mortgaged houses.

They also deal in chambers with arbitration, many family disputes and routine matters. When dealing with arbitration, they can give leave for other people to attend, although this is exceptional.

Other matters dealt with in chambers are pre-trial reviews and interlocutory applications.

Court lists are available for inspection but these do little more than name the parties although they may indicate the nature of the action.

Each court keeps records of proceedings, including the name and address of the defendant, the nature and amount of the claim, and concise minutes of the proceedings, including a note of any judgment, order, or decree. There is no public right of access to the records.

A public register, under the control of the Lord Chancellor's Department, of names, occupations, and addresses of defendants, and amounts in all outstanding county court judgments except for money judgments made in family proceedings, can be inspected on payment (of £4.50 each judgment at the time of going to press) at Registry Trust Ltd, 173/175 Cleveland Street, London, W1P 5PE.

Orders made in bankruptcy and winding-up proceedings are open to public inspection at the court where made (Insolvency Rules 1986 (SI 1986 No 1925) rule 7.27, 7.28).

## High Court

The High Court must, in general, do its work in public but all divisions of the court are entitled to hear some matters in chambers. In these cases, the judge has discretion to give judgment in open court.

Under the Family Proceedings Rules 1991, child cases involving wardship, residence, or contact orders in the High Court or county court must be heard in chambers unless the court otherwise directs. Lady Butler-Sloss said in the Court of Appeal in 1996 that the effect of this was that the courts were bound to hear child cases generally in private. Where issues of public interest arose however it seemed entirely appropriate to give judgment in open court provided, where desirable in the interest of the child, directions were given to avoid identification (*Re P-B (a minor)* [1997] 1 All ER 58).

Any person, on payment of a fee, may inspect and copy at the central office or at a district registry of the High Court the copy of any writ of summons, or other originating process, any judgment or order of the court and, with the leave of the court if there are very cogent reasons, any other document (Rules of the Supreme Court, Order 63, rule 4). In a case transferred to the High Court from the county court, only the summons is open to inspection. There is no right of access to other pleadings or affidavits or judgments and orders given or made in chambers. Obtaining access to court documents by deceit or trickery may be treated as contempt.

## Evidence by written statements

A practice direction in October 1992 dealt with the availability of written statements submitted in place of oral evidence in the Queen's Bench Division.

The direction, issued by a senior master, stipulated that where written statements are to be given the status of evidence in the witness box, the judge can be asked to make those statements available for inspection and to give consent for copies of such statements to be made available.

## Injunctions

Applications for injunctions are heard in chambers (with press and public excluded) in the Queen's Bench Division but are usually heard in open court in the Chancery Division.

In addition, masters and district judges of the High Court deal with many applications and summonses in the course of proceedings in chambers, as in the county court.

In the Family Division chambers hearings are the rule and open court hearings the exception. Most divorce matters are heard privately. In the Queen's Bench Division, interlocutory matters tend to be heard in chambers, but in the Chancery Division they are heard in public.

The Court of Appeal rarely sits *in camera*. When it does so, it is in accordance with *Scott v Scott*, mentioned earlier.

## Divorce

Under rule 48 of the Matrimonial Causes Rules 1977, any person may, within 14 days of a decree nisi being pronounced, inspect the certificate and any affidavit and corroborative evidence filed in support of the petition. Copies may be obtained within 14 days on payment of a fee.

A direction of the senior registrar dated 21 June 1972, says: 'If a matrimonial case is reported it is essential that names and addresses should be reported accurately. In many cases this is not possible unless the associate or court clerk co-operates with the reporter to the extent of confirming the details from the court file.' The direction said the same applied to other matters which were of public record and not confidential, such as the date and place of marriage, the order made by the court and, in the case of divisional court appeals, details of the order appealed from. Though pleadings and other documents should not be shown to reporters, there was no objection to the details referred to being given to them on request.

## Official Secrets Act

The public and press may be excluded when evidence would be prejudicial to national security (section 8, Official Secrets Act 1920).

## Inquests

Rule 17 of the Coroners Rules states that every inquest shall be held in public save that an inquest or part of an inquest may be held *in camera* in the interests of national security.

However, rule 37 allows a coroner to take documentary evidence from any witness where such evidence is likely to be undisputed. It states that the coroner must announce publicly at the inquest the name of the person giving documentary evidence and must read aloud such evidence unless he otherwise directs (see chapter 15).

## Industrial tribunals

Under rule 7 of the Industrial Tribunals (Rules of Procedure) Regulations 1985, an industrial tribunal may sit in private for hearing evidence where it would be against the interests of national security to allow the evidence to be heard in public, or for hearing evidence which in the opinion of the tribunal is likely to consist of (a) information which a witness could not disclose without contravening a prohibition imposed under any Act of

Parliament; (b) information communicated to a witness in confidence or obtained in consequence of the confidence placed in him by another person; (c) information the disclosure of which would cause substantial injury to any undertaking of the witness, or any undertaking in which he works, for reasons other than its effect on negotiations over pay and conditions.

In February 1995, the Queen's Bench Divisional Court held that the decision of an industrial tribunal at Southampton to exclude press and public from hearing salacious or sensitive evidence in a sexual harassment case was unlawful. Mr Justice Brooke said under the rules of procedure tribunal hearings must be in public except in limited circumstances which did not apply in this case.

## Questions

1   On what grounds may press and public be excluded, at common law, from the courts?
2   What does the Magistrates' Courts Act 1980 stipulate about the admission of press and public to summary proceedings?
3   How do the Magistrates' Courts Act 1980 and the Children Act 1989 deal with the right of reporters to attend family proceedings at magistrates' courts?
4   What right has:
    (a)  the public,
    (b)  the press
    to attend youth courts?
5   What provision does the law make for inquests to be held in public? On what grounds may an inquest be held *in camera*?

# 12 Challenging the courts

Court reporters today can sometimes encounter difficulties in their task that did not exist until a few years ago.

In some towns, courts have failed to provide the co-operation needed to ensure that their proceedings are reported properly. Reporters have had difficulty obtaining names and addresses of defendants and courts have made dubious orders in attempts to suppress the publication of such names or addresses.

The High Court has re-emphasised that it is important that the administration of justice should be subject to the spotlight of public scrutiny through reporting of proceedings in the press.

Senior judges, the Home Office, and the Lord Chancellor's Department have urged that defendants' addresses should be easily available.

However, editors and their staffs have often had to challenge orders made by the court suppressing names of defendants and witnesses and other matters.

Often, these orders have seemed contrary to the principle of open justice. Sometimes magistrates also purport to make orders under Acts of Parliament which give them no such power.

Even High Court judges have been known to err in their interpretation of the law affecting reporting.

## What the newspaper can do

This book attempts in various chapters to assess the limits of the courts' power to restrict reporting. Court reporters should know these limits well enough in most cases to recognise where the court has made an order of dubious legality.

## Informal approach

In some cases, all that is needed is for the reporter to make an informal request asking the court to state under which section of which Act the order has been made, and the court will reconsider the matter.

On other occasions, the editor or news editor may have to write to the clerk or to the justices or the judge to achieve the desired result. Details are given in the following pages of High Court decisions on reporting restrictions and where possible case references are provided so that these can be drawn to the attention of the court.

## Judicial review

If these approaches fail, a newspaper can itself initiate proceedings to challenge a court decision, although this can be costly.

Magistrates court orders, especially those made under sections 4 or 11 of the Contempt of Court Act 1981, have been challenged successfully in the Queen's Bench Divisional Court, which has power of judicial review over the actions of all inferior courts.

## Section 159 appeal

Until 1989, orders made by crown courts to restrict reporting could not be challenged in a higher court.

Section 159 of the Criminal Justice Act 1988 provides a right of appeal to the Court of Appeal against a judge's decision to grant or refuse an application either to exclude the press and public at any time or to restrict reporting of a trial on indictment of any related ancillary proceedings.

'Any person aggrieved' (which includes newspapers) may appeal against an order made by a crown court judge:
(a)  under sections 4 or 11 of the Contempt of Court Act 1981;
(b)  restricting admission of the public to the proceedings or any part of the proceedings (*in camera* orders);
(c)  restricting the reporting of the proceedings or part of the proceedings (eg orders under section 39 of the Children and Young Persons Act 1933).

Earlier, after an approach by Tim Crook, a journalist, and others, the European Commission on Human Rights had expressed the view that the lack of a method of appeal against a judge's secrecy order was a potential breach of human rights.

When section 159 came into force, however, it became apparent that it was not as big a step forward towards a more open system of justice as had been thought. The rules of procedure restrict the scope of any appeal.

Any challenge to a judge's ban on reporting must be by way of written representation. The press has no right to appear and argue its case. Leave to make the appeal must first be given by a single judge. The Queen's Bench Divisional Court held in 1993 that leave to appeal or the appeal itself would be decided by the Court of Appeal without a hearing.

The rules give the court, in these appeals, power to restrict the identification of a witness or any other person.

Another drawback is that by the time the Court of Appeal reaches its decision the trial may have finished, although the court does have the power to stop the trial until the appeal is decided. Even if the appeal is successful the newspaper will no longer get its costs. Formerly the Court of Appeal or the Queen's Bench Divisional Court had discretionary power to award costs out of central funds to successful appellants. In 1993 however the House of Lords ruled that there must be specific authority by Act of Parliament; discretionary powers were insufficient.

When the Queen's Bench Divisional Court held in 1995 in the course of judicial review that an industrial tribunal at Southampton had exceeded its powers in excluding reporters from a sexual harassment case, the INS agency and Express Newspapers, who had brought the case, were not awarded their costs, estimated at £10,000 (see chapter 11).

## Invalid orders

Section 4 of the Contempt of Court Act 1981 allows courts to order the postponement of reports if this is necessary to avoid the substantial risk of prejudice. The High Court has emphasised that the risk must be substantial to justify an order being made (see below). Section 11 gives power to the courts, when they withhold a name or other matter from being mentioned in public in their proceedings, to direct that the name or other matter should not be published. (See chapter 17, where the sections are explained, and the full wording of section 4 given.)

There has been criticism that judges and magistrates have, in many cases, been using the 'delaying powers' of section 4 and the 'no names' powers of section 11 unnecessarily, often on an application by defence lawyers seeking to restrict publicity for their client. The press has often successfully challenged these orders.

### Section 4 orders

Mr Justice (later Lord Chief Justice) Taylor in 1988 accepted that he had been wrong in making a section 4 order at Newcastle Crown Court *banning*, rather than postponing, publication of an allegation that a father accused of murdering his daughter's teacher had himself made sexual advances to the girl. The father was said to have believed that the teacher had been his daughter's lover. Counsel for the *Sun* newspaper said: 'It is plain that your lordship has made an order that is a prohibition — not a postponement — and that is not within your jurisdiction.'

The Queen's Bench Divisional Court held in 1992 that any court, including a magistrates court, had discretionary power to hear representations from the press when the court was considering making or continuing a section 4 order. The media were the best qualified to represent the public interest in publicity, which the court had to take into account when performing any balancing exercise in weighing the public interest in open trial against the substantial risk of prejudice (*R v Clerkenwell Metropolitan Stipendiary Magistrates, ex p The Telegraph plc* [1993] 2 WLR 233).

In 1993, the Court of Appeal held that in deciding whether to make a section 4 order, a court should have regard to the competing public considerations of ensuring a fair trial and of open justice. Having identified the risk of substantial prejudice the court should then consider, in the light of the competing public interests, whether an order was necessary to avoid that risk. The Lord Chief Justice said in determining whether publication of matter would cause a substantial risk of prejudice to a future trial, a court should credit the jury with the will and ability to abide by the judge's direction to decide the case only on the evidence before them. The court should also bear in mind that the staying power and detail of publicity, even in cases of notoriety, were limited and that the nature of a trial was to focus the jury's minds on the evidence put before them rather than on matters outside the courtroom (*Ex p The Telegraph plc*, Court of Appeal, [1993] 1 WLR 981 and 987).

Lord Justice Farquharson said in 1991 that the fact that an accused expects to face a second indictment after the hearing of the first one did not in itself justify the making of a section 4 order. It depended on all the circumstances, including the nature of the charges, the timing of the second trial, and the place where that second trial was to be heard. If by an extension of the period between trials, or by the transfer to another court, substantial prejudice to the accused could be avoided then that course should be taken.

Later, Lord Justice Farquharson said if a judge's intention to make a section 4 order was announced suddenly, the press was not generally in a position to make any representations to the judge. The best course was for the judge to make a limited order under section 4 for, say, two days, and thus give the press time to make representations (*R v Beck, ex p Daily Telegraph*, Court of Appeal, 26 October 1991).

Where a court fears that the jury in the current trial would be prejudiced by access to reports of the case which they are hearing, the court should be made aware that the Court of Appeal has acknowledged that there is an *insubstantial* risk of prejudice of a jury by media reports of the day's proceedings (*R v Horsham Justices, ex p Farquharson* [1982] QB 762).

In 1994 Mr Justice Lindsay refused to make a section 4 order postponing reporting of civil cases involving Maxwell pension funds to avoid prejudice to future criminal proceedings. He said : 'By framing (section 4) as it did, the legislature contemplated that a risk of prejudice which could not be described as substantial had to be tolerated as the price of an open press and that if the risk was properly to be described as substantial, a postponement order did not automatically follow' (*MGN Pension Trustees Ltd v Bank of America*, Chancery Division, (1994) Independent, 14 December).

Section 4 cannot be used to restrict reports of events outside the courtroom (*R v Rhuddlan Justices, ex p HTV Ltd* (1985) Times, 21 December). (See also chapter 17.)

## Practice direction

The Lord Chief Justice in a practice direction in 1982 said that a section 4 order must state the precise scope, the time at which it ceased to have effect, and the specific purpose of making the order. Precise written records must be kept of both section 4 and section 11 orders.

The practice direction also said courts would normally give notice to the press that an order had been made and court staff should be prepared to answer any inquiry about a specific case. It would, however, remain the responsibility of reporters and their editors to avoid a breach of an order and to make inquiry in case of doubt. He repeated this guidance in 1990 in the Court of Appeal (*Practice Direction: Contempt of Court Act: Report of Proceedings: Postponement Orders* [1983] 1 All ER 64).

Many magistrates' courts, purporting to make orders restricting reports, appear to have been unaware of the Lord Chief Justice's direction.

The reporter who is in any doubt should, as stated, try to find out from the court under which section of the Act an order has been made, and should then report the matter to his editor so that the validity of the order can be examined.

## Section 11 orders

The Queen's Bench Divisional Court held in 1985 that it was an essential part of British justice that cases should be tried in public and this consideration had to outweigh the individual interests of particular persons (*R v Central Criminal Court, ex p Crook* (1985) Times, 8 November).

In 1987 the divisional court held that, having regard to the principle of open justice, a court was not entitled to make a section 11 order preventing the publication of a defendant's address where the administration of justice did not require such confidentiality. The divisional court granted a declaration that Evesham justices were acting contrary to law in prohibiting the publication of a defendant's address because they felt he might be harassed again by his former wife. Lord Justice Watkins said there were many people facing criminal charges who for all manner of reasons would like to keep their identity unrevealed, their home address in particular. Section 11 however was not enacted for the benefit of the comfort and feelings of defendants (*R v Evesham Justices, ex p McDonagh* [1988] 1 All ER 371, 384, QBD).

In 1985 the divisional court held that a court had no power to make a section 11 order unless it first allowed the name to be withheld from the public during court proceedings. Reporting restrictions imposed by magistrates under section 11 were quashed because the name had been mentioned in open court (*R v Arundel Justices, ex p Westminster Press* [1985] 2 All ER 390).

## Exclusion orders

The powers of the various courts to exclude the press and public are explained in detail in chapter 11, Admission to the courts.

In the first appeals in November 1989 under the section 159 procedure, journalist Tim Crook appealed against decisions by judges in two cases at the Old Bailey to exclude the public during submissions by counsel that the judge should make orders restricting the reporting of the trial itself.

The appeals were dismissed. The Lord Chief Justice said it was wholly appropriate for a judge to sit in chambers to receive information on a procedural matter.

## Section 39 orders

Under section 39 of the Children and Young Persons Act courts have the power to impose a ban on the naming of a juvenile under 18 'concerned in' proceedings in adult courts 'either as being the person by or against or in respect of whom the proceedings are taken, or as being a witness therein' (see chapter 6).

Courts are liable to make section 39 orders unreasonably. Such orders should be challenged.

In the magistrates court, newspapers have sometimes been able to persuade the bench that imposing a section 39 order would merely protect an adult defendant. After Rachel Campey, then editor of the *Express and Echo*, Exeter had successfully asked for such an order to be lifted in 1993, a court in the area later refused a prosecution application for a section 39 order in a case involving a man charged with assaulting his six-month-old son. The chairman of the bench said: 'A six-month-old baby cannot be affected by publicity. We would be protecting the defendant by stopping names going into the paper.'

Crown court judges may be even more open to persuasion. The *Express and Star*, Wolverhampton, in 1993, challenged an order made in the case of a woman who admitted causing grievous bodily harm to her eight-month-old baby. Judge Richard Gibbs lifted the order he had made and said it was doubtful if a report carrying the woman's name would lead to the detriment of the child in the long term.

In 1994, a man was found in a fume-filled car with his two young sons. When he appeared in court at Tavistock in Devon, charged with the attempted murder of his sons, magistrates made a section 39 order forbidding identification of the boys, thus giving anonymity to the accused. At Plymouth Crown Court, however, the judge refused to renew the section 39 order after representations had been made by newspaper and broadcasting organisations. The mother of the boys had also opposed the order, so that the father did not escape publicity.

Some courts tend to make section 39 orders almost automatically when a juvenile is involved but may be open to persuasion.

In 1996 Anne Rothwell, editor of the *Lancaster Guardian*, persuaded a judge at Preston Crown Court to lift a section 39 order banning identification of a 13-year-old girl who had been attacked by a man wielding a rock and who had been named in news stories before her assailant was arrested. After the editor made representations, a court clerk told a reporter that the paper was free to name the girl, but the editor sought, and obtained, a formal lifting of the section 39 order in open court.

In 1997, Martha Roberts, a reporter from *The News*, Portsmouth, successfully challenged an order made at crown court banning the identification of a 12-year-old witness. She accepted that the order might have been appropriate if a witness had received threats. Judge Tom MacKean said he was wrong to have made the order in that withholding the name of the boy from the public was not in the interest of justice.

Each challenge to a section 39 order reinforces the point made by Lord Justice Lloyd in the Court of Appeal in 1992 that such orders should not be made automatically. He said:'There must be a good reason for making an order under section 39 ... If the discretion under section 39 is too narrowly confined, we will be in danger of blurring the distinction between proceedings in the juvenile (now youth) court and proceedings in the crown court, a distinction which Parliament clearly intended to preserve' (*R v Lee* [1993] 1 WLR 110, CA).

In the same case Lord Justice Lloyd said the words 'any proceedings' in section 39 must mean the proceedings in the court making the order and not any proceedings anywhere. His statement indicates that a section 39 order made in the magistrates court does not apply to reports of the case when it reaches crown court. A judge at crown court can make his own section 39 order however.

Procedures which the courts should follow when making section 39 orders were suggested by Lord Justice Glidewell in 1994 (*R v Central Criminal Court, ex p Godwin and Crook* [1995] 1 FLR 132).

He laid down three guidelines:

(1) The court should make it clear what the terms of the order are. If there is any possible doubt as to which child or children the order relates to, the judge or magistrate should identify the relevant child or children with clarity.

(2) A written copy of the order should be drawn up as soon as possible after the judge or magistrate has made it orally. A copy of the order should then be available in the court office for reporters to inspect.

(3) The fact that an order has been made should be communicated to those not present when it is made. For this purpose, court lists should include a reference to the order having been made at an earlier hearing.

Lord Justice Glidewell said a judge had complete discretion to allow those parties with a legitimate interest in the making of, or opposing the making of a section 39 order, to make representations to him about it before he made it.

Courts sometimes make section 39 orders attempting to ban the identification of dead children. In many cases, such a ban would prevent the reporter from covering the case adequately. But over the years several High Court judges have said the courts do not have this power. Discussions between representatives of the Guild of Editors, the Home Office, the Justices Clerks' Society and the Magistrates Association have accepted this finding.

Mr Justice Bristow said at Warwick Crown Court in 1973: 'In my judgment, it (section 39) means that while you can order that the name should not be published if the child who is a victim of an attack is still alive, when the child is dead it does not apply.'

A court however may give *guidance* that publication of the name of a dead child could infringe a section 39 order made to protect living siblings, such as where parents are accused of further charges of cruelty.

In 1991 the Court of Appeal held that section 39 orders could not be used to prohibit the publication of the name of an adult defendant. Lord Justice Glidewell said: 'In our view, section 39 as a matter of law does not empower a court to order in terms that the names of defendants should not be published. It may be that on occasions judges will think it helpful to have some discussion about the identification of particular details and give advice . . . In our view the order itself must be restricted to the terms of section 39(1), either specifically using these terms or using words to the like effect and no more. If the inevitable effect of making an order is that it is apparent that some details, including names of defendants, may not be published because publication would breach the order, that is the practical application of the order; it is not a part of the terms of the order itself' (*R v Southwark Crown Court, ex p Godwin* [1991] 3 All ER 818).

Lord Justice Lloyd said in the Court of Appeal in 1993 that a member of the press who is aggrieved by a section 39 order should go back to the crown court in the event of any changes in circumstances. He also suggested that the press could appeal to the Court of Appeal under section 159 of the Criminal Justice Act 1988 (*R v Lee* [1993] 1 WLR 103). The difficulties of a section 159 appeal are discussed earlier in this chapter.

## Wards of court

The Court of Appeal in 1991 gave guidance to judges on how far injunctions should go in restricting publicity for wards of court. Lord Justice Neill said a distinction could be drawn between cases of mere curiosity and cases where the press was giving information or comment about matters of genuine public interest.

In almost every case, he said, the public interest in favour of publication could be satisfied without any identification of the child to persons other than those who already knew the facts. The injunction had to be in clear terms and had to be no wider than was necessary to achieve the purpose for which it was imposed (*Re M and N (minors) (Wardship) (Publication of Information)* [1991] Fam 211).

In 1989, a weekly newspaper, the *Rutland and Stamford Mercury*, successfully challenged the decision by a High Court judge not to lift an injunction restraining the paper from publishing an interview with a foster mother who had looked after two children since they were babies.

Kensington and Chelsea Borough Council had earlier obtained an injunction to stop the interview being used after social workers had removed the children from the woman and her husband without warning or explanation. Lady Justice Butler-Sloss said the interest of the newspaper was not curiosity but public interest in the exercise of the power of a local authority.

The Court of Appeal ordered that the injunction be reworded so that the story could be used as long as the children, their school, and the family were not identified.

The Court of Appeal urged courts to ban publication of information concerning children only when necessary, to use precise terms, and give decisions in open court when possible. The Master of the Rolls, Lord Donaldson, said if a temporary injunction had been granted in the absence of the other side (the newspaper) a judge should be ready and willing at short notice to consider any application by those affected by it to withdraw or modify it.

Central Television in 1994 successfully appealed in the Court of Appeal against an injunction banning the broadcast, without changes, of a programme on the work of the Obscene Publications Squad. The programme included pictures of a man who had been jailed for offences against boys. The mother of the man's child said this would identify her and the child. Lord Justice Neill said the balancing act between freedom of speech and the interests of the child became necessary only where the threatened publication touched matters which were of direct concern to the court in its supervisory role over the care and upbringing of the child. The press and broadcasters were entitled to publish the result of criminal proceedings. What should be left out was mainly an editorial decision. The court should not restrain publication which was in no way concerned with the upbringing or care of a child but merely affected her indirectly (*R v Central Independent Television* [1994] Fam 192, CA).

## Rape cases

There is no longer any restriction on naming the defendant in a rape case or other sexual offence case (see chapter 8) under either the 1976 or 1992 Sexual Offences (Amendment) Acts and any direction made to ban such identification is obviously invalid. However giving the name of the defendant, although not unlawful itself, could lead to identification of the victim in some cases where other detail is given, for example if a relationship with the victim is stated (see chapter 8).

## Obstructive courts

The court reporter's essential role can be made difficult and sometimes almost impossible if he does not receive minimum co-operation from court officials.

### Magistrates courts

In 1989, the Home Office wrote to justices' clerks commending the practice of making available to the press court lists and, where they are prepared, provisional lists on the day of the hearing. For the details of the Circular see chapter 4. The Circular also recommended that courts supply local newspapers with copies of the court register, when prepared.

The Circular recommends that papers should be charged the full cost.

### Crown courts

In 1989 also, the Lord Chancellor agreed that it was reasonable for the crown court to supply details of a defendant's address if it was available from the court record.

Chief clerks were instructed that where a defendant's address was given in open court the court clerk should note it in the file so that any request for the address, or to confirm it, could be readily dealt with.

Where the address was not given in open court, particular care had to be taken to ensure that it might properly be released, bearing in mind a number of factors. These included whether there was any order restricting reporting, whether the address was readily available, and whether there was confirmation that the address was current. (Reference CS3 (A) DL49/98/01.)

## Data Protection Act

The Act makes it an offence for a data user to disclose information held on a computer to people who are not registered to receive it (see chapter 32).

Some magistrates courts have said they could not provide information for the press for this reason, but there is unlikely to be any difficulty if they have correctly completed the registration form by ticking a box which says: 'Disclosure of data to providers of publicly available information, including press and media'.

The Home Office advised all magistrates courts to register for the purpose of disclosure of data to providers of publicly available information, and journalists having difficulty should refer the clerk to the Circular, which is No 83/1985.

## Questions

1    Under section 39 of the Children and Young Persons Act 1933, may a court order that a juvenile who has been murdered should not be identified?

2    What right does a journalist have to appeal against a decision of a judge at crown court to exclude the press and public or to make an order restricting reporting? What are the drawbacks to the appeal procedure?

3    What direction has been given by the Lord Chief Justice about the making of orders under section 4 of the Contempt of Court Act 1981?

4    May an order under section 11 of the Contempt of Court Act 1981 be made to protect a defendant from harassment? What has been said in the Queen's Bench Divisional Court?

5    What advice has been given on defendants' names and addresses being made available to the press?

# 13 Divorce

Only a small percentage of divorce actions take place in open court, following the changes in divorce law and procedure since 1970, although the decree is pronounced in open court and may be reported.

When cases are heard in public there are restrictions on what a newspaper may report (see the end of this chapter).

The spouse starting the proceedings is known as the petitioner. The petition is served on the other spouse, known as the respondent, who is required to state whether he or she intends to defend. If so, the respondent must file an answer.

## Decree nisi

Divorce actions begin with either the wife or the husband lodging a petition at a county court after one year's marriage. If the petition is, like the vast majority, undefended, evidence of the breakdown of the marriage will be given by affidavit (a sworn written statement) on a printed form. The affidavit will then be considered by a district judge, sitting in chambers, without either party being legally represented.

Later a list of petitioners granted a decree nisi (provisional decree of divorce) will be read out in court.

If, in these undefended cases, the district judge is not satisfied with the evidence in the affidavits and further evidence is not forthcoming, the action will after all be heard by a circuit judge in open court, with witnesses called to give evidence.

Where a divorce petition is contested, the action will normally be heard at a designated county court. Defended divorce cases are seldom tried in the High Court.

Divorce may be granted only on the ground that the marriage has irretrievably broken down. To support this, at least one of five facts must be proved to the satisfaction of the court:

(a) adultery by the respondent, and that the petitioner finds it intolerable to live with him or her;

(b) the respondent behaved in such a way that the petitioner cannot reasonably be expected to live with him or her (unreasonable behaviour);

(c) desertion for two years or more by the respondent. The desertion must be with the intention of ending co-habitation, and would not, for instance, apply where a soldier was posted overseas;

(d) the parties consent to divorce after two years' continuous separation;

(e) the parties have been separated for five years. This allows either side a decree without the consent of the other and without having to prove desertion by either side. A decree may be refused on grounds of grave hardship to the respondent.

A decree nisi does not allow the parties to remarry. They can do this after the decree is made absolute (usually after six weeks) and the marriage is legally dissolved.

Where adultery is relied upon as one of the facts in a defended divorce the alleged adulterer may be named in the petition. If so, he or she is served with the petition and becomes the co-respondent.

A judge can order that the co-respondent's name be struck out of the petition if he feels the evidence does not support the allegation against the co-respondent.

Any person may within 14 days of a decree nisi being pronounced inspect the certificate etc (see chapter 11).

Other decrees which can be awarded by the Family Division of the High Court are listed below.

## Decree of nullity

This is awarded where the court rules there has been no valid marriage and for that reason there cannot be a divorce. A nullity decree may be awarded where there is inability or refusal to consummate the marriage; when a marriage has taken place without the real consent of either party, eg under duress; or when at the time of marriage either party was suffering from a venereal disease in a communicable form; or the wife was pregnant by another man and this was unknown to the petitioner at the time of the marriage.

## Decree of judicial separation

This is usually sought where a man or woman for religious reasons feels there is a stigma in an actual divorce. It does not allow the parties to remarry, but can be granted only on proof of the same facts as a divorce would be. However it is necessary to wait until one year has elapsed from the marriage before filing a petition for judicial separation.

## Decree of presumption of death

This is granted where either side has been absent for seven years or more and adequate efforts to trace him or her have failed. It is also more likely to be sought by those who feel divorce a stigma. If the other party reappears later, the decree still holds good.

## The reporting restrictions

Since the Judicial Proceedings (Regulation of Reports) Act 1926, newspaper reports of actions for divorce, nullity, or judicial separation have had to be confined to four points.

The only permitted particulars are:

(a) names, addresses, and occupations of the parties and witnesses;

(b) a concise statement of the charges (and this can include a concise statement of the 'facts' — one of the grounds which must be proved), the defence, and counter-charges in support of which evidence has been given (ie not abandoned charges or counter-charges);

(c) submissions on any point of law arising in the course of the proceedings and the decision of the court; and

(d) the judgment of the court, and the observations of the judge.

No report can be published until all the evidence has been given in order to comply with (b) above, but once evidence is complete in defended cases, it is possible to publish a report within the restrictions.

Most newspaper stories of defended divorce actions are based on (d) — what is said by the judge — but reports of his remarks must be confined to what he says in giving judgment, rather than what is said during the hearing.

The Act of 1926 also provided restrictions on what may be reported of indecent matter in any type of court. No report of any judicial proceedings may include any indecent matter, or indecent medical, surgical, or physiological details, the publication of which would be calculated to injure public morals.

What would injure public morals in 1926 might not necessarily be held to do so today, were there to be any prosecution.

The Attorney-General must give consent before there can be any prosecution.

So far as is known, neither the restriction on divorce reporting nor that on publication of indecent matter has led to any prosecution; but in 1996 two Scottish newspapers were reported to the Crown Office after complaints

that reports of a divorce case had included matter not permitted under the
Act.

## Questions

1    What particulars may a newspaper report of a divorce action?
2    What is a decree of nullity?

# 14 Bankruptcy and company liquidation

Many bankruptcies are small affairs of limited news value. Others, however, are stories of wild extravagance at the expense of creditors or the accumulation of large bills for unpaid tax and some may involve criminal conduct, although there can be no prosecution for debt alone.

Questions put in the public examination in bankruptcy (sometimes referred to as the bankruptcy court) of Mr John Poulson in 1972 led to the first substantial disclosures of corruption in the affairs of local councils and other public bodies, ending in jail sentences for several men.

Now, a public examination in bankruptcy is not held automatically. A public examination may be held however to give the creditors an opportunity to question the debtor, which they do not have at the meeting of creditors, held earlier.

Reporters should note the different procedures for companies and for individuals who are insolvent. Companies go into liquidation (see later in this chapter) while individuals become bankrupt.

## Bankruptcy

In the case of an individual, either he, or his creditors, can file a petition at the county court for a bankruptcy order to be made by the district judge (formerly known as the registrar) if at least £750 is owed. The Department of Trade has power to raise this figure at any time.

A bankruptcy order will then be granted by the district judge unless the debtor has made an offer which has been unreasonably refused. In place of a bankruptcy order, an individual voluntary arrangement may be made, where the debtor has assets exceeding £2,000 and debts not exceeding £20,000. In this case, the district judge may make only an interim bankruptcy order and refer the matter to a licensed insolvency practitioner from a firm of accountants in the hope of avoiding bankruptcy through voluntary arrangements for payment if the creditors agree.

Otherwise, after a bankruptcy order the official receiver (an officer of the Department of Trade and not of the court) takes over the legal control of all the debtor's property.

With his assistance, the debtor must within 21 days submit a statement of affairs setting out the assets, liabilities, and deficiency. Sometimes, when the prospects of the creditors getting a substantial proportion of what is owed to them are fairly bright, the creditors will appoint a licensed accountant as the trustee in bankruptcy. In this case, he and not the official receiver supervises the sale of any assets and the process of repayment.

Imputations of insolvency may be regarded as defamatory (see chapter 18, What is defamatory) and it is not safe for a newspaper to report the filing of a petition for a bankruptcy order (because of the danger of a libel action should the debtor be found to be solvent). The only exceptions to this occur when the debtor files his own petition, or when a bankruptcy order has been made and is open to public inspection (see chapter 11, 'County courts'), or when the newspaper quotes an announcement in the *London Gazette* that a bankruptcy order has been made, both of which would be protected by qualified privilege.

A creditors' meeting may be held. There is no statutory right for the press to attend. They can be admitted if the official receiver so rules, but the meeting can be a tricky one to report because it is not privileged.

## Reporting bankruptcy court

A public examination in bankruptcy, which, as its name implies, can be attended by anyone, may be held next. The purpose of this is to satisfy the court that the full extent of the debtor's assets and liabilities are known, to establish the causes of his failure, to discover whether there has been any criminal offence, and to establish whether any assets transferred to another person ought to be recovered.

Any transaction in the preceding two years can be declared void, unless it is a normal trading transaction. This can be extended to the preceding 10 years, if intention to deprive the creditors of their money is proved.

The examination usually takes place before the district judge. The debtor is examined by the official receiver or his assistant. If there is a trustee in a bankruptcy, he, or a lawyer representing him, may also ask questions. Otherwise any proven creditor may question the debtor.

Figures reflecting the size of the bankruptcy will emerge during the hearing — the liabilities, the assets, and, most important of all, the deficiency. The liabilities will usually include those due to preferential creditors who, as the name implies, are paid first out of any assets. These include legal and administrative costs of winding up the estate, VAT and national insurance and limited payments due to employees.

It may also be mentioned in the hearing that there are secured creditors, eg banks who have lent money on the strength of security, or those who have provided mortgages on property.

A public examination in bankruptcy may also take place after a judge has made an order following the conviction of a criminal. The purpose of this is to distribute the criminal's assets fairly among the victims of his theft or fraud. Examinations after criminal bankruptcy orders may take place in prison for security reasons.

Normally a public examination is closed, subject to the signing of the shorthand notes (a formality). It may, however, be adjourned for the result of further inquiries. Either way, the outcome at the end of the day is more important in a newspaper story than saying that the debtor was declared bankrupt, as in law he was bankrupt much earlier when the bankruptcy order was made.

A fair and accurate report of a public examination is protected by absolute privilege.

## Effects of bankruptcy

These include the power of the official receiver to assume legal control over all the debtor's property, apart from basic necessities and the tools of his trade, up to £250 in value.

The debtor cannot obtain credit for more than £250 without disclosing that he is an undischarged bankrupt, nor trade under any name other than that in which he went into bankruptcy without disclosing it. He cannot act as a company director nor take part in the management of any company without the leave of the court.

He cannot sit in Parliament or on a local authority, nor take any public office.

## Discharge from bankruptcy

If the court feels the case deserves it, it may make an order for discharge from a first-time bankruptcy after three years. The court may grant a discharge from bankruptcy after two years where the debtor has filed his own petition and unsecured liabilities are less than £20,000.

## Company liquidation

In reporting that a limited company has gone into liquidation, care should be taken to make the circumstances clear.

A *members' voluntary liquidation* takes place where the company is solvent, but the directors decide to close down, possibly in the case of a small firm because of impending retirement, or because of a merger. To imply that such a company is in financial difficulties in this case is clearly defamatory.

A *creditors' voluntary liquidation* takes place for the voluntary winding up to proceed under the supervision of a liquidator.

A *compulsory liquidation* follows a hearing in the High Court or county court of a petition to wind up the company. This is usually because a creditor claims that the company is insolvent, but technically can also arise where a company fails to file its statutory report or hold its statutory meeting on being set up; where it does not start, or suspends, business; or where members of the company are reduced to below the number required in law.

## Questions

1   What are the preliminary stages before a person appears for his public examination in bankruptcy?
2   What is the procedure at the public examination?
3   What are the effects of a person being adjudicated bankrupt?

# 15 Inquests

The office of coroner is one of the most ancient in English law. A coroner must be a barrister, solicitor, or doctor of at least five years' standing.

Although proposals have often been made to reduce the scope of coroners' inquests, they continue to be held to inquire into violent, unnatural, or sudden deaths, or into deaths which take place in some forms of custody.

When an autopsy shows that a sudden death was due to natural causes, however, the coroner has power to dispense with an inquest.

A coroner has the right at common law to take possession of a body until after his inquest has been completed.

An inquest is inquisitorial in its procedure — unlike the criminal court, where the process is accusatorial and is therefore subject to strict rules in the interests of justice. A coroner chooses and questions each witness and can allow or prevent questions being put by others. The Coroners Rules 1984, however, do regulate proceedings at inquests to some extent.

The purpose of an inquest is to find out:
(a)  who the deceased was;
(b)  how, when, and where he met his death;
(c)  the particulars to be registered.

A coroner's jury may not return a verdict of murder, manslaughter, or infanticide against a named person. The Coroners Rules also forbid a rider to the jury's verdict which appears to determine liability in civil law or in criminal law. In 1994 the Court of Appeal ruled that it was not the function of an inquest jury to attribute blame or to express judgment or opinion. To do so would be unfair to those who might face criminal proceedings.

Where a person is suspected of crime in connection with a death, an inquest is usually opened simply to obtain evidence of identity and cause of death, and is adjourned until after these proceedings have been completed.

The Court of Appeal held in 1982 that a coroner must hold an inquest where it was believed that a person had died a violent or unnatural death abroad and the body had been brought back to that coroner's territory.

Inquests are sometimes held into findings of objects containing a substantial proportion of gold and silver or of other valuables where the owner or his known dependants cannot be traced. The purpose of such an inquest is to decide whether the findings should become the property of the Crown.

A jury of at least seven and not more than eleven may sit at inquests. Under the Coroners Act 1988, a jury must be summoned when there is reason to suspect that death occurred in circumstances the continuance or possible recurrence of which is prejudicial to the health or safety of the public. A jury is not compulsory for a road accident inquest.

It has become the convention to report that a coroner's jury returns a verdict and that a coroner sitting without a jury records a verdict.

Fair, accurate, and contemporaneous reports of inquests are protected by absolute privilege.

Rule 17 says that every inquest should be held in public save that any inquest or part of an inquest may be held *in camera* in the interests of national security.

However, another rule, rule 37, allows a coroner to take documentary rather than oral evidence from any witness where such evidence is unlikely to be disputed. The rule provides that the coroner must announce publicly at the inquest the name of the person giving documentary evidence and must, unless he otherwise directs, read aloud such evidence. The effect of this is that a coroner who is so minded can lawfully prevent the press and public from learning the contents of that evidence.

It has been the custom of coroners not to read out suicide notes and psychiatric reports.

A Home Office circular in May 1980 urged coroners to make arrangements to ensure that the press were properly informed of all inquests. A reminder was sent out in 1987.


## Contempt of coroner's court

In 1985, six police officers obtained an injunction to restrain London Weekend Television from broadcasting a filmed reconstruction of events surrounding the arrest and subsequent death in police custody of a Hell's Angel. The injunction was granted on the ground that the broadcast would amount to contempt of an inquest, due to be resumed. In rejecting the television company's appeal against the injunction, the Court of Appeal held that proceedings become active for contempt purposes as soon as a coroner has opened an inquest (see chapter 17).

## Judicial review

There is no direct right of appeal from a verdict at an inquest into a death, but an application may be made to the Queen's Bench Divisional Court for an order to quash a verdict and to order a fresh inquest. This application is sometimes made by relatives aggrieved by a verdict that the deceased took his own life.

## Questions

1   What is the purpose of an inquest?
2   What do the Coroners Rules say about holding inquests in public?
3   What words are used when (a) there is a jury, (b) a coroner sits alone, to indicate how a verdict is reached?

# 16 Tribunals and inquiries

We must now look at the functions of administrative tribunals and ministerial inquiries, and the relationship of the press to them.

## Tribunals

Tribunals are bodies, other than the normal courts we have already studied, that adjudicate in disputes or determine legal rights.

There are about 50 types of tribunals, and about 2,000 tribunals, and the tendency is for them to multiply and to become more important. The ordinary courts often do not have the specialised experience to deal adequately with disputes that arise as a result of developments in the law. Parliament also considers that tribunals can be cheaper, quicker, and less formal.

Tribunals are concerned with a wide variety of matters, including industrial disputes, land and property, national insurance, income support, the National Health Service, transport, and taxation. They vary so much it is difficult to classify them.

Most have an uneven number of members, so that a majority decision can be reached.

Most members are appointed by the minister concerned with the subject, but where a lawyer chairman or member is required the Lord Chancellor generally makes the appointment.

In most cases, members hold office for a specified period.

There is a right of appeal, at least on a point of law, from the most important tribunals to the Divisional Court or Court of Appeal. This enables the individual to challenge ministerial decisions in the courts.

In exceptional circumstances, the Divisional Court or Court of Appeal decisions may be challenged in the House of Lords.

An appeal may also be made to a specially constructed appeal tribunal, to a Minister of the Crown, or to an independent referee (depending upon the standing and the function of the tribunal).

The Council on Tribunals, a permanent body appointed by the Lord Chancellor and the Secretary of State for Scotland, exercises general supervision over tribunals and reports on particular matters. It was set up by Act of Parliament in 1958.

Under the Act, a tribunal must, if requested, furnish a statement of the reasons for the decision reached.

Most tribunals are set up by an Act of Parliament or under a statutory instrument. As a result, a fair and accurate account of the proceedings of those tribunals, even if it contains defamatory statements, enjoys the protection of qualified privilege, subject to a statement by way of explanation or contradiction (see chapter 20, Qualified privilege).

A characteristic of most tribunals is informality. The chairman might not be a lawyer, and the parties might not be represented. As a result, many things might be said during fierce exchanges between the parties that are not strictly relevant to the decision being made and that would not be allowed in an ordinary court.

It is therefore important to remember, when covering the proceedings of tribunals, that qualified privilege does not extend to 'any matter which is not of public concern and the publication of which is not for the public benefit'.

The reporting of some tribunals may be covered by absolute privilege. The Law of Libel Amendment Act 1888 says this covers 'any court exercising judicial authority'.

What of contempt of court? Is it possible for a newspaper to be in contempt as a result of publishing matter that might prejudice proceedings in a tribunal? The question is a difficult one, for judges as well as journalists. The Contempt of Court Act 1981 states that a 'court', for the purposes of the Act, includes any tribunal or body exercising the judicial power of the state.

In *Attorney-General v BBC* (1980), the House of Lords agreed that a local valuation court could not be protected in this way. Although it was called a 'court', its functions were essentially administrative, and it was not a court of law established to exercise judicial power. Unfortunately the judges in the House of Lords gave varying reasons for reaching their conclusion.

In *Pickering v Liverpool Daily Post* (1989), the Court of Appeal agreed that a mental health review tribunal *was* a court.

Lord Donaldson, Master of the Rolls, said the power of the tribunal to restore a person to liberty was a classic exercise of judicial power.

In *Peach Grey & Co v Sommers* (1995) the Queen's Bench Divisional Court decided it had the power to punish contempt of an industrial tribunal which, Lord Justice Rose said, appeared to exercise a 'judicial function'.

A guidance note for the Guild of Editors says: 'It seems that in order to fall within the definition (of a court), a tribunal must wield the state's authority and have the power to resolve controversies, giving binding, authoritative decisions determining the *liability* of the parties.'

Suppose information is disclosed at a tribunal hearing and the publication of that information in a newspaper would prejudice a trial or inquest. If the tribunal is a 'court' under the terms of the 1981 Act it must make a section 4 order to postpone reporting of that information. Otherwise the journalist is free to report – provided he does so bona fide. If the tribunal is not a court it has no power to make a section 4 order, but the journalist risks prosecution if he publishes prejudicial matter (see chapter 17).

The journalist should distinguish between an ordinary tribunal and a tribunal of inquiry set up – though this is rare – under the Tribunals of Inquiry (Evidence) Act 1921. In the latter case, newspaper conduct likely to prejudice the inquiry can lead to contempt proceedings (see chapter 24).

We mention below some of the more important tribunals the reporter may have to attend. In all cases mentioned, a fair and accurate report has privilege, certainly qualified and perhaps absolute.

**Industrial tribunals** provide a large number of good stories relating to such matters as complaints of unfair dismissal, sexual or racial discrimination at work, or exclusion from a trade union; disputes over contracts of employment, redundancy payments, or health and safety at work; and claims to equal pay. The difficulties involved in covering these tribunals are common to many tribunals.

Tribunals sit at 24 permanent centres in England and Wales, or in hired accommodation. About 50 tribunals sit each working day.

It seems likely, in view of the case of *Peach Grey* mentioned above, that a fair, accurate, and contemporaneous report of an industrial tribunal will be covered by absolute privilege. But 'judicial function' is not necessarily the same as 'judicial authority', the requirement in the 1888 Act.

*Procedure* The hearings at industrial tribunals tend to be informal and vary according to the chairman. Some chairmen announce at the start of the hearing the details of the claim and then establish the essential facts, but others plunge straight into matters of detail.

Many fail to ask such basic details as the applicant's first name, age, and address, and sometimes do not read out relevant documents. These details have to be obtained from court officials, who are generally helpful (see Access to information, below), or the parties themselves. It is normal practice for witnesses to confirm their names and addresses before giving evidence.

Sometimes there is an opening speech, similar to that given in a court of law. Note, however, that the case is not necessarily opened by the claimant (or applicant), as it is in a civil law action. In unfair dismissal claims where dismissal is admitted, it is usually up to the employer to prove the dismissal was fair and thus to present his case first. Where the dismissal is denied, the employee usually starts first – although which course is taken is within the discretion of the tribunal.

At the end of the hearing the three tribunal members can either:
(a)   reserve their decision and publish it later;
(b)   give a decision with basic reasons and publish a full reasoned decision later;
(c)   give their decision and reasons in public at once.

Many employers are represented by solicitors or counsel, or possibly by a senior executive. Many applicants bring their cases with the help of their trade union and have their case presented by union officials or solicitors.

There is often considerable bitterness and applicants are sometimes extremely suspicious of the press. Because the parties sometimes have to be approached for follow-up details, reporters may encounter hostility from applicants who think that because they have seen the reporter talking to the employers' representatives he is 'on their side'.

Reports are read with the greatest suspicion and complaints may be made stemming partly from the parties' ignorance of court procedure. For example, where a case has been adjourned and it has been possible to report only one side because only that side has been heard, a complaint may be made that the report was 'one-sided'. Similarly, a small discrepancy in the name of a company (this can arise easily where there is a network of subsidiaries) is pounced upon by the employers.

The safeguard against complaint is, as always, a good shorthand note of the proceedings, accurate transcription of names from lists and from informants when checking, and care in writing.

The tribunal can require a party to provide a written answer to any question.

A tribunal may hold pre-hearing reviews in some cases and if the tribunal considers the arguments of any party have no reasonable prospect of success it may order that party to pay a deposit of up to £150 as a condition of being allowed to bring or to continue to contest the proceedings.

*Admission* Industrial tribunals must normally sit in public, but there are exceptions (see chapter 11, Industrial tribunals).

Tribunals have sat in private where details about a burglar alarm installation would have to be given and where evidence about police reports was necessary.

Pre-hearing assessments (PHAs) before a fully constituted tribunal are not open to the public.

*Access to information* During 1984, instructions were issued to industrial tribunal staff restricting the information they were allowed to give to the press. After representations by media bodies these instructions were amended to provide for staff to give full addresses to a reporter on request on the day of the hearing; and to issue a reserved decision of a tribunal on application by a reporter in respect of a specific case whether or not the reporter was present at the hearing.

*Cases involving sexual misconduct* Under the Trade Union Reform and Employment Rights Act 1993, industrial tribunals have the power to impose temporary anonymity orders (known as restricted reporting orders) in cases involving allegations of sexual misconduct.

Sexual misconduct includes sexual offences, defined in accordance with the Sexual Offences (Amendment) Act 1976 (rape offences) and the Sexual Offences (Amendment) Act 1993 (other sexual offences) and also sexual harassment or other adverse conduct (of whatever nature) related to sex.

An order can be made on an application by a party or on the tribunal's own initiative. It can be made at any time before *promulgation* of its decision (the date the notice announcing the tribunal's decision is sent to the parties).

The tribunal must give 'each party' an opportunity to speak on such an application, but the press has no right to speak and if it wishes to do so must rely on the tribunal's discretion. In 1997, in a case where a policewoman accused a male officer of sexual harassment, the press was banned from identifying the accused, the accuser, and the witnesses. The tribunal at first declined to allow the press to challenge the order, but later heard counsel for the *Yorkshire Evening Post* and agreed that some of the witnesses could be named.

The order must specify the people who must not be identified, who can include any person affected by or making the allegations (which can include alleged perpetrators, witnesses, and complainants).

The order remains in force until the promulgation of the decision unless the tribunal has revoked the order earlier. Promulgation can be weeks or months after the decision is reached.

A notice must be displayed indicating the making of the order and placed on the tribunal's notice board and on the door of the room in which the hearing is being conducted.

Suppose a woman suing for unfair dismissal claims she was indecently assaulted by her employer. The tribunal makes a restricted reporting order prohibiting identification of the woman and her employer. After the promulgation order you can lawfully identify the employer, but remember that you still cannot identify the complainant because she is protected by the Sexual Offences (Amendment) Act 1992, unless she gives her written consent to be named.

Breach of an order will be a summary offence, punishable by a fine.

In addition, in cases that involve sexual offences, tribunals will be able to remove permanently from any documents available to the public any information that would identify any person making or affected by the allegations.

*Cases involving disability* Industrial tribunals can make broadly similar banning orders when considering complaints in respect of unlawful discrimination in employment on disability grounds. The Disability Discrimination Act 1995 says a disability is a physical or mental impairment which has a substantial and long-term effect.

The tribunal can make an order in proceedings in which 'evidence of a personal nature' is likely to be heard, and that means 'any evidence of a medical, or other intimate, nature which might reasonably be assumed to be likely to cause significant embarrassment to the complainant if reported'.

The tribunal can make an order either if the complainant applies for one or on its own initiative. By contrast with cases involving sexual misconduct, in these cases the person or company against whom the complaint is being made cannot apply for an order to be made, but the tribunal has unlimited discretion as to the people it names in the order.

Where the tribunal makes a restricted reporting order and that complaint is being dealt with together with any other proceedings, the tribunal may direct that the order applies also in relation to those other proceedings.

As with cases involving sexual misconduct, the parties must be allowed to make representations before an order is made, but again the press has no *right* to be heard. The order remains in force until it is promulgated.

*Appeals* Appeals from industrial tribunals are heard by the Employment Appeal Tribunal, which sits in London. There are often three 'courts' sitting, each presided over by a High Court judge sitting with lay judges from both sides of industry.

Although still informal compared with a normal court of law, the appeal tribunal hearings are more set in procedure, and parties are more likely to be represented. The court gives reasons for its decisions.

Appeal tribunals frequently produce interesting stories, because the cases tend to be ones regarded as important or difficult.

Under the Employment Protection Act 1975, Schedule 6, the appeal tribunal can sit in private in the same circumstances as industrial tribunals.

**Rent assessment committees** hear appeals against fair rents fixed by a rent officer for regulated tenancies and can determine a market rent in certain circumstances for assured and assured short-hold tenancies.

Regulated tenancies are, broadly speaking, those lettings by non-resident private landlords that began before 15 January 1989. Assured and assured short-hold tenancies are such lettings that began on or after that date. Hearings are open to the public unless for 'special reasons' – which are not defined – the committee decides otherwise.

**Rent tribunals** register reasonable rents for restricted contract lettings. These are, broadly, lettings by private landlords living on the same premises as the tenant that were created before 15 January 1989. If the tribunal is asked by one of the parties to sit in public, it has discretion whether or not to do so.

**Valuation tribunals** hear appeals against the valuation of non-domestic property assessed by valuation officers and against the valuation of domestic property by listing officers – the same people wearing different hats. Upon these valuations are based payments to the local authorities. People may appeal if they believe that their property has been wrongly valued, that they are not liable to pay, that their property should not give rise to council tax, that discounts have been calculated wrongly, or that they have been wrongly penalised by their local authority. These tribunals must sit in public unless satisfied that a party's interests would thereby be prejudiced.

**Social security appeal tribunals (SSATs)** consider cases relating to national insurance, income support, and family credit. They decide appeals against decisions given by adjudication officers (AOs). They also decide claims and questions referred to them by AOs. Hearings are in public, unless the claimant requests a private hearing or the chairman is satisfied that intimate personal or financial circumstances may have to be disclosed or that considerations of public security are involved. A tribunal can exclude the public while it is deliberating on its decision or discussing any questions of procedure.

**Medical appeal tribunals** decide appeals on medical questions from medical boards on claims for mobility allowance and industrial injuries and industrial disablement benefits. The rule on open hearings is the same as for SSATs.

**Attendance allowance boards** hear questions referred from adjudicating officers. The rule on open hearings is the same as for SSATs.

**Pensions appeal tribunals** determine appeals from decisions by the Secretary of State for Social Services on claims to pensions in respect of war service injuries suffered in the Second World War, war injuries suffered by civilians in the Second World War, and service injuries since the Second World War. The hearing is held in public unless the chairman directs otherwise.

**Family health services committees** are set up by family practitioner committees to handle complaints about self-employed health practitioners who are accused of breaking the terms of their contracts with the National Health Service. Proceedings must be in private.

**National Health Service tribunals** hear representations from the service committees (see above) if a committee decides that the practitioner should no longer be included on the NHS approved list. Proceedings are in private unless the practitioner applies for the inquiry to be in public.

**Mental health review tribunals** hear applications for discharge from patients detained under the Mental Health Act 1983. Proceedings are in private unless a patient requests a hearing in public and the tribunal is satisfied this would not be contrary to the interests of the patient.

**General Medical Council** decides matters relating to complaints against doctors. The professional conduct committee sits in public but can exclude the public if it considers this is in the interest of justice, or desirable having regard to the nature of the case or the evidence. It must, however, give its decision in public.

**Solicitors' disciplinary tribunals** must, in general, hear allegations of professional misconduct in public. But the tribunal may exclude the public from all or any part of the hearing if it appears that 'any person would suffer undue prejudice from a public hearing or that for any reason the circumstances and nature of the case make a public hearing undesirable'.

**Bar Council** hears allegations against barristers in private unless the barrister asks for a public hearing. The decision must be announced publicly.

## Local inquiries

Local inquiries ordered by ministers are comparable to administrative tribunals. Some Acts of Parliament provide that a public inquiry must be held, and objections heard, before a minister makes a decision affecting the rights of individuals or of other public authorities.

An inquiry might be held, for example, before land is compulsorily acquired for redevelopment or the building of a housing estate and also before planning schemes are approved.

An inquiry is conducted by an inspector on behalf of the minister. In some cases, the inspector decides the matter at issue. In others he must report to the minister, who subsequently announces his decision and the reasons for it.

Some statutes under which inquiries, local or otherwise, may be held stipulate that they must be held in public. In others, this is discretionary.

By the Planning Inquiries (Attendance of Public) Act 1982, evidence at planning inquiries held under the Town and Country Planning Act 1971 must be given in public. But the Secretary of State can direct that evidence shall not be heard in public if this would result in the disclosure of matters relating to national security or measures taken to ensure the security of property, and if that disclosure would be contrary to the national interest.

Proceedings are, again, not so formal as in an ordinary court of law. Qualified privilege is available as a defence for a fair and accurate report.

The findings of a public inquiry are usually made available to the press.

## Questions

1   What protection applies to a fair and accurate report of the proceedings of a tribunal set up by an Act of Parliament or a statutory instrument?
2   What difficulties does the reporter face in reporting proceedings of an industrial tribunal?
3   An industrial tribunal, hearing a case where a person complains of sexual harassment, may make a restricted reporting order. What can such an order cover? How long does the order last?
4   For what purposes might a local inquiry be held?

# 17 Contempt of court

The main concern of the law of contempt of court is to preserve the integrity of the legal process rather than to safeguard the dignity of the court.

A journalist can fall foul of the law of contempt in a number of ways. The greatest risk is in the publication of material which might prejudice a fair trial, such as extraneous information that might tend to sway a juror's mind.

The journalist can also be in contempt by publication of anything which interferes with the course of justice generally (for example, by naming a blackmail victim at the end of the trial, which would deter future blackmail victims from coming forward, or by vilifying a person for having acted as a witness at a trial, which might deter future potential witnesses).

An editor and a newspaper company can also be in contempt if material is published in breach of an undertaking given to a court, or in breach of an order of the court (although breaches of orders made by magistrates courts under an Act of Parliament are treated as a breach of that Act rather than contempt).

Another way in which a journalist can be in contempt is by conduct other than publication. An example of this would be seeking to find out about the discussions that had gone on in the privacy of the jury room while a verdict was being reached (see chapter 7). A further example would be if a journalist were to pay or offer to pay a person, due to be a witness in a coming trial, for information to go into a background article for use after the trial, and the amount of that payment were to vary according to whether the accused was eventually found guilty.

There has been an offence of contempt of court for centuries, but until 1981 it was almost entirely governed by the common law, that is by rules made by the judges rather than Acts of Parliament.

At common law, a newspaper was always at risk of being in contempt when proceedings were 'pending or imminent'.

Until 1981, the common law had regarded contempt by publication as an offence of *strict liability.*

This meant the prosecution had to establish only that the contempt had been committed. It was not considered necessary for the prosecution to prove that there had been an intent to commit the offence, as is usual in the criminal law.

The Contempt of Court Act 1981 limited the operation of this strict liability rule. It provides that a person can be guilty of contempt by publication, regardless of intent, only in cases where:

(a) the publication creates a substantial risk of serious prejudice or impediment to particular proceedings; and

(b) proceedings are active.

A contempt prosecution for a prejudicial publication may still be possible *at common law* outside these two conditions, for example if proceedings are not active. But specific intent must be proved. It is possible that if a person was heedless to the obvious risk of prejudice this might be equated with intent. But in 1991 Lord Justice Bingham (later Lord Bingham of Cornhill, Lord Chief Justice) cast doubt on this view when he said that proof of recklessness was not sufficient.

The subject is further dealt with later in this chapter (Contempt at common law).

## The 1981 Act

The Act says any writing, speech, broadcast, or other communication addressed to any section of the public may be treated as contempt of court, regardless of intent.

Proceedings for contempt under the strict liability rule can be taken only by a crown court or higher court, by the Attorney-General, or by some other person with his consent.

Magistrates do not have power to punish contempt of court by publication.

They can however jail for a month or impose a fine of £2,500 on anyone insulting them, or any witness, lawyer, or officer of the court, or on anyone who interrupts the proceedings or misbehaves.

Any contempt of a magistrates court by prejudicial publication (although none appears to have been recorded) would have to be dealt with by the High Court.

### Substantial risk

The first criterion, 'substantial risk of serious impediment or prejudice', has been found to give a little more latitude to journalists than was previously the case, especially for material published either months before a trial or distributed in parts of the country far away from the jury catchment area of the court of trial.

This should not be interpreted as giving leave to publish anything whatever at an early stage. Contempt is still possible even then, especially in assuming the guilt of the accused, in disclosing his previous convictions or other information derogatory of him, or in the publication of a photograph of him if identity is to be an issue at his trial or at a police identity parade. There is a particular danger of contempt arising from the publication of matter which might be said to interfere with the course of justice while a trial is actually in progress and the jury is thus more vulnerable to outside influences (see later in this chapter).

There have been a number of cases in the 1990s where judges have abandoned trials because of the possible effect of this pre-trial publicity even though publication took place some time before the trial . Other trials have been delayed or moved to a less convenient place to lessen the likelihood of potential jurors being influenced.

However, most judges in England and Wales have accepted that pre-trial publicity which is merely prejudicial, rather than meeting the higher test of a substantial risk of serious prejudice, is not to be treated as a contempt under the strict liability rule.

## Effect on the jury

As long ago as 1969, Mr Justice (later Lord Justice) Lawton said: 'I have enough confidence in my fellow-countrymen to think that they have got newspapers sized up … and they are capable in normal circumstances of looking at a matter fairly and without prejudice even though they have to disregard what they have read in a newspaper …. It is a matter of human experience and certainly a matter of experience for those who practise in the criminal courts first that the public's recollection is short, and secondly, that the drama, if I may use that term, of a trial almost always has the effect of excluding from recollection that which went before.' (*R v Kray* [1969] 53 Cr App Rep 412.)

More recently, some senior judges have taken the view that a jury when instructed by the judge is capable of looking at the evidence fairly even though they may have to disregard what they have read or heard.

The Court of Appeal in April 1996 dismissed an appeal by Rosemary West against her convictions for murder. One of the grounds of the appeal was that adverse press coverage about Fred and Rosemary West meant that she could no longer get a fair trial. The Lord Chief Justice, Lord Taylor, rejected this argument. He said that to hold that view would mean that if allegations of murder were sufficiently horrendous as to shock the nation, the accused could not be tried. That would be absurd. 'Moreover provided the judge effectively warns the jury to act only on the evidence given in court, there is no reason to believe that they would do otherwise,' he said.

Three months later the Queen's Bench Divisional Court refused to hold five national newspapers in contempt through reports they had carried after the arrest of Geoff Knights on a charge of wounding a cab driver. Knights' trial at Harrow Crown Court had been abandoned in October 1995 by Judge Roger Sanders, who accepted submissions that Knights could not get a fair trial.

Lord Justice Schiemann gave the Queen's Bench Divisional Court's reasons for not finding the newspapers in contempt (*Attorney-General v MGN Ltd* (1996) 31 July, unreported). He said it was difficult to see how any of the articles complained of created any greater risk of serious prejudice than that which had already been created by publicity about Knights before the incident with the cab driver. However, he accepted that there could be circumstances where it was proper to stay a trial on the grounds of prejudice even though no individual was guilty of contempt.

## Principles of the strict liability rule

Lord Justice Schiemann set out the principles for the application of the strict liability rule. He said each case must be decided on its own merits and the court would test matters as they were at the time of publication. The mere fact that by reason of earlier publications there was already some risk of prejudice did not in itself prevent a finding that the latest publication had created a further risk. The court would not convict of contempt unless it was sure that the publication in question had created some substantial risk that the course of justice would not only be impeded or prejudiced but seriously so. In assessing this, the court would consider the likelihood of the publication coming to the attention of a potential juror, the likely impact on an ordinary reader and, crucially, the residual impact on a notional juror at the time of the trial.

In assessing substantial risk a small risk multiplied by a small risk resulted in an even smaller risk, as when the long odds against a potential juror reading the publication was multiplied by the long odds of any reader remembering it.

## Risk less than substantial

In 1994, Mr Justice Lindsay giving judgment in the Chancery Court said the legislature contemplated that a risk of prejudice which could not be described as substantial had to be tolerated as the price of an open press (*MGN Pension Trustees v Bank of America National Trust and Savings Association and Credit Suisse* (1994) Independent, 14 December).

He said the authorities were almost unanimous in the respect they paid to a jury's ability to put out of mind that which should not be in mind. He quoted Lord Denning, Master of the Rolls, who in 1982 said that the risk of juries being influenced was so slight it could usually be disregarded as insubstantial.

Next he quoted Sir John (later Lord) Donaldson, Lord Denning's successor as Master of the Rolls, who said that trials by their nature served to cause all concerned to become progressively more inward-looking, studying the evidence given and submissions made, to the exclusion of other sources of enlightenment.

Finally, Mr Justice Lindsay quoted Lord Taylor, Lord Chief Justice, as saying in 1993 in the Court of Appeal (*Ex p The Telegraph* [1993] 1 WLR 987): 'In determining whether publication of matter would cause a substantial risk of prejudice to a future trial, a court should credit the jury with the will and ability to abide by the judge's direction to decide the case only on the evidence before them. The court should also bear in mind that the staying power and detail of publicity, even in cases of notoriety, are limited and that the nature of a trial is to focus the jury's minds on the evidence put before them rather than on matters outside the courtroom.'

In May 1994, when prosecutions for contempt against Independent Television News, the *Daily Mail*, *Daily Express*, *Today*, and the *Northern Echo* (Darlington) failed, the Queen's Bench Divisional Court decided that there was no more than a remote risk of serious prejudice actually occurring.

The court held that no contempt had been established because of the length of time between publication and trial, the limited circulation of copies of the papers which contained the offending material, and the ephemeral nature of a single ITN broadcast.

The material complained of had been used within two days of the arrest of two Irishmen on charges of murdering a special constable and the attempted murder of another police officer.

ITN had said in its early evening news bulletin that one of the arrested men, Paul Magee, was a convicted IRA terrorist who had escaped from prison while serving a life sentence for the murder of an SAS officer. Next day, three national newspapers used similar stories and a fourth gave information about Magee's past without actually mentioning his conviction for murdering the SAS officer.

Lord Justice Leggatt said it was of overriding importance that the lapse of time between the publications and the trial was likely to be nine months, and in the event was.

He was not persuaded that viewers of the ITN broadcast would have retained the information for that time. Different considerations would have applied if the information had been repeated. In the case of the newspapers, the risk of serious prejudice occurring was diminished; in the case of one newspaper, the *Northern Echo*, it was annulled because only

146 copies of the paper were on sale in London where Magee's trial was to take place. Although the possibility of leakage of the previous conviction through a juror having heard about it indirectly by word of mouth did exist, the risk was so slight as to be insubstantial.

The risk of prejudice could never be excluded but the requirement for strict liability contempt was the criminal standard of proof beyond all reasonable doubt. ITN had been extremely careless and the newspapers had behaved erroneously. The broadcast should never have taken place nor the articles been published but, as stated, no contempt had been committed.

Some editors have taken the *Northern Echo* judgment to mean that regional newspapers may be allowed to report more widely on crime which is to be tried at a great distance from their circulation area.

The lapse of time was a factor in assessing the substantial risk of serious prejudice in a contempt case in 1986. The cricketer Ian Botham had issued a writ for libel against a newspaper which had published allegations about his activities during the MCC tour of New Zealand. The libel case was set down for trial not before March 1987, but in 1985 another newspaper, the *News of the World*, published similar allegations linked to a tour in the West Indies.

The Court of Appeal held that because of the lapse of time between the publication of the *News of the World* article and the trial due to take place before a jury at least ten months later, the test of a substantial risk of serious prejudice was not satisfied and therefore the *News of the World* was not in contempt of court.

## When proceedings are active

A writer, editor, publisher, proprietor, director, or distributor of any publication may be held to be in contempt regardless of intent only if proceedings are active at the time of publication. The Act says criminal proceedings are deemed to be active from the relevant initial step — if a person has been arrested, or a warrant for his arrest has been issued, or a summons has been issued, or if a person has been charged orally.

However, the reporter may not know whether a person who is with the police, after a crime has been committed, has actually been arrested or is merely 'helping the police with their inquiries'. If he is at the police station against his will, he is, in law, under arrest, whether or not the proper arrest procedures have taken place. There are many cases where journalists do not know if a person has willingly gone to the police station and is to go home later, or is to be detained. The Police and Criminal Evidence Act 1984 provides that where a person attends voluntarily at a police station without having been arrested, he is entitled to leave at will unless placed under arrest. (Quite apart from the contempt issue, there may also be a libel risk in naming a person who is helping the police with their inquiries — see chapter 2.)

In some cases, where the police have other suspects in mind, they may not wish to disclose that they have arrested one person.

Often, the press do not know a warrant has been issued. If a journalist is not certain whether proceedings are active or not, he should use extreme caution.

As a result of a case in 1985, proceedings are also active if an inquest has been opened, even if the evidence given was merely formal, and even if the inquest was adjourned, without a date being fixed (see chapter 15).

## When proceedings cease to be active

Under the Act the risk ceases to apply if:
(a) the arrested person is released without being charged (except when released on police bail);
(b) no arrest is made within 12 months of the issue of a warrant;
(c) the case is discontinued;
(d) the defendant is acquitted or sentenced; or
(e) he is found unfit to be tried, or unfit to plead, or the court orders the charge to lie on file.

The Act leaves open the possibility that the journalist and his newspaper may be liable for contempt even though a jury has returned a guilty verdict and the defendant is merely awaiting sentence by the judge. In the past, judges have expressed differing views as to whether they could be affected by anything that appeared in a newspaper (for example, background stories about the accused and the crime) once the jury has discharged its duty. A carefully-written background article may seem unlikely to create a substantial risk of serious prejudice to the sentencing process. Additionally it may be protected by the defence of a discussion in good faith of public affairs under section 5 of the Act (see later this chapter).

The Act provides that if an appeal is lodged liability for contempt resumes from the lodging of the appeal and ends again when hearing of the appeal is completed unless a new trial is ordered or the case remitted to a lower court. Thus there is a free-for-all time (the words of Sir Michael Havers when Attorney-General) between sentence and the lodging of any appeal.

Often a lawyer announces at the end of a case that his client will appeal but liability for contempt does not resume until the appeal is lodged formally.

Appeals to the Court of Appeal from crown court trials may be lodged at a crown court office. Appeals on a point of law to the Queen's Bench Divisional Court from a crown court appeal hearing must be lodged at the

Royal Courts of Justice in London. Appeals from magistrates court summary trials may be lodged at a local crown court office.

## Police appeals for press assistance

Sometimes when the police have obtained a warrant for a person's arrest, they seek the help of the press and television in tracing him. Technically, a newspaper publishing a police message which links the wanted man with the crime could be at risk of contempt. But the Attorney-General said in the House of Commons during the debate on the Contempt Bill in 1981:

> It is plainly right that the police should be able to warn the public through the press that a particular suspect is dangerous and should not be tackled, or it may simply be that they issue a photograph or some other identification of the wanted man. The press has nothing whatever to fear from publishing in reasoned terms anything which may assist in the apprehension of a wanted man and I hope that it will continue to perform this public service.

There is no known case of a newspaper being held in contempt after publishing a police appeal, but a judge could still decide it was contempt.

The Attorney-General's comments would not apply to information supplied by the police and published or repeated after an arrest had been made as this could not be said to be information published to assist in tracing a wanted man.

## Defence in not knowing proceedings were active

Section 3 of the Act provides a publisher with a defence for contempt of court under the strict liability rule if, at the time of publication, having taken all reasonable care, he did not know and had no reason to suspect that relevant proceedings were active. The burden of proof, however, in establishing that all reasonable care was taken is upon the publisher accused of contempt. To avail his newspaper of this defence, therefore, a journalist reporting a crime story must check with the police to make sure no suspect is to hand. He should make a habit of noting the time and the name of the police informant.

## Contempt in court reporting

One of the greatest dangers of being in contempt of court through creating prejudice can arise in what is published when a jury has started to try a case.

It has long been recognised that there are some circumstances in which even a fair and accurate report of proceedings in open court, though privileged against an action for defamation (see chapter 20), could nevertheless prejudice a fair trial and thus be contempt of court.

For example, it may be contempt to report details of proceedings in any court which take place after the jury is sent out during legal submissions. These submissions may be on the admissibility of a witness's evidence or about matters incriminating the defendant. To make it possible for the jury to read such submissions in a newspaper or hear them in a broadcast before the end of the trial would defeat the purpose of the jury being sent out.

A newspaper which adds extraneous information to a report of an ongoing trial before a jury may also be held in contempt. Even information which has previously been in the public domain is not exempt from this. In 1981, the *Guardian* was fined £5,000 for contempt because during a trial it recalled that two of the accused had previously escaped from custody. The jury had not been told of their escape. The trial had to be abandoned and held afresh in the following year.

In several cases, judges have taken a stern view when journalists have reported even the actual proceedings in the court before the jury has been brought in. Sometimes, a defendant facing a number of charges will plead guilty to some but deny others, and then the jury will be brought in to try him on the charges he has denied. If a newspaper carrying a report before the end of the trial mentions that the defendant has pleaded guilty to some offences, the judge may feel it necessary to stop the trial and to order a re-trial before a fresh jury in another town at great expense to public funds.

In 1981, before the 1981 Act took effect, four evening newspapers were each fined £500 for contempt of court arising in this way. In no case had the judge indicated to reporters present that they should not report the guilty pleas made before the jury was brought in.

The 1981 Act gives the courts power to rule that some matters should not be reported for the time being. Section 4(2) says:

> The court may, where it appears to be necessary for avoiding a substantial risk of prejudice to the administration of justice in those proceedings, or in any other proceedings, pending or imminent, order that the publication of any report of those proceedings or any part of those proceedings be postponed for such period as the court thinks necessary for that purpose.

Section 4 of the Act also provides that when publication of a report is ordered to be postponed, eventual publication of it will be treated as contemporaneous for purposes of privilege against a libel action if the report is published as soon as is practicable after the order expires.

The Act says, however, that subject to any such court order a person is not guilty of contempt of court under the strict liability rule in respect of a fair and accurate report of legal proceedings held in public published contemporaneously and in good faith.

In 1982, the Attorney-General said this provision did not apply to reports of licensing magistrates and other administrative tribunals as these were not courts within the meaning of the Act. Therefore newspapers risked contempt proceedings if they published reports of such hearings that might prejudice pending criminal trials.

In reporting courts generally, it might be assumed from this provision that if a court inadvertently omits to make an order banning immediate publication of statements made in open court which could prejudice a fair trial (eg legal submissions made in the middle of a crown court trial during the absence of the jury), a journalist and his paper would not be in contempt in reporting these statements.

However, one view is that if a court failed to make an order prohibiting publication of a report of proceedings in the absence of the jury and a journalist reported these matters, a judge might hold him in contempt on the ground that he had not acted in good faith as required by the Act.

In February 1985 during the trial of Clive Ponting, a civil servant, on a charge under the Official Secrets Act, the judge discussed with counsel in the absence of the jury the instructions he should give to the jury on their return to court. The *Observer* published a report of these discussions, while the trial was still in progress.

The judge said afterwards that he had not issued a directive under section 4 prohibiting publication because it had never occurred to him that the discussions would be publicised before the end of the trial.

He referred the matter to the Attorney-General who later announced that he had decided not to prosecute the *Observer* for contempt.

It is permissible to indicate in a general way that the jury were excluded during legal submissions and to report anything about the submissions that is said before the jury is sent out of court or after they return.

It is permissible to report details after the defendant has been tried.

It should be noted that the Act empowers any court, for example a magistrates court, to order postponement of a report. A magistrates court can make such an order delaying a report of a preliminary hearing of an indictable offence, or part of it, even if the defendant has chosen to have reporting restrictions lifted under section 8 of the Magistrates' Courts Act 1981. In November 1981 the Queen's Bench Divisional Court ruled that such an order should be no wider than was necessary to prevent the possibility of prejudice.

## Tainted acquittals

If a person is convicted of an offence involving intimidation of a witness and the court believes that a fresh trial may now take place of a person who was acquitted because of that intimidation, a section 4 order may be made postponing reporting of the proceedings against the person guilty of the intimidation offence. Once the court dealing with the intimidation offence grants a certificate as a first step towards a new trial of the person originally acquitted, proceedings for the new trial are treated as if they were pending or imminent for the purposes of making a section 4 order. This new provision, in the Criminal Procedure and Investigations Act 1996, makes an inroad into the principle that a person once acquitted by a jury cannot be tried again for the same offence.

## Reporting of section 4 orders

Is it permissible to report that a section 4 order has been made and the terms of the order? Lord Justice Mann said in the Queen's Bench Divisional Court in 1992 that if the courts were minded to make orders preventing the public from knowing what was going on in a public court, those orders should be drafted and made public in such a way that it was crystal clear what the press could or could not do.

## Section 11 orders

Section 11 of the Contempt of Court Act also gives power to the courts when they allow a name or other matter to be withheld from the public, to prohibit the publication of that name or matter in connection with the proceedings, as appears to the court to be necessary for the purpose for which it was withheld. The power is intended to prevent the names of blackmail victims or people involved in national security from being revealed and secret processes from being disclosed.

There has been criticism that the courts have, in many cases, been using both the 'delaying powers' of section 4 and the 'no names' powers of section 11 without good cause. A number of regional papers have successfully challenged in the Queen's Bench Divisional Court orders made in magistrates courts, and orders made at crown court can now be challenged in the Court of Appeal.

See also chapter 12, Invalid orders.

## Crime stories

One of the most common situations where a journalist could find himself in contempt of court arises in crime reporting.

It has been argued that the 'substantial risk of serious prejudice' test for strict liability contempt has created a more liberal climate for some stories published at the time of the arrest.

Before proceedings become active because of an arrest, or the issue of a warrant for arrest, there will normally be no danger under the strict liability rule of the 1981 Act, but there is still a possibility of contempt at common law, as already explained.

Once proceedings become active, the crime can still be reported but the story must be carefully worded lest it should suggest in any way that those in police hands are indeed the culprits.

Thus, one can report a post office robbery and say that later a man was arrested, but not *the* man was arrested. It would also be prejudicial to describe the appearance of three men who raided a bank as being tall or dark-haired or bearded, lest those arrested answered to that description. To publish such matter would be to curtail the ability of the defence to contest identity.

There are dangers too in publishing interviews with a witness to a crime once an arrest has been made, where the witness makes contentious statements. A witness who sees his account published in a newspaper or on television may be less receptive to questions put in cross-examination or examination-in-chief and feel obliged to stick to his story, even when wrong.

Interviewing witnesses with a view to publication of material after the trial, though probably permissible in most cases, should be handled with care, lest even this might be said to influence a witness in sticking to the account he gave to the journalist when he comes to give evidence.

It could also be contempt to publish background material about an accused person. In particular, any statement implying that an arrested man has a previous criminal history is likely to be treated as a serious contempt.

A Scottish daily newspaper was fined £20,000 and its editor £750, in 1979, for contempt of court arising from an article published at the time of the arrest of four people on drugs charges. The article referred to three of the four as having escaped from custody in the Netherlands. It said they set up a registered company and imported chemicals and that a large quantity of drugs was seized from a bungalow they occupied.

Some matter will be common ground, not creating a substantial risk of serious prejudice, and in each case the decision on whether to publish it must be taken in the light of the effect it might have on the mind of a potential juror or magistrate.

Journalists should also be aware that it is possible to prejudice proceedings in favour of the accused, as well as against him. Newspaper campaigns to secure an acquittal could be held to be contempt.

## Discussion of public affairs

Section 5 of the Contempt of Court Act was introduced because of complaints that freedom of expression in the United Kingdom had been unnecessarily restricted by a ruling given in a case in 1974. The *Sunday Times* wanted to publish an article raising important issues of public interest on the way the drug thalidomide had been marketed at a time when civil actions were pending against the manufacturers, Distillers Company (Biochemicals) Ltd, on behalf of children affected by the drug before their birth.

The House of Lords ruled in an appeal that the proposed article would be contempt, because the public interest in the proper administration of justice outweighed the public interest in discussion of the matters raised in the article.

Commenting on the decision, the Government-appointed Phillimore Committee said in 1974:

At any given moment many thousands of legal proceedings are in progress, a number of which may well raise or reflect such issues (matters of general public interest). If, for example, a general public debate about fire precautions in hotels is in progress, the debate clearly ought not to be brought to a halt simply because a particular hotel is prosecuted for breach of the fire regulations.

The European Court of Human Rights in 1979 held that the Lords' ruling violated Article 10 of the European Convention on Human Rights, which affirmed freedom of expression.

The Government's response to the Phillimore Committee and the Court was to introduce a new defence. It is that a publication made as, or as part of, a discussion in good faith of public affairs is not to be treated as contempt of court under the strict liability rule if the risk of impediment or prejudice to particular legal proceedings is merely incidental to the discussion. The time of liability for contempt in civil proceedings was also changed (see later in this chapter).

Two newspapers were prosecuted in 1981 for contempt arising from comments published during the trial of Dr Leonard Arthur, a paediatrician accused of murdering a Down's Syndrome baby. The *Sunday Express* admitted contempt in an article by John Junor, the editor. The article complained of the trial taking five weeks and said if the Down's Syndrome baby had been allowed to live so long he might have found someone apart from God to love him. The editor was fined £1,000 and Express Newspapers £10,000.

The *Daily Mail*, however, denied contempt. When the case was heard in the Queen's Bench Divisional Court, the court rejected a submission put forward by the *Daily Mail* that its article, by Malcolm Muggeridge, was a discussion in good faith of public affairs under section 5 and that the risk of prejudice was merely incidental.

On appeal, the House of Lords held that the article did create a substantial risk of serious prejudice to the trial of Dr Arthur. But it ruled that the article did meet the criterion of being written in good faith and because it was written in support of a pro-life candidate at a by-election it was a discussion of public affairs.

Lord Diplock said the article made no express mention of the Arthur case and the risk of prejudice would be properly described as merely incidental.

A television company and the proprietors of a free newspaper accused of contempt of court in 1989 failed when they pleaded that the offending item was a discussion in good faith of public affairs, under the terms of section 5.

Lord Justice Lloyd said in the Queen's Bench Divisional Court that one test of section 5 was to look at the subject matter of the discussion and see how closely it related to particular legal proceedings. 'The more closely it relates, the easier it will be for the Attorney-General to show that the risk of prejudice is not merely incidental to the discussion.'

TVS Television Ltd was fined £25,000 and H W Southey £5,000 for carrying reports which caused a trial at Reading Crown Court to be stopped and re-heard later, at an estimated additional cost of £215,000.

TVS had screened an investigation 'The New Rachmans' while one of the landlords identified in the programme was on trial accused of conspiracy to defraud the DSS. The free newspaper carried a story based on a TVS press release.

Lord Justice Lloyd also rejected a submission that the new 'Rachmanism' had been the subject of a public discussion in Reading for many years and therefore did not create a substantial risk of prejudice. The judge said publication in the middle of a trial would have had a very different impact since it dealt with a matter with which the jury were very closely concerned.

## Time of liability for contempt in civil proceedings

The Act says that civil proceedings are deemed to be active for contempt purposes when the case is set down for trial, or when a date is fixed for the case to be heard. 'Setting down for trial' is a technical stage when the case enters a waiting list where it may remain for months. Liability lasts until the case is disposed of, abandoned, discontinued, or withdrawn. Contempt of court by publication is less likely in civil proceedings however. Juries are rarely used apart from in actions for defamation, false imprisonment, or malicious prosecution.

## Tape recordings

It is contempt of court under section 9 of the 1981 Act to use or take into court for use, any tape recorder (except by permission of the court), or to make any recordings.

*Tribunals*

See chapter 16.

*Interviewing jurors*

See chapter 7.

**Pictures**

Publication of a photograph can in general be contempt just as much as an accompanying story.

The rule is that publication of the photograph of a defendant is not likely to be contempt provided there is no argument about his identity. But if the case hinges on witnesses identifying the defendant, in court or at an identity parade, as a man who committed the crime, to use a picture of the man would clearly be contempt.

In 1994, a record fine for contempt of court of £80,000 was imposed by the Queen's Bench Divisional Court on the *Sun* which published a photograph of a man accused of murder. This picture was published six weeks before a police identity parade, in which he was picked out by witnesses. Kelvin MacKenzie, editor at the time of publication, was fined £20,000. Lord Justice Steyn said two witnesses who saw the photograph in the *Sun* and who picked out the accused man at the identity parade were cross-examined at the trial. He said that not surprisingly the defence were able to argue that their identification was unreliable. Kelvin MacKenzie had said that the *Sun* did not know an identity parade was imminent when the photograph was published.

**Contempt at common law**

As stated, it remains possible for a journalist to be prosecuted for common law contempt, outside the provisions of the Contempt of Court Act, eg when proceedings are not yet active.

But the prosecution has to prove the journalist intended to create prejudice. The court can infer intent from all the circumstances, including the foreseeability of the consequences of the conduct. Nor need it be the journalist's sole intention. In legal terms intent is not the same as motive or desire.

If an armed man against whom no proceedings were active were in a house holding police at bay, it could be contempt of court to publish or broadcast a list of his previous crimes. It could be argued that the editor must have realised that the eventual proceedings were bound to be prejudiced and the court could infer from this that he intended this result, even if he did not desire it.

In 1988 the *Sun* was fined £75,000 for contempt at common law. The newspaper offered to fund a private prosecution of a doctor on a charge of raping an eight-year-old girl, and then published two articles with details of the allegation.

The newspaper said that at common law no offence was committed unless the proceedings were 'pending or imminent', but Lord Justice Watkins rejected this argument. Contempt could be committed if proceedings were not imminent, he said.

He said intent was proved because the editor must have foreseen that the articles he published and the steps he announced he was taking to assist the mother to prosecute would incur a real risk of prejudicing the fairness of the doctor's trial.

But in 1991 the *Sport* newspaper and its editor were cleared of contempt at common law after they published previous convictions of a rapist being sought by police for questioning about a missing schoolgirl. No warrant had been issued, so the case was not active under the strict liability rule of the 1980 Act.

The editor said he had ignored police requests not to publish because the rapist was 'on the run and a danger to other women'. The court held the Attorney-General had not proved intent beyond reasonable doubt.

The two judges in this case disagreed as to whether Lord Justice Watkins was right in saying (above) that contempt could be committed when proceedings were not yet imminent, so the law on this point remains unclear.

In 1987 the *Sunday Times* and the *Independent* were found guilty of contempt of court for publishing material from Peter Wright's book *Spycatcher* at a time when injunctions were in force against the *Observer* and the *Guardian* (see chapter 23).

The injunctions were interim (temporary), intended to prevent publication of confidential information until the issues could be argued at trial, and lawyers said there would be little point having a trial if the confidential material had already been published by other papers and so was no longer confidential. Thus the administration of justice would be impeded.

The cases against the *Observer* and the *Guardian* were not active because they had not been set down for trial.

The strict liability rule of the Act applies only to publications likely to affect particular proceedings. A publication interfering with the course of justice generally without affecting particular proceedings, such as an article after a trial which vilified witnesses for coming forward to give evidence, could not be treated as strict liability contempt. Proceedings would no longer be active and the article would not create prejudice to particular proceedings. Therefore it could be dealt with only at common law.

# Appeals

Under section 13 of the Administration of Justice Act 1960, a right of appeal is provided for a person held to be in contempt. Appeals from the High Court (except from the Divisional Court) and the county court go to the Court of Appeal, and appeals from the Divisional Court and the Court of Appeal go to the House of Lords.

## Report of hearings in private

Section 12 of the 1960 Act laid down that publication of information about proceedings held *in camera* or in chambers shall not in itself be contempt. It is, however, contempt to report proceedings involving mental health, national security, or secret processes; wardship of court, cases under the Children Act 1989, and others relating wholly or mainly to the maintenance or upbringing of children (see chapter 6).

In *Pickering v Liverpool Daily Post* (1991), a man convicted of a number of sexual attacks and ordered to be detained in a secure mental hospital wanted to prevent the press publishing details of his application to a mental health tribunal for discharge. The House of Lords said the press could report that a named patient had applied to a tribunal. That was not 'information relating to the proceedings' within section 12.

The essential privacy protected by the exceptions in section 12 attached to the substance of the matters that the court had closed its doors to consider. The press could report that the tribunal would sit, was sitting, or had sat on a certain date, time, or place behind closed doors. It could report the decision of the tribunal to discharge, absolutely or conditionally. But it could not report the recorded reasons for the decision because these disclosed the evidence and other material on which it was based.

The Lord Chief Justice said in 1971, during an espionage trial, that speculation about what had gone on in court while it was sitting *in camera* was potentially contempt of court.

There is nothing to prevent a newspaper reporting the outcome of applications made to a judge in chambers for bail or for a bill of indictment, provided no order has been made under section 4 of the Contempt Act.

## Scandalising the court

The courts have often held that the conduct of the judges in court and decisions of the court are matters of legitimate concern, and the press has a right, and even a duty, to criticise in good faith within reasonable limits.

Lord Atkin said in the Appeal Court in 1936: 'Justice is not a cloistered virtue. She must be allowed to suffer the scrutiny and respectful, even though outspoken, comment of ordinary men.'

He said, however, that there must be no imputing of improper motives to those administering justice.

What is prohibited is scurrilous abuse of a judge and attacks upon the integrity or impartiality of a judge or court. In 1928, an article in the *New Statesman* saying that Dr Marie Stopes, the birth control pioneer, could apparently not hope for a fair hearing before Mr Justice Avory was held to be a contempt and the magazine was ordered to pay costs.

Today, a newspaper may be more likely to be sued for defamation by a judge whose good faith is questioned than it is to be prosecuted for contempt of court.

## Questions

1　In what circumstances may an article be treated as contempt of court under the 1981 Act's strict liability rule? What is meant by that rule?
2　How can an article be in contempt of court even though it does not prejudice a particular trial?
3　If a newspaper is in contempt who may be proceeded against?
4　Who may take action for an alleged contempt of court under the strict liability rule?
5　When does the risk of contempt of court start in the case of a newspaper article? How is this starting point defined, for criminal proceedings, by the Contempt of Court Act 1981? How long does the risk last for criminal proceedings?
6　A warrant is issued for a man's arrest and the police seek the help of a newspaper in tracing him. Explain the newspaper's liability for contempt.
7　How long does liability for contempt of court last if a warrant for arrest is issued and the man is not arrested?
8　If a jury at crown court returns a guilty verdict but sentence is postponed, what is a newspaper's position in the law of contempt should it wish to comment on the case?
9　If a court finds a defendant guilty and his solicitor then says it is his intention to appeal, what is a newspaper's position in the law of contempt?
10　What defence does a journalist have under the Contempt of Court Act 1981 if he is accused of contempt after the publication of a crime story, but did not know that an arrest had been made?
11　How can a fair and accurate report of court proceedings be in contempt? What powers do the courts have to stop a newspaper from publishing a report of court proceedings?

12 How can a court stop a newspaper publishing the name of someone involved in court proceedings? In what circumstances are such powers likely to be used?

13 How must a crime story be made safe once the police arrest a suspect?

14 Explain how publication of a picture could be held to be contempt of court.

15 Detail the defence a newspaper might have if it publishes a general news story on some social issue when a trial is about to take place involving such an issue.

16 At what time does risk of contempt of court start when a civil case is to be tried?

# 18   Defamation

## The Defamation Act 1996

The Defamation Act 1996 made significant changes. Some of these changes, as recorded in the following chapters, were implemented on 4 September 1996. Others were expected to be implemented in 1997, but the date had not been announced when this edition of *McNae* went to press in May. For that reason, the book covers the provisions of the Act and also states the previous law.

## Dangers of defamation

For the journalist, the publisher, and distributor of newspapers – indeed, for anyone who earns his living with words – the law of defamation presents one of the greatest perils.

The law exists to protect the reputation of the individual (both his moral reputation and his professional reputation) from unjustified attack. Such an attack may be dealt with either as a civil or as a criminal matter. In civil law it is a tort – that is, a civil wrong for which monetary damages may be claimed.

The principle is the same as that involved in an action for damages brought by a man who has been physically injured as a result of another's act, whether through negligence or premeditated attack. He may sue for damages and, if successful, will be awarded a sum of money by way of compensation.

As we have seen (in chapter 1), the law of defamation tries to strike a balance between the individual's right to have his reputation protected and freedom of speech, which implies the freedom to expose wrongdoing and thus to damage reputation.

So the law provides certain defences for the person who makes a defamatory statement about another for an acceptable reason.

Newspapers, however, are sometimes reluctant to fight defamation actions even when they seem to have a strong defence. There are various reasons for this.

The first is the uncertainty involved in libel actions. For example, the statement that seems to one person quite innocuous may, equally clearly, be defamatory to another. It is often difficult, therefore, even for lawyers skilled in the law of defamation to be able to forecast the jury's decision (see 'What is defamatory', next section).

Then even if a journalist and his newspaper are convinced of the truth of his story, he may be unable to prove it in court (see 'Justification' in chapter 20).

Because the outcome of a case may be unpredictable, a newspaper has to consider very carefully indeed the money involved if it loses. Again, the matter is difficult to assess. In personal injury cases a judge decides the damages to be paid to a successful plaintiff. He can assess the value of a limb, or an eye, or even a life by the application of certain standards, such as a person's age and earning capacity.

In libel cases, however, damages are normally determined by a jury. We do not know how they reach their decision, but there is little doubt that in general they find it a difficult and confusing job and some have awarded huge sums. Until recently the Court of Appeal had no power to vary awards, and judges were prevented from advising juries, except in the most general terms, on how to estimate the worth of a man's good reputation, or the extent to which it was in danger of being damaged by a false statement or unfair criticism.

In 1990 the Court of Appeal was given the power to vary jury awards, and in 1995 the court reduced to £75,000 a jury award of £350,000 to the singer Elton John for an article in the *Sunday Mirror* which had described his behaviour at a Hollywood party and said he was hooked on a bizarre diet which involved chewing food, then spitting it out without swallowing it. He had argued the words implied he was lying when he said he had overcome his bulimia.

In its judgment in this case, the court said that in future libel actions judges and counsel would be allowed to draw the attention of juries to the level of awards in personal injury cases and could suggest the level of award they would consider appropriate in a particular libel action.

It is too soon to assess the effect of these changes. However, it seems likely that awards will continue to be substantial. Five days after the Court of Appeal's ruling, a judge used the new powers when summing up in a libel action brought by David Ashby MP against the *Sunday Times*, which had alleged he shared a double bed with another man during a holiday. The judge said damages of less than £50,000 would be niggardly, but more than £120,000 would be extravagant. (In the event, the jury found for the newspaper.)

In 1996 a hospital consultant won £625,000 damages against the *Daily Mirror*, which had referred to him as 'Dr Dolittle' for failing to find a hospital bed for a patient who later died. The judge had merely told the jury not to go mad and to keep their feet on the ground.

Very large sums have been awarded not only against wealthy tabloid newspapers but also against small publications whose continued existence has been threatened. And they have been awarded not only for stories of sex and scandal but also for articles in which the media erred while trying to fulfil their traditional role as the public's watchdog.

But the damages award, large as it often is, is frequently exceeded by the legal costs, which are generally met largely by the loser. In 1994 the BBC was ordered to pay an estimated £1.5 million costs in a case where a judge, rather than a jury, had heard the case and awarded £60,000 damages. The libel was contained in a Panorama programme, 'The Halcion nightmare', which reported that, long before the sleeping drug was banned in the United Kingdom, evidence existed that it might have had serious adverse side effects.

The dilemma that may be faced by an editor who wishes to publish material he believes to be in the public interest, such as a warning against a powerful organisation, was illustrated graphically in 1981 by the Moonies case, *Orme v Associated Newspapers Ltd*. Dennis Orme, leader of the Unification Church (the Moonies) in Britain, sued over an article in the *Daily Mail* which said the church was a sinister organisation that brainwashed young people into economic servitude, broke up families, and left parents in despair.

The case lasted 100 days, and the jury heard 117 witnesses, many from overseas. The jury found for the newspaper, and Orme was ordered to pay costs estimated at about £400,000.

Sir David English, the editor, recalled after the case that he had asked the paper's lawyers how much it might cost if the paper were to fight and lose. He was told: 'It might be as much as a million pounds.'

He was told that if the paper won it might still have to pay 'up to half a million' because the *Daily Mail* could not be sure of getting back its costs from the Unification Church.

It is not surprising that, faced with that kind of decision, even the more ardent campaigning papers sometimes decide either not to carry the story or, having carried it, to apologise and settle out of court by payment of damages. The alternative may be the extinction of the paper.

Indeed, the vast majority of libel cases are settled out of court, without any publicity, and for this reason the cost of libel to newspapers is often underestimated.

The Defamation Act 1996 introduced a summary procedure for trying defamation cases, which it was hoped would reduce the cost of smaller-scale libel actions. It was expected that this change in the law would be implemented during 1997. Under the new procedure a party to a defamation action can apply to a court for the matter to be heard by a judge alone, or the judge himself can decide to deal with the case in this way. The judge can dismiss the plaintiff's claim if it has no realistic prospect of success. If, however, there is no realistic defence to the claim, the judge can give judgment for up to £10,000 in damages, a declaration that the statement complained of was false and defamatory, an order preventing the matter complained of being further published and an order that the defendant publish a suitable correction and apology.

In the remainder of this chapter, we shall be looking at the classic definitions of defamation, in the next chapter what a plaintiff has to prove, and in the next defences available to anyone who finds himself facing an action for damages.

But first a word of warning. Because the law of defamation is so complex, this book can provide nothing more than a rough guide, an indication that a newspaper can sometimes go further, in safety, than many journalists suppose, and ought sometimes, in prudence, to stop and reflect before taking a dangerous course of action. In this way it may help to preserve a balance between excessive caution and unreasonable risk.

Beyond this it cannot claim to go. The golden rule for the journalist is that if publication seems likely to bring a threat of libel, take professional advice first.

This does not mean that the editor must necessarily take the lawyer's advice. At some time or other every editor must decide whether to play for safety or to obey his conscience and 'publish and be damned'.

The newspaper's role in exposing wrongs is an extremely important one. As Lord Justice Lawton (then Mr Justice Lawton) said in a case in 1965:

> It is one of the professional tasks of newspapers to unmask the fraudulent and the scandalous. It is in the public interest to do it. It is a job which newspapers have done time and time again in their long history.

It is a job which frequently cannot be done without risk and therefore requires a considerable degree of courage on the part of the journalists involved.

Sometimes, however, publication of the words that cause the problem are not the result of a conscious decision but the result of an innocent error. There will be a solicitor's letter from 'the other side' which may lead eventually to the High Court.

Again, this is the moment to take legal advice. Libel should not be a matter for the editorial office amateur to play with, for the dangers of aggravating the offence by mishandling are too great.

A too fulsome apology can, in certain circumstances, be as dangerous as an inadequate correction. On the other hand, the correct legal steps, taken promptly, can remove the sting from an action and save perhaps thousands of pounds.

If these comments make the subject seem rather alarming, remember that the most common cause of libel actions against newspapers is the journalist's failure to apply professional standards of accuracy and fairness.

The best protection against getting your newspaper involved in an expensive action is to make every effort to get the story right and to ensure that the 'other side' has its say.

## What is defamatory?

The law of the United Kingdom recognises in every man a right to have the estimation in which he stands in the opinion of others unaffected by false and defamatory statements and imputations.

Defamatory statements may be made in numerous ways. Broadly speaking, if the statement is written or is in any other permanent form, such as a picture, it is libel; if it is spoken or in any other transient form it is, with two exceptions, slander.

The exceptions are (i) a defamatory statement broadcast on radio or television, or in a cable programme, which by the Broadcasting Act 1990 is treated as libel, (ii) a defamatory statement in a public performance of a play, by virtue of the Theatres Act 1968.

The journalist's job in recognising and avoiding libellous statements would be simpler if there were a comprehensive definition of defamation, but no one has yet devised a definition which covers every case.

There are, however, certain definitions that judges often use when they are trying to explain defamation to juries. In a libel case, the judge rules whether the words complained of are *capable* of bearing a defamatory meaning. If the answer is yes, a jury must decide whether in the circumstances in which they were used the words *were* in fact defamatory. It is not the job of the judge when sitting with a jury to say whether words complained of *were* defamatory.

Judges tell juries that a statement about a person is defamatory of him if it tends to do any one of the following:
(a)  expose him to hatred, ridicule, or contempt;
(b)  cause him to be shunned or avoided;
(c)  lower him in the estimation of right-thinking members of society generally; *or*
(d)  disparage him in his business, trade, office, or profession.

Notice the words 'tends to', which are important. The person suing does not have to show that the words actually did expose him to hatred or whatever.

Judges tell juries that in deciding whether statements are defamatory they should use as their measuring stick the standard of intelligence and judgment of a completely hypothetical creature they refer to as the 'reasonable man'.

The test is whether, under the circumstances in which the statement was published, reasonable men and women to whom the publication was made would be likely to understand it in a defamatory sense.

In 1988 two lawyers sued the *Sunday World*, Dublin, for an article that said they argued in a shop about which of them first saw the last chocolate éclair. The newspaper admitted the story was not true but denied it was defamatory; it was a humorous story which made the lawyers look human.

One of the lawyers told the jury: 'I was hugely embarrassed to see myself canvassed as an ass.' The jury decided the words were defamatory and awarded the lawyers £50,000 each.

In definition (c), notice the phrase 'right-thinking members of society generally'. It is not enough for a plaintiff in a libel action to show that the words of which he complains have lowered him in the estimation of a limited class in the community who may not conform with that standard.

For example, it is not defamatory to say of a member of a club that he gave information to the police, leading to the conviction of officials of the club for keeping a gaming machine on the premises, even if that statement lowers his reputation in the eyes of members of the club. 'Right-thinking members of society' would *expect* a person to give information to the police in the circumstances.

It *is* defamatory to say of a person that he is insolvent or in financial difficulties – even though this may impute no blame to him at all.

## Meaning of words

Many statements are capable of more than one meaning. An apparently innocuous statement may carry an inference that, in the ordinary and natural meaning of the words, is defamatory. The inference is understood by someone without special knowledge who 'reads between the lines in the light of his general knowledge and experience of worldly affairs'.

The test of what the words mean is again the test of the reasonable person. It is *not* the meaning intended by the person who wrote the words, nor indeed the meaning given to them by the person to whom they were published. The point is illustrated by the following three cases.

In a case in 1988 against *Stationery Trade News*, the Charles Freeman Group, a firm of envelope importers, sued for an article that carried the headline 'Counterfeits – retailers warned'.

The article reported that retailers and wholesalers had been asked to boycott counterfeit stationery products from overseas, which were causing concern among British manufacturers. It gave examples of products imitating well-known brands and illustrated one of the products using the captions 'Impostor' and 'Real thing'.

The last two paragraphs of the article dealt with another issue. They read:

> In the envelope market, there have been similar problems involving foreign envelopes being marketed here under a British-sounding brand name.
>
> The envelope makers' association, EMMSA, recently won an origin marking victory over Charles Freeman which was selling, under its own name, the Great West range of envelopes. These products were not British as the marketing implied, but mainly from Germany. The company was required by the Trading Standards Office to include the country of origin on the label. 'This is not just a protectionist measure towards a British industry,' said Eric Smith, EMMSA chairman, 'consumers have a right to know what they are buying.'

Charles Freeman said the article, the headline, and the pictures were defamatory. The words meant 'in their natural and ordinary meaning' first that the company was guilty of marketing counterfeit envelopes and that retailers and wholesalers were being asked to boycott the company's products. In addition the company said the article meant it was marketing rubbish and had been dishonestly marketing its products as British.

The magazine denied the article bore any of these meanings – and indeed nowhere in the article can one find any of these specific allegations. However, the jury found for the envelope distributors and awarded £300,000 against the magazine (which had a controlled circulation of fewer than 9,000).

In a case the same year against Radio City, the judge said the meaning of the words was of crucial importance. The Liverpool radio station had put out a one-hour programme in which four local people strongly criticised holidays provided at a site in France by a holiday company run by another local man, David Johnson, and his wife.

The interviewer told Johnson, during the broadcast: 'We have spoken to literally dozens of people who bought holidays off you during the last two years and they have described you as a con man.'

Radio City said the broadcast meant the Johnsons knowingly or recklessly deceived 'some at least of their customers', made promises to them that they could not keep and displayed a callous indifference to the distress that such behaviour caused. And it said those allegations were true.

By contrast Johnson said the broadcast meant he was *habitually* dishonest or cynical, but the great majority of his customers were well-satisfied. The judge told the jury they must decide whether the words did in fact mean conduct towards 'at least some' customers or whether they meant 'habitual' conduct. The jury found for Johnson and awarded £350,000.

In 1989 £470,000 was awarded against the *Mail on Sunday* for libelling a food retailer and his firm in the course of an award-winning series revealing the extent to which the public was being sold food after the sell-by date. The article read in part:

Backstreet spaghetti mountain!

Eleven thousand cans of spaghetti have been discovered in a backstreet warehouse – yet another example of the thriving trade in secondhand food.

The cans were originally destined for Sainsbury's but somewhere along the complicated chain of food dealers their labels have been ripped off and replaced with the obscure brand name Samantha…

As the law stands it is perfectly legal to deal in secondhand food but health officers and consumer watchdogs are increasingly concerned about the multi-million pound business. They are particularly worried about the growth in sales of repackaged food that is near to or beyond the sell-by date stamped on the products. Food withdrawn from supermarket shelves is turning up in corner shops repacked and, in some cases, not fit for human consumption…

It was true the spaghetti had been intended originally for Sainsbury's. The *Mail on Sunday* said the article meant the company sold secondhand food of uncertain origin which was or might be unfit for human consumption, and it claimed that was true. The company said the article meant it knowingly repackaged and sold food past its sell-by date. The jury found for the food wholesalers.

The eminent judge Lord Reid summed up the question of the meaning to be given to words in this way:

Ordinary men and women have different temperaments and outlooks. Some are unusually suspicious, and some are unusually naive. One must try to envisage people between these two extremes and say what is the most damaging meaning they would put on the words in question.

The words must be read in full and in their context. As a result, a statement that might be innocuous standing alone can acquire a defamatory meaning as a result of *juxtaposition* with other material.

In the case against the *Mail on Sunday*, the judge reminded the jury the article about the 'spaghetti mountain' appeared on a page carrying the strapline: 'Exclusive Mail on Sunday Investigation: The scandal of sell-by food'. Above the article about the spaghetti was a piece carrying the headline: '"Change the law" call – shoppers want a binding date stamp' and there was a rag-out of the front-page article from the previous week's paper carrying the headline: 'The great food racket – old and unfit to eat, but it's still for sale'.

Referring to the strapline, the judge said: 'There it is at the top of the page with the black line [a six-point rule] round everything in the page. You may think the sub-editor's headline ... provides a setting for everything which appears in the page which is surrounded by that thick black line.'

Juxtaposition is a constant danger for journalists, and particularly for sub-editors and those dealing with production.

Just as a defamatory meaning may be conveyed by a particular context, so a defamatory meaning may be removed by the context. A judge said in 1835 that if in one part of a publication something disreputable to the plaintiff was stated, but that was removed by the conclusion, 'the bane and the antidote must be taken together'.

The House of Lords applied this rule in 1995 (*Charleston v News Group Newspapers Ltd*), when it dismissed a case in which Ann Charleston and Ian Smith, two actors from the television serial Neighbours, sued the *News of the World* over headlines and photographs with captions in which their faces had been superimposed on models in pornographic poses.

The main headline read: 'Strewth! What's Harold up to with our Madge?' The text said:

> What would the Neighbours say ... strait-laced Harold Bishop starring in a bondage session with screen wife Madge. The famous faces from the television soap are the unwitting stars of a sordid computer game that is available to their child fans ... The game superimposes stars' heads on near-naked bodies of real porn models. The stars knew nothing about it.

The actors' lawyers conceded that a reader who read the whole of the text would realise the photographs were mock-ups, but said many readers were unlikely to go beyond the photographs and the headlines.

Lord Bridge, one of the judges, said it was often a debatable question, which the jury must resolve, whether the antidote was effective to neutralise the bane. The answer would depend not only on the nature of the libel a headline conveyed and the language of the text that was relied on to neutralise it but also on the manner in which the whole of the material was set out and balanced. In this case, no reader could possibly have drawn a defamatory inference if he had read beyond the first paragraph of the text.

Lord Nicholls, another of the law lords, warned that words in the text of an article would not always be efficacious to 'cure' a defamatory headline. 'It all depends on the context, one element in which is the layout of the article. Those who print defamatory headlines are playing with fire.' The ordinary reader might not notice words tucked away low down in an article.

## Innuendoes

A statement may be innocuous on the surface, but be defamatory to *those with special knowledge*.

A famous judge once said that there were no words so plain that they might not be published with reference to such circumstances and to persons knowing those circumstances so as to have a meaning very different from that which would be understood by the same words used differently.

For example, for a newspaper to say of Mr Smith that he is a socialist is not obviously defamatory; but if the paper's readers know that he is a member of the Conservative Party such a statement might be held to be defamatory because it imputes he is politically dishonest.

Such a hidden meaning is referred to as an *innuendo*, from the Latin word meaning *to nod to*.

The plaintiff who claims that he has been defamed by an innuendo must show not only that the special facts or circumstances giving rise to the innuendo exist, but also that these facts are known to the people to whom the statement complained of was published.

For example, if Mr Smith wants to sue the newspaper, he must show not only that he is a member of the Conservative Party, but also that some of the newspaper's readers know this. Otherwise, they could not understand the statement in anything other than its innocent sense.

In 1986 Lord Gowrie, a former Cabinet Minister, received 'substantial damages' after suing over a newspaper article which implied that he took drugs.

The previous year he had resigned as Minister for the Arts and the *Star* newspaper, under the headline 'A lordly price to pay', stated: 'There's been much excited chatter as to why dashing poetry-scribbling Minister Lord Gowrie left the Cabinet so suddenly. What expensive habits can he not support on an income of £33,000? I'm sure Gowrie himself would snort at suggestions that he was born with a silver spoon round his neck.'

Lord Gowrie's counsel said: 'The reference to Lord Gowrie's expensive habits, the suggestion that he was unable to support those habits on his ministerial salary, the use of the word "snort" and the reference to a "silver spoon around his neck" all bore the plain implication, to all the many familiar with the relevant terminology, that Lord Gowrie was in the habit of taking illegal drugs, in particular cocaine, and had resigned from the Cabinet because his ministerial salary was insufficient to finance the habit.'

## Changing standards

It might be easier for journalists to cope with the law of libel if the 'reasonable man' was consistent, but the standards of public opinion which this hypothetical individual is supposed to reflect are not fixed and unchangeable, but vary from time to time depending upon public attitudes in the country.

Imputations which were defamatory a hundred years ago may not be defamatory today, and vice versa.

For example, in the reign of Charles II it was held to be actionable to say of a man that he was a papist and went to mass. In the next reign similar statements were held not to be defamatory.

During the 1914-18 war a court decided that it was a libel to write of a man that he was a German.

Is it defamatory to call someone homosexual? It certainly used to be. In the case *of Ashby v Sunday Times*, referred to above, where a paper claimed an MP shared a double bed with another man, the paper's counsel argued this allegation was no longer defamatory. It is not clear what view a jury would take on that argument, but such statements are dangerous because in such cases the plaintiff generally argues that the allegation carried other defamatory inferences. Ashby argued the statement meant he was a liar and a hypocrite in denying that he had left his wife because of a homosexual affair.

## Product testing

Can a publication defame a person or a firm by disparaging goods? It is an increasingly important question as product testing becomes commonplace in newspapers and magazines.

The answer is yes. But consider first the statement that any words which disparage a person in the way of his business, trade, office, or profession are defamatory.

To fall within this category it is not sufficient that the statement should simply affect the person adversely in his business; it must impute to him discreditable conduct in his business, or else tend to show that he is ill suited or ill qualified to carry it on because he has some characteristic or lacks some other characteristic.

For example, it is defamatory to write of a businessman that he has been condemned by his trade association or of a bricklayer that he does not know how to lay bricks properly.

It is not defamatory to report incorrectly that a businessman has retired, even though such a report may result in substantial loss to the person referred to. Such a statement does not impute any misconduct or suggest that the person is in any way unsuited to carry on his trade; nor does it reflect upon his reputation in any way. (However, the wronged person may have an action for malicious falsehood: see chapter 21.)

From the above it follows that any statement in disparagement of goods or their quality is defamatory if it reflects on the owner or manufacturer in his character as a person or as a trader. Not all words that criticise a person's goods are defamatory. For example, a motoring correspondent could criticise the performance of a certain make of car without reflecting upon the character either of the manufacturer or the dealer. (Again, the statement might give rise to an action for malicious falsehood: see chapter 21.)

The imputations that give most problems are dishonesty, carelessness, and incompetence.

In a case in 1994 in which a jury awarded £1.485 million damages to the manufacturer of a yacht, Walker Wingsail Systems plc, an article in *Yachting World* contrasted the manufacturer's striking claims for the yacht's performance with the drastically poorer performance of the boat when tested by the journalist. Even the plaintiff's expert witness, who tested the boat, found the performance figures substantially worse than claimed by the manufacturer. The article also revealed that the company's claims of impressive sales 'deals' referred to returnable deposits rather than firm contracts.

The manufacturer said the article meant it had *deliberately* misled the public by its publicity material. The sales director, wife of the managing director, told the court: 'Effectively [the article] called my husband and myself charlatans and liars.' *Yachting World* denied the article meant the manufacturer had been dishonest, but said the firm had made its misleading claims carelessly and irresponsibly, and it said that was true.

We are not allowed to know which meaning the members of the jury attached to the words (see chapter 17, Juries), but the vital decision they had to make in the privacy of the jury room was what were the motives of the manufacturer in making its claims.

As we shall see in chapter 20 (Fair comment) the imputation of improper motives is a common libel risk, and very difficult to prove to the satisfaction of a jury.

In the case, also in 1994, in which the BBC had to pay £60,000 damages (with an estimated £1.5 million costs) to the makers of the drug Halcion (see above), the judge was not asked to adjudicate on the question of the safety of the drug but upon whether there had been *intentional concealment* of information relating to its safety.

So the journalist must be keenly aware of the dangers in such articles. This does not mean that articles highly critical of products cannot be published. On the contrary, the journalist has a duty to his readers to expose false claims. But he must be sure when doing so that he has protection under one of the defences explained in chapter 20 before going ahead.

One important defence is justification, which means truth. You must be careful you have your facts right. Bovril, the meat extract, collected damages in 1985 from the publishers of a book which said the product contained sugar. The statement (which was incorrect) implied the company was lying when stating the contents of its product.

The other important defence is fair comment, which allows people to give their honest views on matters of public interest. The facts upon which the comment is based must be correct. In the *Yachting World* case, the manufacturer claimed the magazine, in making its criticisms, had failed to point out that the boat when tested by the magazine was far heavier than it had been when the manufacturer's performance claims were originally made, and in addition its bottom had become badly fouled. (As stated, we have no means of knowing whether the jury accepted that argument, which the magazine strongly rejected.)

The defence also fails if the person suing can show the journalist was motivated by malice, a legal concept explained in chapter 20. The judge told the jury in the *Yachting World* case that this did not necessarily involve telling lies. He continued:

> If someone publishes defamatory matter by way of comment recklessly, without considering or caring whether it be true or false, that defendant is treated as if he or she knew it was false.

Earlier he had asked the editor of the magazine why, when he realised his journalist's performance figures were so drastically different from the firm's, he did not check back. 'Why not, in the extraordinary circumstances, before sanctioning the publication of the article, pick up the telephone and say, "Hey, this looks extraordinary. Is there any explanation?"'

But the editor said the manufacturer had already had opportunities to explain the discrepancies and the magazine's technical editor said it was policy not to 'enter into negotiations or ask for explanations'. If he did so, pressure would be put upon him and this would strike at the credibility of the magazine. 'Our readers want to see what a fair report says on the day.'

Journalists tend to accept without question the long standing journalistic policy of declining to show copy to the subjects of investigations but it could be that this approach appears less than fair to judges and juries. (Again, we do not know the attitude of the *Yachting World* jury.)

*Which* magazine, publisher of perhaps the greatest number of product tests, always sends the factual results of its tests to the subjects before publication but never the comments. Thus it can be, and is, highly critical of products while minimising the danger that its defence of fair comment will be lost as a result of challenges on facts.


## Who can sue

In addition to individuals, a corporation (see Glossary) can sue for a publication injurious to its trading reputation. And, in general, a corporation, whether trading or non-trading, can sue in libel to protect its reputation – if it has a corporate reputation distinct from that of its members which is capable of being damaged by a defamatory statement.

In the case against *Yachting World*, referred to above, the jury awarded £1 million to the firm, £450,000 to the managing director, and £35,000 to the sales director.

But in an important decision in 1993 (*Derbyshire County Council v Times Newspapers*), the House of Lords held that institutions of local or central government could not sue for defamation in respect of their 'governmental and administrative functions' because this would place an undesirable fetter on freedom of speech. They can still sue for libels affecting their property, and they can still sue for malicious falsehood over articles concerning their governmental and administrative functions if they can show malice.

Note that it will still be possible for individual members or officers of the council to sue. A judge in the House of Lords said:

> A publication attacking the activities of the authority will necessarily be an attack on the body of councillors which represents the controlling party, or on the executives who carry on the day-to-day management of its affairs. If the individual reputation of any of these is wrongly impaired by the publication any of these can himself bring proceedings for defamation.

As a general rule, an association, such as a club, cannot sue unless it is an incorporated body, but words disparaging an association will almost invariably reflect upon the reputations of one or more of the officials who, as individuals, can sue.

The Bill of Rights 1689 reserved jurisdiction in all matters relating to proceedings in Parliament to Parliament itself, and this had the effect that an MP was unable to sue a newspaper for allegations about his conduct in the House. The Defamation Act 1996, in a provision that took effect in September 1996, allows Parliamentarians to waive their parliamentary privilege in defamation actions and thus sue. The change enabled Neil Hamilton MP to continue an action against the *Guardian* over allegations that he had accepted cash for asking parliamentary questions. In October that year he abandoned his case.

## Questions

1   Why are newspapers sometimes reluctant to fight defamation cases, even when they seem to have a good case?
2   In what circumstances, if any, do you consider a newspaper should decide to 'publish and be damned' in spite of the risk of a libel action?
3   Give four definitions of a defamatory statement.
4   What standard do judges use in deciding whether a statement is capable of having a defamatory meaning?
5   What is meant, in the law of libel, by an innuendo? How does it differ from an inference?

6    Do views of what is libellous change over the years? If so, give examples.

7    Is it defamatory to report, incorrectly, that a famous pop star has become a member of a closed order of monks?

8    Could it be defamatory to report that wine sold in a local store 'cannot be the wine it is represented to be'? Or that other wine sold in the store, of a particular vintage, is not good wine?

9    What disadvantages follow from the policy of magazines and newspapers of not informing manufacturers, before publication, of the results of product testing?

# 19 What the plaintiff must prove

To succeed in an action for defamation, a person must prove three things about the statement:
(a)  it is defamatory;
(b)  it has been reasonably understood to refer to him;
(c)  it has been published to a third person.

It is almost as important for the journalist to remember what the defamed person does *not* have to prove.

Most important of all, he does not have to prove that the statement is false, although, as we shall see, if the statement is true *and the journalist can prove it is true* he has a defence.

Secondly, the plaintiff does not have to prove intention: it is normally no use the journalist saying, 'I didn't mean to discredit him.' (Intent is, however, relevant in the defence of 'unintentional defamation', under the Defamation Act 1952, and the 'offer of amends' defence, under the Defamation Act 1996: see next chapter. It is also relevant upon the issue of damages.)

Thirdly, the plaintiff does not have to prove that he has been damaged in any way. He needs to show only that the statement *tends* to discredit him. A person may, in fact, sue for libel even though the people to whom the statement was published knew it to be untrue. The court will presume damage.

## Identification

The plaintiff must be able to prove that the words of which he complains identify him as the person defamed.

Some journalists believe they can play safe by not naming the person about whom they are making the defamatory statement, but such an omission may prove no effective defence.

The test of whether the words identified the person suing is whether they would reasonably lead people *acquainted with him* to believe that he was the person referred to.

A judge said in 1826: 'It is not necessary that all the world should understand the libel; it is sufficient if those who know the plaintiff can make out that he is the person meant.' That is still the law today.

In 1987 a former Royal Navy lieutenant, Narendra Sethia, was awarded £260,000 damages against the publishers of the *Mail on Sunday* over allegations that he had stolen a log from HMS *Conqueror,* the nuclear powered submarine which sank the Argentinian cruiser the *Belgrano* during the Falklands conflict. The article did not name Sethia, but said the missing log had been recovered from a former *Conqueror* officer living in the West Indies.

His counsel argued that friends, relatives, and former naval colleagues understood this to refer to Sethia. (The matter was later settled out of court for £120,000.)

During the late 1980s and 1990s the Police Federation, representing junior police officers, made good use of this aspect of the libel law in many actions against newspapers on behalf of their members. During the 33 months to March 1996 the federation fought 95 libel actions, winning all of them and recovering £1,567,000 in damages. (A case the federation did not win, *Bennett v The Guardian* (1997), is referred to below and in the next chapter.)

Many of the officers were not named. In a characteristic case, the *Burton Mail* paid £17,500 compensation plus legal costs to a woman police constable who featured anonymously in a story following a complaint about an arrest. The original complaint was investigated by the Police Complaints Authority, but rejected.

Note well that in this type of case the test of identification is not whether the general reader knew who was referred to, but whether some individuals, such as the officer's colleagues (and family), did.

In *Morgan v Odhams Press Ltd* (1971), a journalist sued successfully over an article in the *Sun* newspaper which neither named him nor described him. A person reading the article carefully would have noted various details which were inconsistent with a reference to Mr Morgan. However, the court said ordinary people often skimmed through such articles casually, not expecting a high degree of accuracy. If, as a result of such reading, they reached the conclusion that the article referred to the plaintiff, then identification was proved.

In the 1981 Moonies case, mentioned in chapter 18, the *Daily Mail* article did not give the name of Dennis Orme, the British leader of the Unification Church, who sued. The paper argued that the libel was not actionable at his suit.

The judge, however, said Mr Orme was well-known as the leader of the church. The charges contained in the article were capable of referring to him if only on the basis that people might well say that he must have known what went on. Later, the jury decided that the words did refer to him after the judge told them: 'Orme says he is the church in the United Kingdom. It is a case of *l'Etat c'est moi.*'

The lesson this case has for journalists is that it is important they understand that derogatory comments about an institution can reflect upon the person who heads that institution. For example, many newspapers have in recent years had to pay damages to head teachers, who were not named in the paper, for reports which criticised schools. These reports are generally based on complaints by parents. Accounts of bad teaching and discipline at a school must reflect on the head teacher, who is responsible, and imply that he is incompetent or negligent. Journalists can generally defend themselves, when challenged over such reports, only by proving the statements are true or fair comment (see next chapter).

It is dangerous to make a half-hearted effort at identification. In *Newstead v London Express Newspapers Ltd* (1940), the *Daily Express* reported that 'Harold Newstead, 30-year-old Camberwell man', had been sent to prison for nine months for bigamy.

The paper was successfully sued by another Harold Newstead, who worked in Camberwell, and who claimed that the account had been understood to refer to him.

The plaintiff claimed that if the words were true of another person, which they were, it was the duty of the paper to give a precise and detailed description of that person, but the paper had 'recklessly struck out' the occupation and address of the person convicted.

As a result of the *Newstead* case, and others like it, the 1952 Defamation Act introduced a defence called 'unintentional defamation', replaced in the 1996 Act by the 'offer of amends' defence, a provision expected to be implemented in 1997. How these defences may be invoked is described later. Here it is only necessary to stress that any lack of reasonable care by the paper or a member of its staff resulting in publication of the libel would rule out the defence of unintentional defamation, so it seems it would not have been available to the newspaper in the *Newstead* case. (There is no similar requirement of reasonable care in the offer of amends defence.)

So not naming may not protect you. Indeed, greater trouble is often caused by failing to identify properly the person whose reputation is being attacked because another person may say the words referred to him. A newspaper quoted from a report by the district auditor to a local council criticising the council's deputy housing manager. The paper did not name him. But a new deputy manager had taken over, and he issued a writ claiming he was thought to be the offending official.

It is sometimes wrongly assumed that there is safety in generalisations. There seldom is. Again, dangers may be increased.

For example, the statement 'I know of at least one member of Blanktown Council who is there only because of the contracts that come his way' is clearly defamatory of *someone*.

Almost certainly the councillor the writer has in mind will find plenty of friends to identify him as the member concerned, and if there are two or three other members who also have (legitimately) obtained contracts from the council, the paper may face actions for libel by all of them.

It must be stressed, as was illustrated in the Newstead case, that the fact that a defamatory story is true of one person does not give you any protection if your story is understood to refer to someone else.

The principle was illustrated in the case *Bennett v The Guardian* referred to above. In 1992 the *Guardian* newspaper was running stories about an investigation into allegations of corruption at Stoke Newington police station made by people convicted or accused of drug offences. Scotland Yard issued a press statement saying that eight Stoke Newington officers, whom it did not name, had been transferred to other stations, and the paper's crime correspondent wrote two pieces about the transfer of the officers, whom he did not name, together with background material he had accumulated during his investigation.

Five officers sued, saying the story meant *they* were involved in planting and dealing drugs, a meaning denied by the *Guardian*, which had no idea of the identity of the men when it published the story.

When the case came to court in 1997, five years later, the newspaper sought to show that its story was true, but it was not allowed to bring any evidence of allegations made against police officers *other than* the five who were suing. (The jury found for the newspaper by a majority.)

Subject to what we shall learn about the defences of justification and fair comment, it is safer to be specific, and to pin critical comment fairly and squarely on the person meant, by naming him.

Another common danger arises from *juxtaposition*, mentioned in the previous chapter. A person may be defamed because a reference to him is juxtaposed with other material. The other material may or may not be defamatory, but in combination the two have this effect.

A meat porter collected damages from *Titbits*. He won a meat-carrying race during the Smithfield centenary celebrations and the magazine used the picture to illustrate an article about Christmas thieving. Always consider the implications when using library pictures to illustrate stories and features.

Notice that in the *Stationery Trade News* case described in the previous chapter the magazine accurately reported the counterfeiting of stationery products and named some of those responsible. The company which won huge damages in the case was named in what the magazine considered to be a separate part of the article, dealing with another issue, but the jury found the allegations referred to the plaintiff company as well.

The copy referring to the envelope manufacturers was sandwiched between the allegations of counterfeiting and the *pictures* illustrating counterfeiting, and no doubt this additional juxtaposition helped to persuade the jury.

## Publication

The plaintiff must also prove that the statement has been published. With the exception of criminal libel (see chapter 21) there is no defamation if the words complained of, however offensive or untrue, are addressed, in speech or writing, only to the person about whom they are made.

To substantiate defamation, they must have been communicated to at least one other person.

In the case of newspapers, there is no difficulty in proving this: publication is assumed.

A libel contained in a letter is another matter. Here, if the letter were written to the plaintiff and posted in an envelope addressed in such a way that it should be opened only by the plaintiff personally, there would be no publication to a third person.

On the other hand, a postcard would be 'published' to the postman delivering it, because he had an opportunity to read it, and the law would presume that he did!

It is important to remember that, as the lawyers put it, every repetition of a libel is a fresh publication and creates a fresh cause of action.

Some journalists are reluctant to accept this. If they are told that a statement in their copy is libellous they reply, 'But *we* are not making that statement: the chairman of the council (or some other important local figure) is.'

Certainly the person who originated the statement may be liable, but anybody who repeats the allegation may be sued also.

Indeed, one of the most common causes of libel actions is repeating statements made by interviewees without being able to prove the truth of the words.

In 1993 the *Western Daily Press* had to pay damages for libellous comments made by the chairman of an NHS hospital trust when commenting upon the resignation of a doctor (see next chapter, Privilege).

In 1993 and 1994 also papers had to pay damages to defendants in the Birmingham Six case, who had been sentenced to prison for terrorism but later cleared on appeal. Former West Midlands police officers were accused of fabricating evidence in the case, but their prosecution was abandoned. After the abandonment of the case, the *Sunday Telegraph* reported one of the three officers as referring to the Birmingham Six and saying: 'In our eyes, their guilt is beyond doubt.' The matter was settled out of court. The paper had to carry a prominent apology and the plaintiffs were reported to have received £250,000.

The *Sun* newspaper published an article based upon the *Sunday Telegraph*'s interviews. It later carried an apology and was reported to have paid £1 million.

In the past it has not even been safe to repeat a defamatory allegation made by a head of state. In 1976 Princess Elizabeth Bagaya of Toro, the former foreign minister of Uganda, collected substantial damages from several publications which had repeated libellous allegations of immoral conduct made about her by General Amin, dictator of Uganda. However, under a provision of the Defamation Act 1996 expected to come into effect in 1997, journalists will have privilege for a fair and accurate copy of or extract from matter published by or on the authority of a government anywhere in the world. (The privilege, however, does not apply to matters which are of no public concern and where publication has no public benefit.)

Journalists on local newspapers need to be alert when handling the bygone days column, because a defamatory statement is actionable even if it is repeated many years later.

A doctor received damages for statements published in 1981 in the 'Looking Back' column of the *Evening Star*, Ipswich. The statements, repeated from an article published 25 years previously, had gone unchallenged then.

Live broadcasts can prove dangerous. A member of a television audience made allegations against a vet during a studio discussion. In 1996 the broadcaster, Anglia TV, accepted that the claims were entirely untrue. The company said it had no prior knowledge of what was to be said, and did nothing to endorse the allegations, but it had to pay damages. The comments made on television were later reported in *Our Dogs* magazine, which also had to pay damages. All three – the member of the audience, the television company, and the magazine – had 'published' the defamatory words.

Suppose a journalist in writing defamatory allegations makes it clear that they are only rumours, or goes further and says he does not believe them?

As we saw in the last chapter, words must be read in their context and it is possible that the 'bane' of a defamatory statement may be cured by the 'antidote' of a disclaimer or explanation. The House of Lords dismissed a case in which two actors from Neighbours sued the *News of the World* over headlines and photographs with captions in which their faces had been superimposed on models in pornographic poses.

An entire article must be read to judge whether the contents are defamatory, but a disclaimer or explanation of defamatory matter may not negate the sting of the libel if it is placed in a less than obvious position where the reasonable, average reader may not read it. Every case that comes before a court will be different.

In 1987, during the General Election campaign, David Steel, the Liberal leader, accepted a 'very substantial' settlement from the *Star* newspaper for allegations about himself and a woman friend. The newspaper's counsel said the article contained a strong denial of the allegations by Steel's agent, and was published in an attempt to inform those who had heard the rumours that they were untrue.

In 1993 the *New Statesman* paid damages to John Major, the Prime Minister, after the cover of an issue carried the headline 'The curious case of John Major's "mistress"', and an article within discussed rumours which it said had been circulating. When sued, the magazine said the article was never intended to assert that an affair, let alone an adulterous relationship, had ever taken place.

The *New Statesman* was also in trouble for repeating a story from another publication. In a satirical column it repeated the allegation, for which the *Guardian* had already paid damages, that the Conservative politician Lord Tebbit had once said 'No one with a conscience votes Conservative.'

A person who has been defamed may sue the reporter, the sub-editor, the editor, the publisher, the printer, and the distributor. All have 'published' the words.

In John Major's case against the *New Statesman*, referred to above, the damages paid by the magazine were only £1,001, but the Prime Minister and the woman named in the article, who also sued, received £60,000 from the printers and distributors.

The actual cost to the magazine was estimated to be £250,000, including the damages, legal costs, indemnities to printers and distributors, and the cost of the issue containing the words, which had to be withdrawn.

In the past, a newsvendor or bookseller could usually put forward a defence of innocent dissemination. A defendant could use this defence when he was merely the conduit for the passage of the words complained of and was thus not responsible for them.

The Defamation Act 1996 (in a section that came into effect in September 1996) extended this defence, and it now applies to anyone who was not the author, editor, or publisher of the statement complained of, who took reasonable care in relation to its publication, and who did not know and had no reason to believe that whatever part he had in the publication caused or contributed to the publication of a defamatory statement.

A court deciding whether a person took reasonable care, or had reason to believe that what he did caused or contributed to the publication of a defamatory statement, shall have regard to:
(a) the extent of his responsibility for the content of the statement or the decision to publish it,
(b) the nature or circumstances of the publication, and
(c) the previous conduct or character of the author, editor, or publisher.

The list of categories of people who are not authors, editors, or publishers for the purposes of the new defence includes broadcasters of live programmes who have no effective control over the maker of the statement complained of and providers of Internet services over which the statement complained of is transmitted by a person over whom they have no effective control.

## Questions

1   What must a plaintiff prove to succeed in an action for defamation?
2   Is it possible to libel someone without naming him? Illustrate your answer by examples.
3   What dangers does the press risk by juxtaposing material that otherwise would be safe?
4   Explain the implications of the legal principle that 'Every repetition of a libel is a fresh publication.'
5   Your story begins: 'There is understood to be no truth in the rumour that ....' What are the dangers?

# 20 How much protection

It must often seem to journalists that the law of libel is weighted against newspapers, but it has been amended (in 1888, 1952 and 1996) to try to protect the legitimate functions of a free press while still protecting the reputation of the individual.

No one will argue that the efforts that have been made to reconcile two apparently opposed interests are wholly satisfactory. On the one side there have been attempts to introduce a law of privacy, which would give the individual greater protection against the press and particularly against intrusion (see chapter 31).

On the other hand, there have been attempts to give the newspapers greater protection than they have at present. Those calling for such protection pointed to the career of the newspaper proprietor Robert Maxwell, who, it was claimed after his death in 1991, had effectively gagged the press by manipulating the libel laws, using numerous writs and injunctions to conceal his wrongdoing.

Nevertheless, the existing law provides a greater degree of protection than journalists always fully appreciate. Indeed, if you are just beginning to study the law of defamation you will find it instructive to examine a copy of your daily newspaper and pick out the defamatory material. You will probably be surprised to see how much of what is published is clearly defamatory, within the definitions you have just been studying. How can the papers get away with these stories?

The remainder of this chapter will answer that question by explaining the various defences available in an action for defamation.

Again, it is emphasised that no journalist should try to be his own lawyer: when trouble looms, it is essential to take expert advice.

But if the journalist knows the defences for which the law provides, he can use them to test the safety or otherwise of what he intends to publish.

Just as in the last chapter we listed some matters the plaintiff in an action does **not** have to prove, so we note here two defences that do **not** exist – though many students and some journalists appear to believe they do.

It is no defence to show that your story was published in the public interest. Think how easy it would have been for the editors of the newspapers to publish the stories about Robert Maxwell that many of them had in their in-trays if they could have put forward such a defence, instead of embarking on the hazardous exercise of trying to prove the truth of their stories.

You will see when you read the sections on fair comment and privilege that the question of public interest arises, but there is no defence of public interest as such.

Nor is there a defence of 'fairness'. Some journalists believe that if they publish a defamatory statement about someone and then offer the defamed person the opportunity to reply the report is 'fair' and they have a defence. But if they are sued they will have to prove the truth of the allegation.

The *Daily Telegraph* reported a press conference in which defamatory allegations were made about the firm of solicitors who had acted for paratrooper Lee Clegg, convicted of murdering a woman in a stolen car. The reporter put the claims to the lawyers, and when they faxed him a reply rejecting the criticisms he incorporated it in his story and added the word 'emphatically' to their rejection of the allegations to demonstrate the forcefulness of their feelings.

When the case came to court in 1996 he said, 'I submitted my copy in a form I thought gave me protection.' But the lawyers' counsel told the court: 'It's no good saying including a denial weakens the sting of a libel. The only thing that takes the sting out of a libel is to withdraw it.' The jury awarded the solicitors £130,000 damages.

Journalists may wonder how this ties in with the statement of the judge, referred to in the previous chapter ('Meaning of words'), that if in one part of a publication something disreputable to the plaintiff was stated, but that was removed by the conclusion, 'the bane and the antidote must be taken together'.

The word 'removed' is important. Notice that in the case where the *News of the World* published pictures of well-known actors whose faces had been superimposed on models in pornographic poses no one reading the newspaper could have finished by concluding that the two actors had actually been indulging in pornographic activity; the antidote cured the bane by *removing* the defamatory meaning, the sting. In the case above, no rebuttal by the firm of solicitors, however vehement and however prominent, could have removed the implication of incompetence.

You will see when you read the section on privilege that the question of fairness arises, but there is no defence of fairness as such.

All the defences to a libel action are explained in this chapter. If your story is not covered by one of the defences mentioned, you do not have a defence.

The main defences are:
(a) justification;
(b) fair comment;
(c) privilege;
(d) accord and satisfaction;
(e) unintentional defamation;
(f) offer of amends.

## Justification

It is a complete defence to a libel action (with the limited exception arising under the Rehabilitation of Offenders Act 1974: see chapter 22) to prove that the words complained of are true.

But it is a difficult defence to advance because, as stated previously, in a libel action it is not the task of the plaintiff to show the words were untrue, but of the defendant to show that they were true. Other reasons why the defence is so difficult are explained below.

The name of the defence is justification, a misleading name because the defendant does not have to show he had any moral or social reason for publishing the defamatory words. It is sufficient if they are true. It has been suggested that the defence should be renamed truth.

The defence applies to statements of fact. If the words complained of consist of a statement of fact they must be proved to be true, but if they are an expression of opinion they may be defended as fair comment (see next section).

The journalist must persuade the jury that his story is true 'on the balance of probabilities', which is a lower requirement than 'beyond all reasonable doubt', the standard in criminal cases.

The *Sun* successfully used the defence when sued in 1994 by Gillian Taylforth, the television actress, and her boyfriend after the paper published a front-page splash headlined 'TV Kathy's "sex romp" on A1' saying the couple had indulged in oral sex in a parked car.

The *Sun* obtained confirmation from the police press office that the boyfriend had been cautioned for indecency, and when sued the paper joined the police in the defence, with the result that the main defence witness was the officer who claimed he saw the incident.

Taylforth and her boyfriend denied the story and the court arranged a reconstruction of the event in which the judge, jury, and journalists watched as the couple showed what position they said they had been in and then two *Sun* journalists simulated the paper's version. The jury found for the paper 10-2.

The costs of that case, which Taylforth and her boyfriend had to meet, were estimated at £500,000. Had the paper lost, it would have had to pay the bill, in addition to damages, another illustration of the point made in chapter 18 that the cost of proving the truth of a story may sometimes be prohibitive for a small or impecunious paper, which will therefore choose not to publish the story or, having published, to apologise and settle out of court.

Cost is not the only factor that makes justification a difficult defence. Cases in which the media pleads justification can be extremely complex, as the following two examples show.

In 1992 Scottish Television (STV) successfully defended a libel action brought by Antony Gecas, the former platoon commander of a Lithuanian police battalion under German occupation who settled in Edinburgh after the 1939-45 war. In a 1987 programme called 'Crimes of War' STV accused him of involvement in the murder of thousands of Jews.

When sued, STV was faced with the task of proving its account of events that had happened nearly half a century before. Its researchers visited many countries to find new evidence. Some of the witnesses were too old or fragile to go to Scotland for the trial, so the court sat in Lithuania to hear some of the evidence.

At the end the judge (who heard the case without a jury, as is the practice in Scotland) found for STV. He said Gecas had participated in many operations involving the killing of innocent Soviet citizens, including Jews, in particular in Byelorussia during the last three months of 1941, and in doing so committed war crimes against Soviet citizens who included old men, women and children. The case cost an estimated £1.5 million.

The BBC also was faced with proving the truth of its account of events that had happened many years before in a case in 1994. It was sued by Upjohn, the American manufacturer of the sleeping drug Halcion, and its British subsidiary, over a Panorama programme 'The Halcion nightmare'. The programme reported that evidence had been accumulating since as early as 1972 that the drug had serious adverse side effects, including amnesia, paranoia and violent behaviour, and it claimed that Upjohn had intentionally distorted, suppressed or falsified the data of clinical trials to conceal this evidence from regulators.

The drug, which had been available in Britain for 12 years, was banned here in 1993.

The BBC claimed its allegations were true. The judge (who tried the case alone, without a jury) said Upjohn had made 'serious errors and omissions' in the reporting of a clinical trial to regulators and, in relation to disqualified investigators, had acted recklessly, but he rejected the allegation of dishonesty. The corporation was ordered to pay £60,000 damages, and its costs were estimated at £1.5 million.

According to the judge, paperwork before the court amounted to 36,000 sheets of paper. The case lasted 62 days in court (in addition to six days spent out of court by the judge reading papers), and the court considered evidence from 100 witnesses, 30 of them in live testimony. The action was combined with others involving Upjohn, and the total cost was estimated at £3 million.

Another reason that the defence of justification is so difficult is that it entails proving not only the precise truth of each defamatory statement (subject to the exception provided for in the 1952 Defamation Act, mentioned below) but also any reasonable interpretation that may be understood of the words complained of and any innuendoes lying behind them.

As stated in chapter 18, *Yachting World* was sued for libel over statements in a critical boat test it had published. It claimed that the facts contained were true, and there was no doubt that there was a wide difference between the performance of the boat as claimed in the manufacturer's publicity material and the figures recorded by experts who tested the boat after litigation began. But the magazine accepted that the words carried the implication that the firm had made its misleading claims carelessly and irresponsibly, and the jury found against it.

In 1987 Jeffrey Archer, the politician and novelist (later Lord Archer), was awarded £500,000 against the *Star* newspaper, which said that he had paid a prostitute for sexual intercourse. He also sued the *News of the World* for a story headlined 'Tory boss Archer pays off vice girl'. It was true that Archer had paid £2,000 to the prostitute to go abroad to avoid scandal but he claimed the article implied he had had a sexual relationship with her. The paper said it had never intended such a suggestion, but it had to pay Archer £50,000 damages in an agreed settlement.

In *Lewis v Daily Telegraph*, and *Lewis v Associated Newspapers Ltd* (1964) two national newspapers stated that the City of London Fraud Squad was inquiring into the affairs of a company. The statement was true, but Lewis said the words meant he and the company were guilty of fraud, or at least were suspected of fraud, and heavy damages were initially awarded against the newspapers. On appeal, the House of Lords ruled that the words were not capable of meaning that fraud had been committed, but they were capable of meaning that the plaintiffs were *suspected* and that whether they had this meaning or not should be left to a jury.

The matter was settled out of court without a new trial, and it remains unclear whether it is defamatory of a person to say the police are investigating his activities.

Such a statement may safely be reported if it is based on an official police statement (see the section Privilege, later in this chapter). Even so, journalists must be very careful in straying outside the strict wording of the statement. In the case *Bennett v The Guardian,* referred to in the last chapter under Identification, the paper's story was based upon a Scotland Yard press statement saying that eight Stoke Newington officers, whom it did not name, had been transferred to other stations. The paper's crime correspondent accurately reported the statement, but added background material he had accumulated during his investigation. Five officers sued, saying the story *meant* they were involved in planting and dealing drugs, a meaning denied by the *Guardian*. As stated, the jury found for the newspaper by a majority. Had they not done so the paper would have faced huge damages and costs.

To say of A 'He is a thief' may be true in the simple meaning of the words. But if the basis for the assertion is one conviction for stealing a packet of bacon from a self-service store a defence of justification to any action for defamation brought by A might fail.

For A would argue that the words contained the meaning that he was a persistent thief, and was a person whom no one should trust, whereas he was essentially an honest man who had had a single lapse.

A jury might well take the view that A's reputation, though not exemplary, had been made blacker by the description applied to him.

The principle is an important one. Many libel actions result from the journalist implying habitual conduct from a single incident. In the *Radio City* case referred to in chapter 18 the broadcast company said it was true that the holiday firm's proprietor made promises to holidaymakers that he could not keep and was indifferent to the distress caused. Nineteen witnesses gave evidence in support of the programme. But the proprietor said the implication was he did this *habitually*, and he called 21 witnesses who gave glowing or favourable accounts of their holidays with him. The jury found in his favour.

The defence of justification is not only difficult; it is dangerous. If it fails the court will take a critical view of the newspaper's persistence in sticking to a story which it decides is not true, and the jury may award greater damages accordingly.

In the Archer case (see above) the *Star* newspaper claimed its story that Archer had sexual relations with the prostitute was true. The case lasted three weeks. The £500,000 damages were awarded after the judge told the jury that the newspaper had carried the case through to the bitter end and if they found in Mr Archer's favour the damages should be sufficiently large to 'send a message to the world that the accusations were false'.

## The investigative journalist

The examples given make it clear that the journalist embarking on an investigative story must not only be sure of his facts. He must be able to prove them in court. A number of stories for which newspapers paid damages later proved to be true, but too late to prevent the damage to the paper; as a general rule, courts are very reluctant to overturn decisions or agreed settlements when new facts come to light.

If the journalist is relying on a witness to back up his case, no one but the witness will be able to tell the jury his account of a particular incident. The journalist's account of the witness's story is hearsay – that is, an account of someone else's statement put forward to prove the truth of what it claims. It is inadmissible – unless it was made in the presence and hearing of the plaintiff.

Journalists find this difficult to accept. A newspaper may receive a visit from parents outraged by drug taking or bullying in a school. The story is clearly defamatory. The children rather than the parents have experienced the drug taking or bullying, so the parents' account of what their children told them is hearsay and therefore (with exceptions under the Civil Evidence Act, see below) inadmissible.

Supposing, on another story, the witnesses' evidence is admissible; are the witnesses going to be available to give evidence when the case comes to court, which may be years after the events described in the story? The journalist must be sure he keeps track of them, noting their various changes of address.

Are they going to be willing to give evidence?

How convincing will their version of events sound when tested by clever cross-examination? What impression will they make on the jury? In particular, will the jury believe their version of events in preference to the version of the person suing? The libel action that Jeffrey Archer brought against the *Star* (see above) resolved itself into a clash of evidence on whether he had in fact resorted to a prostitute. The jury accepted the account of the leading Conservative politician in preference to that of the prostitute.

English juries are said to be likely to accept the word of a police officer. In the case brought by the TV actress Gillian Taylforth against the *Sun* (see above) the newspaper had the rare experience of having its story backed by police evidence.

Reference has been made (see previous chapter, Identification, and previous section in this chapter) to the numerous cases brought in recent years on behalf of police officers for allegations of bad conduct such as brutality and harassment. Local editors may see it as their duty to publish such stories in the public interest but they must be aware of the strong likelihood that the jury will accept the denial of the officer rather than the allegation of the source, who, in the nature of things, will often be a person of low social standing, perhaps with a criminal record. In the case of *Bennett v The Guardian*, in 1997 (see above), the sources of allegations printed in the *Guardian* included a convicted person (later cleared on appeal); a man who had been charged with drug dealing, but against whom charges had been dropped; and the solicitor of a convicted drug dealer.

If the journalist is working on a story where he expects his version may be challenged in court, he would do well to persuade his witness to make a signed statement at the time.

This could be a signed statement or tape recording of any witness willing to testify against the plaintiff. It could be a note written by the journalist in his notebook and signed by the witness.

Better, it could be a statutory declaration from any such witness. That is a more formal statement made before a JP and it carries greater weight in court.

Best, it could be an affidavit, more formal still and sworn on oath. Both this and a statutory declaration put the deponent at risk of perjury if he is not telling the truth.

If the worst happens and the journalist's vital witness decides when the case comes for trial he does not want to give evidence, but the journalist has a signed statement, the reluctant person can be summoned to court by subpoena and forced to answer questions; if he changes his story, he may be cross-examined.

If the journalist has a statement, whether written or tape recorded, from a witness who dies or goes abroad before the trial the statement itself can be produced in evidence.

The Civil Evidence Act 1968 makes hearsay evidence acceptable in court subject to certain conditions. For practical purposes, where the statement comprises, or is contained in, a document, it **must** be signed to make it admissible.

What is the value of a photocopy of a document? Suppose, for example, you are running a story about council workmen fiddling their expenses and you derived your facts from the photocopy of a confidential council document that included false expenses claims.

If you can explain why the original is not available, that makes the copy available for evidence. But you would have to persuade the court that the document is authentic – eg by evidence from someone within the council. The libel plaintiff would no doubt challenge its authenticity.

Often the paper's case is weakened because the journalist himself has failed to observe the basic editorial discipline of keeping his notebook in good order. When the journalist is required to give evidence, a court will attach weight to a shorthand note properly dated. By contrast, the court may attach significance to the lack of any such note. In the case in which Jeffrey Archer sued the *Star* (see above) the judge asked the jury if they did not find it odd that none of the journalists had produced a note of what they had been told by Archer.

In 1997 the *Sunday Times* was attempting to prove the truth of a story about Albert Reynolds, the former Irish Prime Minister. The reporter who wrote the story said he could produce no notes because 'I was not in note-taking mode.' The jury found for Reynolds.

Tape recordings must be kept too. In 1992 Jason Connery, the actor, sued over an article in the *Sun* which carried comments attributed to him and which, he said, meant he would be afraid to fight for his country in the Gulf War. He denied making any such comments.

The journalist, in her evidence, said she had tape recorded a conversation with Connery, but had destroyed the tape after she had taken notes from it to prepare her copy. The jury awarded £35,000 damages.

The time factor is important. Until the law was changed in September 1996 plaintiffs had three years within which to issue their writs, and for tactical reasons their lawyers often delayed. In the case referred to in the last chapter in which the *Burton Mail* was sued over its report of an arrest,

the arrest was in 1991 and the writ was issued in 1993. In the 1997 case of
*Bennett v The Guardian*, referred to above, the writ was issued in 1995 a
week before the end of the three-year period.

The Defamation Act 1996 reduced the limitation period to one year. But
it may still be another year or two before the matter eventually comes to
court.

If there is a plea for special damages to compensate for actual loss
caused by the damaging publication, the delay may well be necessary for
the plaintiff to accumulate proof.

But for the defendant newspaper, the delay poses enormous difficulties.
Witnesses may have died or disappeared: in any event, they can hardly be
expected to remember the details. In the *Mail on Sunday* case referred to
in chapter 18, the writ was issued in 1984 but the matter did not come to
trial until 1989; by that time much of the evidence had been destroyed as
a danger to health and journalists' notes had been disposed of.

One curious hurdle placed in the path of investigative journalists was
removed by the Defamation Act 1996. In defamation actions, a conviction
of an individual was conclusive proof that he had committed the crime for
which he was convicted. If the newspaper published a story alleging that
a police officer had fabricated evidence to obtain convictions, the officer
could argue that the conviction was conclusive proof of guilt, and therefore
the evidence could not have been fabricated. Under a section of the Act that
came into effect in September 1996, convictions are conclusive proof only
in respect of offences committed by *the plaintiff*.

Suppose a plaintiff asks a court to grant him an injunction preventing
a newspaper publishing defamatory material. The court will always refuse
an injunction once a newspaper says it is going to plead the defence of
justification.

## Section 5 defence

Before the 1952 Defamation Act was passed, to succeed in a plea of
justification it was necessary to prove the precise truth of every defamatory
statement in the offending article. Now the law says (in section 5 of the
Act) that a defence of justification shall not fail merely because the article
contains some inaccuracies.

This is the actual wording:

> In an action for libel or slander in respect of words containing two
> or more distinct charges against the plaintiff, a defence of justification
> shall not fail by reason only that the truth of every charge is not
> proved, if the words not proved to be true do not materially injure the
> plaintiff's reputation, having regard to the truth of the remaining
> charges.

The section 5 defence was used successfully in 1992 in the case mentioned above in which Antony Gecas sued STV. The programme said Gecas used his pistol to 'finish off' Jews and others who had been shot and thrown into pits but were still alive.

The judge said he did not consider STV had proved the allegation but in his opinion the inclusion of the allegation in the programme did not materially injure Gecas's reputation over and above the injury to his reputation arising from the allegations that had been proved.

## Fair comment

Newspapers faced with an action for defamation rely much more frequently on the defence of fair comment made honestly on a matter of public interest.

### *Only comment*

Notice that the defence applies only to comment. It does not provide a defence for the publication of defamatory facts. But the comment must be based upon facts that are either stated or indicated in the story complained of. And these facts must be true.

A judge gave an example of fair comment. He said that if you accurately report what some public man has done and then say 'Such conduct is disgraceful', that is merely an expression of your opinion, your comment on the person's conduct.

So also if, without reporting the man's action, you identify the conduct by a reference to it that readers will understand. In either case, you enable your readers to judge for themselves how far your opinion is well founded.

But, the judge said, if you assert that the man has been guilty of disgraceful conduct and do not state what that conduct was, this is an allegation of fact for which there is no defence other than truth or privilege (see next section).

It is no use going to court and saying: 'This comment would have been fair if we had not been misinformed.' The only acceptable defence is: 'The facts are true and the comment upon those facts is fair.'

There is an exception where the comment is based on privileged material, such as a report of judicial proceedings. In that case, the defence will still succeed even if the facts mentioned in the privileged report later turn out to be untrue.

The law does not require the 'truth' of the comment itself to be proved; by its nature it cannot be. Comment may be responsible or irresponsible, informed or misinformed, constructive or destructive; but it cannot be true or false.

Nor does the law require that the defendant pleading fair comment should carry the court with him. It is not necessary to persuade either the judge or the jury to share his views.

## Honest opinion

What a defendant must do is satisfy the jury that his comment upon established facts represents his honestly held opinion.

The law was expressed by Lord Diplock (then Mr Justice Diplock) in his summing up to the jury in a case in which Lord Silkin unsuccessfully sued Beaverbrook Newspapers for certain statements by 'Cross Bencher' in the *Sunday Express*. He said:

> People are entitled to hold and express strong views on matters of public interest, provided they are honestly held. They may be views which some or all of you think are exaggerated, obstinate, or prejudiced.
>
> The basis of our public life is that the crank and the enthusiast can say what he honestly believes just as much as a reasonable man or woman.
>
> It would be a sad day for freedom of speech in this country if a jury were to apply the test of whether it agrees with a comment, instead of applying the true test of whether this opinion, however exaggerated, obstinate, or prejudiced, was honestly held.

The name of this defence does not help the young journalist to understand its nature; indeed the Faulks Committee on Defamation described it in 1975 as 'seriously misleading having regard to the actual nature of the defence, which in reality protects unfair comment'.

Clearly, the opinion of a person with prejudiced or exaggerated views may be extremely unfair if viewed objectively by a balanced person. It is better to emphasise that the comment must be *honest*. The committee recommended that the defence should be renamed simply 'comment'.

## Without malice

If the defence is to succeed, it is essential that the defamatory statement was made without malice. Malice in law means much more than spite or ill-will, although these are included in the definition. It means any dishonest or improper motive.

The reason behind this limitation on the defence is that fair comment is intended to allow freedom of speech to people with something to say about matters of public interest, but this freedom must not be abused by people for the wrong reasons.

For example, if it could be shown that the editor of a newspaper had published critical comment to discredit a public figure because of a personal grudge this would constitute malice, and the defence of fair comment would fail. The defence would probably fail also if the editor had launched a sensational attack, couched in immoderate terms, merely in the hope of increasing his paper's circulation.

If the journalist makes a comment based upon facts he knows to be untrue, this is prima facie evidence of malice. It may also be evidence of malice if a journalist comments upon facts recklessly, not caring whether they are true or false.

Suppose a journalist reports an interview with a councillor, in which the councillor strongly criticises another member of the council on a matter of public interest. Unknown to the journalist, the interviewee has a grudge against the person criticised, and that is the reason for the attack. Does the malice 'infect' the story written by the reporter, so that he cannot put forward a plea of fair comment? Is the malice transferred?

The answer to this question is not clear, even though Lord Denning said in *Egger v Chelmsford* (1964) that 'it is a mistake to suppose that, on a joint publication, the malice of one defendant infects his co-defendant.'

### Imputing improper motives

An important limitation of the defence occurs where the journalist not only criticises a person's actions, but also imputes corrupt or dishonourable motives to him.

Lord Chief Justice Cockburn said in 1863:

> One man has no right to impute to another, whose conduct may be fairly open to ridicule or disapprobation, base, sordid, and wicked motives, unless there is so much ground for the imputation that a jury shall find not only that he had an honest belief in the truth of his statements, but that his belief was not without foundation.

The imputation of improper motives is another common cause of libel actions. Notice how this applies to some of the cases we have considered.

In the case against *Yachting World* the argument was over the motives of the manufacturer. It seems the jury did not accept the magazine's assessment.

The motives of the manufacturer of Halcion were at the root of the case against the BBC. Upjohn had certainly failed to notify the regulators about some side-effects of the drug. But the judge refused to accept this had been done dishonestly.

In both these cases the defendants had tried to plead fair comment, in addition to justification.

A more everyday example appeared in a woman's page article that gave recipes for home-made stuffing. It stated:

> Although Mr X [a well-known chef] tried to cajole us in television advertisements to buy some branded packets, I am quite sure that neither he nor any other cook who fancies their reputation would dream of using any but a home-made stuffing.

Mr X claimed this was an attack on his probity and was defamatory. He said he used and liked the branded packet of stuffing that he advertised on television. The claim was settled by the publication of a letter written by Mr X, but the newspaper incurred legal costs. (The case is reported in *A Practical Look at Libel* by Peter Carter-Ruck.)

In 1996 two England cricketers, Devon Malcolm and Phillip DeFreitas, accepted damages from *Wisden Cricket Monthly* for an article which, according to Malcolm's solicitor, suggested that England players of overseas origin (particularly West Indian or Asian), would lack real commitment to the England team, being instead motivated solely by a desire for personal advancement and achievement.

## Invective

Though the limits of fair comment are wide, it is possible to go over the top. A judge has said that the language in which the comment is couched must not 'pass out of the domain of criticism itself'. A jury awarded the actress Charlotte Cornwell damages after the journalist, Nina Miskow, commenting on her performance in a television show, depicted her as 'Wally of the Week'. She wrote: 'She can't sing, her bum is too big, and she has the sort of stage presence that jams lavatories.'

## Privilege

The law recognises that there are occasions when the public interest demands that there shall be complete freedom of speech without any risk of proceedings for defamation. We say that these occasions are privileged.

Privilege exists under the common law (see Privilege at common law, later in this section). But journalists in most cases rely on privilege granted by parliament – that is, statutory privilege. Both at common law and under statute, there are two kinds of privilege, absolute and qualified.

*Absolute privilege*, where it is applicable, is a complete answer and bar to any action for defamation. It does not matter whether the words are true or false. It does not matter that they were spoken maliciously. If they are protected by absolute privilege, that is a complete bar to any action.

But though a journalist may be reporting what is said on an occasion that is privileged absolutely it does not follow that his report is similarly protected.

Take the proceedings of Parliament. These enjoy absolute privilege under the common law. A Member may say whatever he wishes in the House of Commons without fear of an action for defamation. But the reports of parliamentary debates published in a newspaper enjoy only qualified privilege which, as we shall see later in this chapter, introduces a question of the motive in publication.

The official daily reports of parliamentary proceedings (in Hansard) have absolute privilege; so have reports published by order of Parliament (such as White Papers). But their publication in a newspaper, in full or in part, enjoys only qualified privilege.

We are on safer ground, however, when we come to consider court reporting. It is generally considered that a fair and accurate report of judicial proceedings in a court within the United Kingdom, published contemporaneously, enjoys absolute privilege, under the Law of Libel Amendment Act 1888.

The Defamation Act 1996, under a provision expected to come into effect in 1997, removes any doubt and makes it clear the defence is absolute. The Act also extends the protection to reports of the European Court of Justice, or any court attached to that court, the European Court of Human Rights, and any international criminal tribunal (a war crimes tribunal) established by the Security Council of the United Nations or by an international agreement to which the United Kingdom is a party.

Privilege for court reports constitutes a most valuable protection for newspapers because what is said in court (especially a criminal court) is often highly defamatory.

Without such protection, court reporting as we know it would be impossible, and the protection is given because the law recognises the vital part that newspapers must play in the administration of justice.

However, there are still precautions which must be taken if it is not to be forfeited.

The law specifies that the report must be 'fair and accurate'. This does not mean that the proceedings must be reported verbatim: however abbreviated the report, it will still be 'fair and accurate' if it presents a summary of both sides, contains no inaccuracies, and avoids giving disproportionate weight to one side or the other.

The unfair or inaccurate report, however, forfeits the protection of privilege. Should this happen, the newspaper is in a dangerous position, for it is unlikely that any other defence is available to it.

In 1993 the *Daily Sport* paid substantial damages to a police officer acquitted of indecent assault. The paper reported the opening of the case by the prosecution and the main evidence of the alleged victim, but did not include her cross-examination by the defence, which began on the same day.

Later the paper briefly reported the officer's acquittal. The officer's solicitor said the alleged victim made a number of admissions under cross-examination that weakened the evidence-in-chief given by her.

Trials may last for days, weeks, or months and statements made by the prosecution in criminal cases or by the plaintiff in civil cases may subsequently be shown by the defendant to be wrong. However, it is established that where a trial lasts more than one day the proceedings of each day may be published separately at the time.

Evening papers and broadcasters regularly publish accounts of that part of a day's trial that has been heard by their time of publication. Had the *Daily Sport* case gone to court the outcome is uncertain. It may have been in a less strong position than an evening paper because it had ample time to publish details of the cross-examination in its report of the day's hearing.

The safest journalistic practice is that if the newspaper has reported allegations made by the prosecutor that are later rebutted those rebuttals also should be carried.

Turning to accuracy, all allegations in court reports must be attributed because a report that presents an allegation as if it were a proved fact is inaccurate. Do not write 'Brown had a gun in his hand' but 'Smith said Brown had a gun in his hand.'

A newspaper is left with no protection at all if, whether or not by carelessness, it identifies as the defendant someone who is only a witness or unconnected with the case. This may happen because of similarities of name and address. In county court cases reporters sometimes confuse the names of the plaintiff and the defendant.

Newspapers must avoid wrongly reporting that the defendant has been convicted when he has in fact been acquitted. In 1993 the *Hendon and Finchley Times* had to pay substantial damages to a man acquitted of conspiring to smuggle drugs. The man's solicitor told the court that although the story reported the man had been acquitted, it did so in terms that conveyed the impression he was in fact guilty as charged and ought not to have been cleared.

Other mistakes that the court reporter can make include wrongly reporting the defendant has been found guilty of a more serious offence than the correct one, and giving the wrong address for the defendant – which can lead to a complaint by the person living at that address.

The law also requires, for absolute statutory privilege to attach, that the report should be published contemporaneously with the proceedings. For all practical purposes this means publication in the first issue of the paper following the hearing, or while the hearing is proceeding.

An evening paper might begin reporting a case in its early editions, continue to add to its report as later editions appear, and perhaps conclude it the following day.

However, care should be taken in 'holding over' court matter from one issue to another, as weekly newspapers sometimes do.

Sometimes the report of court proceedings has to be postponed in accordance with the law. In that case, says the Defamation Act 1996 (in a provision due to be implemented in 1997), the story is treated as if it were published contemporaneously if it is published 'as soon as practicable after publication is permitted'.

Non-contemporaneous reports of court proceedings, if fair and accurate, still enjoy qualified privilege at common law (see next section).

In general, privilege extends only to the actual report of the proceedings. It does not protect defamatory matter shouted out in court which is not part of the proceedings. Nor does it protect matter gleaned from documents presented to the bench but not read out in open court. The Defamation Act 1996, in a provision expected to take effect in 1997, extends qualified privilege to a fair and accurate copy of or extract from a document made available by a court and this may for the first time give protection to information from charge sheets; *may* rather than *will* because it is not clear what meaning courts will attach to the words 'made available by a court'. Previously, such information has not been privileged unless read out during the proceedings.

Headlines and introductions lead to many complaints. Particular care should be used in writing them to avoid any misrepresentation or exaggeration.

Journalists working on free publications should see the section 'Free publications' later in this chapter.

*Qualified privilege* is available as a defence to the journalist on certain occasions where it is considered important that the facts should be freely known in the public interest. In general, qualified privilege affords just as much protection to a newspaper as absolute privilege, provided certain conditions are observed.

These are that the report is:

(a)  fair and accurate; *and*
(b)  published without malice.

But qualified privilege does not protect the publication in a newspaper of matter which is not of public concern and the publication of which is not for the public benefit.

Just as the court reporter must take care not to lose his privilege by reporting matter which is not part of the proceedings, so the reporter who has attended, say, a council meeting must be careful not to hazard the protection which the law allows to that report by including matter which is not privileged.

For example, there is no privilege for a report of defamatory statements made by a councillor after the meeting when he is asked to expand on statements made during the meeting.

When considering fair comment, we saw that the reporter might lose his defence because of the malice of the person he was reporting. Fortunately, it is established that he cannot similarly lose his defence of privilege. That is, if on a privileged occasion he reports a speaker who, it later transpires, was actuated by malice, the reporter can still succeed in maintaining the defence of privilege, provided he himself was not actuated by malice.

There is a long-standing privilege at common law for the publication of defamatory statements in certain circumstances (see next section). But the journalist has relied in his everyday work not upon the common law but upon the provisions of the 1888 Act mentioned above and the 1952 Defamation Act. The 1952 Act, for example, gives journalists protection in covering council meetings and statements from police spokesmen. The 1996 Act, in a provision expected to be implemented in 1997, considerably extends this statutory protection.

The schedules to the Acts of 1952 and 1996 give in Part I a list of statements having qualified privilege and in Part II a list of statements privileged 'subject to explanation or contradiction'.

This means that, if required to do so, an editor who has published a defamatory statement upon an occasion mentioned in Part II must publish a 'reasonable letter or statement by way of explanation or contradiction'.

Failure to publish such a statement, or failure to do so in 'an adequate or reasonable manner having regard to the circumstances', would destroy the defence of qualified privilege.

Legal advice should be taken if any statement that the complainant asks to be published gives rise to any difficulty, such as the risk of libelling another person by contradicting what he has been reported as saying.

The schedules to both Defamation Acts are reproduced below. Reference to them will show what action is appropriate in any particular circumstances. Attention is drawn particularly to paragraph 9 of the 1952 schedule and paragraph 12 of the 1996 schedule, which provide a legal definition of a 'public meeting'.

It is very wide, covering almost any kind of meeting that a reporter will be required to attend. Note that it refers to a lawful meeting held for the furtherance or discussion of a matter of public concern, whether admission to the meeting is general or restricted. A press conference is not a public meeting.

Whether a meeting is 'lawful' within the meaning of this Act is a matter for the judge to decide if the matter goes to court.

Note also that paragraph 10 of the 1952 schedule and paragraph 11 of the 1996 schedule cover meetings held in public by local authorities or by justices of the peace 'acting otherwise than as a court exercising judicial authority'. This provision extends the protection of qualified privilege to the proceedings of justices' licensing meetings.

Paragraph 8 of the 1952 schedule and paragraph 14 of the 1996 schedule gives protection to reports of findings and decisions of a wide variety of bodies. The 1996 Act extends this protection to reports of the findings and decisions of associations formed to promote charitable objects 'or other objects beneficial to the community'. Note the protection does not apply to a report of the *proceedings* of such bodies.

The Local Government (Access to Information) Act 1985 in effect amended paragraph 10 of the 1952 Act to extend qualified privilege to reports of the sub-committee meetings of a number of authorities, including county councils and district councils. There has been no statutory qualified privilege for reports of the sub-committees of other authorities, notably town councils. This omission was remedied by paragraph 11 of the 1996 Act, which includes in its definition of local authorities any authority or body to which the Public Bodies (Admission to Meetings) Act 1960 applies.

Paragraph 12 of the 1952 schedule and paragraph 9 of the 1996 schedule are very important. In previous editions of *McNae* the editors have suggested that young reporters could usefully learn paragraph 12 by heart. It gives protection for a copy or fair and accurate report or summary of any notice or other matter issued for the information of the public by or on behalf of any government department, officer of state, local authority, or chief officer of police. The term 'local authority' was defined by a later Act to include health authorities.

Paragraph 9, due to come into effect in 1997, repeats and extends the protection but does so in a way which does not easily lend itself to rote learning. It gives privilege, subject to explanation or contradiction, to a fair and accurate copy of or extract from a notice or other matter issued for the information of the public by or on behalf of:

(a) a legislature in any member state (that means, a member of the European Union) or the European Parliament;

(b) the government of any member state, or any authority performing governmental functions in any member state or part of a member state, or the European Commission;

(c) an international organisation or international conference.

Any authority performing governmental functions clearly includes local authorities, and the Act states that the phrase also includes 'police functions'.

There will be many occasions when a reporter will wish to report the misdeeds of a person but may be inhibited by the fear of a libel action. The answer is often to obtain the information in the form of an official statement by a police or local authority spokesman.

But notice that the lists in both schedules are very precise. It is tempting to assume they cover all statements by people in authority, but they do not cover, for example, statements by the spokesmen of NHS hospital trusts, British Telecom, a gas board, a water board, British Rail, London Regional Transport, British Airport Authority or other bodies created by statute that are involved in providing day-to-day services to the public.

Suppose a reporter telephones the spokesman of one of the bodies mentioned in the Act and puts questions to him: is the report of the spokesman's comments protected? In *Blackshaw v Lord* (1983), Lord Justice Stephenson said that it would unduly restrict the privilege contained in paragraph 12 to confine it to written handouts.

> It may be right to include ... the kind of answers to telephoned interrogatories which Mr Lord [a *Daily Telegraph* reporter], quite properly in the discharge of his duty to his newspaper, administered to Mr Smith [a government press officer]. To exclude them in every case might unduly restrict the freedom of the press ... But information which is put out on the initiative of a government department falls more easily within the paragraph than information pulled out of the mouth of an unwilling officer of the department ... not every statement of fact made to a journalist by a press officer of a government department is privileged.

In chapter 2 we saw the danger of giving information about people 'helping police with their inquiries', but paragraph 12 of the 1952 schedule and paragraph 9 of the 1996 schedule have the effect that the reporter is safe if he publishes a fair and accurate report of any notice issued by the police for the information of the public.

The two paragraphs also give privilege to press reports of council documents, but note well that the documents must be 'issued for the information of the public'. The privilege would not cover a report based on a document leaked to the press.

There is privilege under paragraph 6 of the 1952 schedule for a fair and accurate copy of or extract from, among other things, a document which is required by the law of any part of the United Kingdom to be open to inspection by the public. Under paragraph 5 of the 1996 schedule this protection is no longer limited to the United Kingdom.

Note that the protection does not cover other legal documents which are not publicly available. This provision gives protection, for example, to the reporting of defamatory statements that are *endorsed on* a libel writ, but the protection does not cover any accompanying documentation.

As stated above, the 1996 Act greatly widens the categories of situations where privilege applies. The 1952 schedule does not cover reports of foreign courts, foreign legislatures or public inquiries appointed by governments (unless they operate within 'Her Majesty's dominions'). But the 1996 schedule gives privilege to a fair and accurate report of such proceedings in public anywhere in the world.

The 1996 Act also greatly extends qualified privilege with respect to the reporting of company affairs. Until now only reports relating to proceedings at general meetings of public companies carried qualified privilege. The Act (in a provision expected to come into effect in 1997), extends privilege to documents circulated among shareholders of a UK public company with the authority of the board or the auditors or by any shareholder 'in pursuance of a right conferred by any statutory provision'. Such documents may well be very critical of board members.

The Act gives the Government the power to extend privilege to the reports of statements by bodies, officers or other people designated by them. This power would enable the Government to extend privilege to quangos and other such non-governmental bodies. This provision was expected to be implemented in 1997.

Journalists working on free publications should see the section Free publications later in this chapter.

Here are the schedules to the 1952 Act and the 1996 Act in full.

**Defamation Act 1952**

**Newspaper statements having qualified privilege**

PART I: STATEMENTS PRIVILEGED WITHOUT EXPLANATION OR CONTRADICTION

(1)    A fair and accurate report of any proceedings in public of the legislature of any part of Her Majesty's dominions outside Great Britain.

(2)    A fair and accurate report of any proceedings in public of an international organisation of which the United Kingdom or Her Majesty's Government in the United Kingdom is a member, or of any international conference to which that government sends a representative.

(3)    A fair and accurate report of any proceedings in public of an international court.

(4)    A fair and accurate report of any proceedings before a court exercising jurisdiction throughout any part of Her Majesty's dominions outside the United Kingdom, or of any proceedings before a court-martial held outside the United Kingdom under the Naval Discipline Act, the Army Act, or the Air Force Act.

(5)    A fair and accurate report of any proceedings in public of a body or person appointed to hold a public inquiry by the government or legislature of any part of Her Majesty's dominions outside the United Kingdom.

(6)    A fair and accurate copy of or extract from any register kept in pursuance of any Act of Parliament which is open to inspection by the public, or of any other document which is required by the law of any part of the United Kingdom to be open to inspection by the public.

(7)    A notice or advertisement published by or on the authority of any court within the United Kingdom or any judge or officer of such a court.

PART II:   STATEMENTS PRIVILEGED SUBJECT TO
EXPLANATION OR CONTRADICTION

(8)    A fair and accurate report of the findings or decision of any of
the following associations, or of any committee or governing body
thereof, that is to say—
(a)  an association formed in the United Kingdom for the purpose of
     promoting or encouraging the exercise of or interest in any art,
     science, religion or learning, and empowered by its constitution
     to exercise control over or adjudicate upon matters of interest or
     concern to the association, or the actions or conduct of any
     persons subject to such control or adjudication;
(b)  an association formed in the United Kingdom for the purpose of
     promoting or safeguarding the interests of any trade, business,
     industry or profession, or of the persons carrying on or engaged
     in any trade, business, industry or profession, and empowered
     by its constitution to exercise control over or adjudicate upon
     matters connected with the trade, business, industry or profession,
     or the actions or conduct of those persons;
(c)  an association formed in the United Kingdom for the purpose of
     promoting or safeguarding the interests of any game, sport or
     pastime to the playing or exercise of which members of the
     public are invited or admitted, and empowered by its constitution
     to exercise control over or adjudicate upon persons connected
     with or taking part in the game, sport or pastime; being a finding
     or decision relating to a person who is a member of or is subject
     by virtue of any contract to the control of the association.
(9)    A fair and accurate report of the proceedings at any public
meeting held in the United Kingdom, that is to say, a meeting bona
fide and lawfully held for a lawful purpose and for the furtherance
or discussion of any matter of public concern, whether the admission
to the meeting is general or restricted.
(10)    A fair and accurate report of the proceedings at any
meeting or sitting in any part of the United Kingdom of –
(a)  any local authority or committee of a local authority or local
     authorities, and any sub-committee of the authorities listed in
     the Local Government (Access to Information) Act 1985 [see
     chapter 28];
(b)  any justice or justices of the peace acting otherwise than as a
     court exercising judicial authority;
(c)  any commission, tribunal, committee or person appointed for
     the purposes of any inquiry by Act of Parliament, by Her
     Majesty or by a Minister of the Crown;
(d)  any person appointed by a local authority to hold a local inquiry
     in pursuance of any Act of Parliament;

(e) any other tribunal, board, committee or body constituted by or under, and exercising functions under, an Act of Parliament; not being a meeting or sitting admission to which is denied to representatives of newspapers and other members of the public.

(11) A fair and accurate report of the proceedings at a general meeting of any company or association constituted, registered or certified by or under any Act of Parliament or incorporated by Royal Charter, not being a private company within the meaning of the Companies Act 1948.

(12) A copy or fair and accurate report or summary of any notice or other matter issued for the information of the public by or on behalf of any government department, officer of state, local authority or chief officer of police.

**Defamation Act 1996**

**Statements having qualified privilege**

PART I: STATEMENTS PRIVILEGED WITHOUT EXPLANATION OR CONTRADICTION

1 A fair and accurate report of proceedings in public of a legislature anywhere in the world.

2 A fair and accurate report of proceedings in public before a court anywhere in the world.

3 A fair and accurate report of proceedings in public of a person appointed to hold a public inquiry by a government or legislature anywhere in the world.

4 A fair and accurate report of proceedings in public anywhere in the world of an international organisation or an international conference.

5 A fair and accurate copy of or extract from any register or other document required by law to be open to public inspection.

6 A notice or advertisement published by or on the authority of a court, or of a judge or officer of a court, anywhere in the world.

7 A fair and accurate copy of or extract from matter published by or on the authority of a government or legislature anywhere in the world.

8 A fair and accurate copy of or extract from matter published anywhere in the world by an international organisation or an international conference.

PART II: STATEMENTS PRIVILEGED SUBJECT TO EXPLANATION OR CONTRADICTION

9(1) A fair and accurate copy of or extract from a notice or other matter issued for the information of the public by or on behalf of—

(a)  a legislature in any member state or the European Parliament;
(b)  The government of any member state, or any authority performing governmental functions in any member state or part of a member state, or the European Commission;
(c)  an international organisation or international conference.

(2)  In this paragraph 'governmental functions' includes police functions.

10  A fair and accurate copy of or extract from a document made available by a court in any member state or the European Court of Justice (or any court attached to that court), or by a judge or officer of any such court.

11(1)  A fair and accurate report of proceedings at any public meeting or sitting in the United Kingdom of –
(a)  a local authority or local authority committee;
(b)  a justice or justices of the peace acting otherwise than as a court exercising judicial authority;
(c)  a commission, tribunal, committee or person appointed for the purposes of any inquiry by any statutory provision, by Her Majesty or by a Minister of the Crown or a Northern Ireland Department;
(d)  a person appointed by a local authority to hold a local inquiry in pursuance of any statutory provision;
(e)  any other tribunal, board, committee or body constituted by or under, and exercising functions under, any statutory provision.

(2)  *This sub-paragraph defines 'local authority' in England and Wales, Scotland, and Northern Ireland.*

(3)  A fair and accurate report of any corresponding proceedings in any of the Channel Islands or the Isle of Man or in another member state.

12(1)  A fair and accurate report of proceedings at any public meeting held in a member state.

(2) In this paragraph a 'public meeting' means a meeting bona fide and lawfully held for a lawful purpose and for the furtherance or discussion of a matter of public concern, whether admission to the meeting is general or restricted.

13(1)  A fair and accurate report of proceedings at a general meeting of a UK public company.

(2)  A fair and accurate copy of or extract from any document circulated to members of a UK public company –
(a)  by or with the authority of the board of directors of the company,
(b)  by the auditors of the company, or
(c)  by any member of the company in pursuance of a right conferred by any statutory provision.

(3)  A fair and accurate copy of or extract from any document circulated to members of a UK public company which relates to the appointment, resignation, retirement or dismissal of directors of the company.

(4)   *This sub-paragraph defines 'UK public company'.*

(5)   A fair and accurate report of proceedings at any corresponding meeting of, or copy of or extract from any corresponding document circulated to members of, a public company formed under the law of any of the Channel Islands or the Isle of Man or of another member state.

14   A fair and accurate report of any finding or decision of any of the following descriptions of association, formed in the United Kingdom or another member state, or of any committee or governing body of such an association –

(a)   an association formed for the purpose of promoting or encouraging the exercise of or interest in any art, science, religion or learning, and empowered by its constitution to exercise control over or adjudicate on matters of interest or concern to the association, or the actions or conduct of any persons subject to such control or adjudication;

(b)   an association formed for the purpose of promoting or safeguarding the interests of any trade, business, industry or profession, or of the persons carrying on or engaged in any trade, business, industry or profession, and empowered by its constitution to exercise control over or adjudicate upon matters connected with the trade, business, industry or profession, or the actions or conduct of those persons;

(c)   an association formed for the purpose of promoting or safeguarding the interests of a game, sport or pastime to the playing or exercise of which members of the public are invited or admitted, and empowered by its constitution to exercise control over or adjudicate upon persons connected with or taking part in the game, sport or pastime;

(d)   an association formed for the purpose of promoting charitable objects or other objects beneficial to the community and empowered by its constitution to exercise control over or to adjudicate on matters of interest or concern to the association, or the actions or conduct of any person subject to such control or adjudication.

15(1)   A fair and accurate report of, or copy of or extract from, any adjudication, report, statement or notice issued by a body, officer or other person designated for the purposes of this paragraph–

(a)   for England and Wales or Northern Ireland, by order of the Lord Chancellor, and

(b)   for Scotland, by order of the Secretary of State.

(2) An order under this paragraph shall be made by statutory instrument which shall be subject to annulment in pursuance of a resolution of either House of Parliament.

*Privilege at common law* applies in certain circumstances where the law affords protection to defamatory statements that are untrue for 'the common convenience and welfare of society', as a judge said in 1834.

One such circumstance is where a person makes a defamatory statement in the performance of a legal, moral, or social duty to a person who has a corresponding duty or interest in receiving it.

For example, suppose someone is seeking a job. His potential employer writes to his former employer to ask for a reference. The former employer can reply frankly. He cannot be sued for libel for what he says, even if the facts are wrong, provided he is not motivated by malice.

Can newspapers benefit from this form of privilege? In a case in 1960 the *Times* successfully used the defence. It was sued over its accurate report of a defamatory remark made by a defendant in a foreign court case. The English court that tried the libel action found that the foreign case was so closely linked with the administration of justice in the United Kingdom that the readers of an English paper had a legitimate and proper interest in the matter and the paper had a duty to inform them.

Later many newspapers tried to use this defence but none succeeded until 1996, when the Court of Appeal decided that the *Independent* newspaper had qualified privilege at common law for a sentence that carried the inference that a Ghanaian politician was involved in killings and should have been prosecuted. The court held that part of the story had statutory qualified privilege; common law privilege applied to the other sentence because the facts given were 'part of the matters relating to the proceedings which the public were entitled to know'.

Generally this defence fails because the court takes the view that the readership of a newspaper is too wide for the purpose of communicating the defamatory statement to those with a duty to receive it.

The point was illustrated in 1993 in a case where the *Western Daily Press* was sued for defamatory remarks made by the chairman of an NHS hospital trust. As stated above, such a body is not covered under paragraph 12 of the schedule to the Defamation Act 1952 or paragraph 9 of the schedule to the 1996 Act.

The matter was clearly one of great public interest. Junior doctors at a hospital participated in a local television programme in which they said staff shortages and long waiting lists had put patients' lives at risk and two had died.

The paper, following up the story, interviewed the chairman, who made defamatory remarks about the doctor in charge, who sued both the chairman and the paper.

The paper claimed it had a duty to publish the story to its readers, who were either patients or potential patients at the hospital or were otherwise legitimately interested in the provision of health care services at the hospital. It pointed out that if the statement had come from a health authority (a local authority, under both schedules) reporting would have been protected and indeed before 1990 newspapers had a statutory privilege in reporting information put out by authorities managing hospitals.

But at first instance a master of the High Court struck out the defence saying that the regional newspaper's circulation was far too wide for it to be able to claim the defamatory words would be published to those who had an interest in receiving it. To suppose that a judge or jury would accept that argument was 'so preposterous as to be beneath consideration'.

A judge on appeal agreed with the master. He said the paper must have been published to a very, very large number of people who were not patients at the hospital and were very unlikely to be potential patients.

There is also qualified privilege at common law for a defamatory statement made by a person in reply to an attack upon his character or conduct. There would be no privilege for any response wider than necessary to meet the specific allegations. A newspaper carrying a lawful response would share in the privilege. In the *Western Daily Press* case mentioned above the NHS hospital trust chairman and the newspaper attempted unsuccessfully to use this defence.

Finally, there is qualified privilege at common law for fair and accurate reports of judicial proceedings in this country and reports of the proceedings of Parliament. If a journalist refers to court proceedings that are not contemporaneous his report does not attract absolute privilege but he may still be able to plead qualified privilege for any defamatory statements in his report.

**Free publications** have differed from paid-for newspapers with respect to privilege, but the Defamation Act 1996 (in a provision expected to be implemented in 1997) ends the distinction. As we have seen, this protection is largely derived from statute; previous statutes have extended privilege only to 'newspapers', and have defined newspapers in various ways.

Like paid-for newspapers, free publications benefit from the common law qualified privilege for fair and accurate reports of parliamentary and judicial proceedings.

Free newspapers also benefit from absolute privilege for fair and accurate court reports, provided they are published contemporaneously, because the Law of Libel Amendment Act 1888 covers newspapers printed for sale and published at intervals not exceeding 26 days, and also 'printed matter' published as frequently and containing 'only or principally advertisements'.

But the Act does not cover, say, a weekly newspaper distributed freely to the employees of a firm and carrying few if any advertisements or a commercially run monthly magazine targeted at members of a profession or trade. (The relevant section of the 1888 Act will be repealed when the 1996 Act is fully implemented.)

This apparent lack of protection is not as important as it may seem because of the existence of the common law qualified privilege mentioned above, but the position of free publications under the Defamation Act 1952 has been more significant because so much of the work done by reporters, particularly on local papers, comes under the Act's umbrella.

The Act's provisions apply only to publications printed for sale.

What, therefore, is the position of a journalist working on a free publication who reports defamatory remarks made at a council meeting or by a police spokesman, or the decision of a professional or sporting association on a disciplinary matter?

There has been no reported decision on this issue.

One view is that the Defamation Act (and, before it, the 1888 Act) codified the position of newspapers at common law, and that if a free newspaper were sued for a defamatory statement made, say, at a council meeting then the inclusion of such reports in the schedule to the Act indicates this is the kind of statement a court would be likely to regard as privileged even when published in a free newspaper.

What is the position of a free publication in relation to the qualified privilege, mentioned in the preceding section, for statements made by those with a duty to make them to those with a duty or interest to receive them?

In the case of a newspaper it seems the readership will nearly always be too wide. The position of a specialist journal might be different, however. In *Star Gems v Ford* (1980), *Retail Chemist* was sued for publishing a reader's defamatory letter alleging various business malpractices on the part of a wholesale firm that dealt with chemists.

The publication was sent free to every chemist or manager of a chemist's shop. In addition there were a number of subscribers who paid for a copy. The journal claimed it was covered by qualified privilege because when the editor received the letter he had a duty or interest to communicate its terms to those who might be affected by the dubious sales practices alleged, and they had an interest to receive this information.

The judge agreed. He said the publication was a specialist journal subject to qualified privilege. (However, in this case the privilege was lost because of the editorial staff's 'malice' or recklessness in failing to check the facts.) Whether the Appeal Court would have reached the same decision is uncertain and great caution is advised.

All privilege conferred by the 1996 Act applies to any form of publication, and not merely to newspapers.

## Accord and satisfaction

This is a plea that the matter has been otherwise disposed of, for example by the publication of a correction and apology which has been accepted by the plaintiff in settlement of his complaint.

## 'Without prejudice'

A complaint to a newspaper may be made by a telephone call to the editor or another member of the staff; by a letter from the complainant direct, or from his solicitors.

A solicitor writing on behalf of a client demanding a correction and apology will always avoid suggesting that this action by a newspaper will be enough in itself to settle the dispute and will make it clear that the request is made 'without prejudice' to any other action that may become necessary.

The journalist, through ignorance, may fail to safeguard his interests in this way, particularly in the early stages of a complaint, before he has had the chance to take legal advice. He should not do anything that will prejudice the outcome of any legal action.

In any letter or conversation arising from the complaint the journalist should make it clear that what is said or written is 'without prejudice'. This identifies the exchange of views as merely exploratory. The words should be typed at the top of any letter, or introduced into the conversation. If they are omitted, what is said or written may be taken as an admission, can be used in evidence, and may defeat any effort by the lawyers to put up a defence.

Anything said without prejudice is legally off the record, and the contents of any statement or letter made or written without prejudice normally cannot be referred to in evidence if proceedings follow.

## Care with corrections

It is no defence for a newspaper to publish a correction and apology not accepted by the plaintiff. Such a publication may be found by a court to constitute an admission that the matter was wrong and possibly that it was defamatory.

It may even be thought to make matters worse. In the *Stationery Trade News* case referred to in chapter 18 the magazine, after receiving a complaint from the envelope importers, carried an article on the front page of the following month's edition saying:

> Referring to our lead story last month, 'Counterfeits – retailers warned', envelope distributor Charles Freeman has asked us to point out that its Great West range, which is mentioned in one section of the story, is a 'high quality line' and not in the same category as the counterfeit notepads from China, also mentioned. The envelopes, which come from Ireland and Germany, are now origin marked to that effect and therefore there is no question of the consumer being misled.

The company said the correction made matters worse. The judge said the wording was curious and might be taken by the ordinary reader to mean the company had been counterfeiting and now was not, having origin-marked the envelopes.

On the other hand, if the jury finds for the plaintiff, the fact that the newspaper took prompt and adequate steps to correct the error, and to express regret, will provide a plea in mitigation of damages – that is, it will tend to reduce the size of damages awarded.

And an aggrieved person may be prepared to sign a waiver – that is, a statement saying he waives his right to legal redress in exchange for the publication of a correction and apology – and such a waiver will provide a complete defence.

The defence of accord and satisfaction does not depend upon the existence of any formal written agreement, but clearly the newspaper has a stronger case if it can produce a signed paper (known as a waiver) in the following terms:

I confirm that the publication of an apology in the terms annexed in a position of reasonable prominence in the next available issue of the (name of paper) will be accepted in full and final satisfaction of any claim I may have in respect of the article headed (give headline) published in the issue of your newspaper for (date).

A practical danger for an editor who asks a complainant to sign a waiver is that the reader may not have realised previously that he has a claim for damages and, thus alerted, he may consult a lawyer. The waiver is therefore most useful when the complainant has already threatened to consult a lawyer.

Journalists should take care that in correcting one libel they do not perpetrate another. For example, to say that allegations contained in a speech by X about Y were untrue could amount to calling X a liar – a damaging allegation and likely to be costly.

Newspaper editors are often asked to publish a correction of a statement made in judicial proceedings and reported in the paper. The mistake was not the newspaper's – the account was a correct report of the proceedings and is therefore privileged (see Privilege, above). The correction, however, carries no statutory privilege, and if it is defamatory the newspaper's only defence may be qualified privilege at common law (see Privilege at common law, above), which is likely to be difficult to mount.

An editor receiving such a request should suggest to the aggrieved person that by arrangement with the magistrates he or his solicitor should make a statement in open court. This statement can then be safely reported, under the cloak of privilege.

A final word of advice on corrections. Inexperienced reporters will sometimes try to avoid the consequences of their errors without referring them to their editor. They may be approached directly by the person making the complaint and try to shrug it off. Or they may incorporate a scarcely recognisable 'correction' (without apology) in a follow-up story.

Either course of action is highly dangerous. It may further aggravate the offence and annoy the person concerned, and he may well take more formal steps to secure satisfaction. In such circumstances the reporter should immediately tell his editor so that he may deal with the matter promptly and correctly.

*Payment into court*

Another way to 'satisfy' a plaintiff is by payment into court. This means that the newspaper lodges a sum of money with the court and the plaintiff can take out this money at any time to end the litigation. If he does not accept it, however, the action continues.

Neither the judge nor the jury is told at the trial how much money has been paid in. If the award is less than, or the same as, the amount paid in, the plaintiff will usually be ordered to pay his own and the defendant's costs after the date the money was paid in. This legal device, intended to keep down the number of libel claims, is generally considered an important inhibition preventing people of modest means from suing newspapers.

**Unintentional defamation**

Before the 1952 Defamation Act was passed, a newspaper was in constant peril of libelling someone unintentionally. The danger still exists but the consequences were lessened by the Act and by the Act of 1996.

There are various ways in which unintentional defamation can occur. The classic example was the case of Artemus Jones. Here a journalist introduced a fictitious character into a descriptive account of a factual event in order to provide atmosphere.

Unfortunately the name he chose was that of a real person, a barrister. Stung by the comments of his friends, who either genuinely or for fun associated him with the report, the real Artemus Jones sued and recovered substantial damages.

There are other circumstances equally dangerous. One is the case where an account relating to one person is understood to refer to another. We considered the case of Harold Newstead in the section on identification.

Another is the case where a statement is on the surface innocuous but, because of circumstances unknown to the writer, is defamatory. A well-known case where this happened was *Cassidy v Daily Mirror*. Cassidy, at the races, was photographed with a woman he described as his fiancée, and this was the way she was described in the caption to the photograph used by the newspaper. But Cassidy was already married, and his wife sued on the ground that people who knew her would assume she had been 'living in sin'.

And then there is the situation where a character in a fictional work is accidentally identifiable with a real person.

A person can still be defamed in these various circumstances, but under the 1952 Act the newspaper has a defence if the words complained of were published innocently and an offer of amends is made in accordance with the Act.

To establish innocent publication the publisher must show that he did not intend the words to refer to the plaintiff and knew of no circumstances by which they might be understood to refer to him *or* that the words were not prima facie defamatory and that he knew of no circumstances by which they might be defamatory of the plaintiff.

The defendant newspaper must publish a suitable correction and apology and take reasonable steps to notify people to whom the defamatory words have been published that they are alleged to be defamatory.

The publisher must be able to show that he exercised 'all reasonable care'. The offer of amends shall be made 'as soon as practicable'.

## Offer of amends

'Offer to make amends' is the title given in the Defamation Act 1996 to the defence introduced to replace that described above, known in the 1952 Act as 'unintentional defamation'. The latter is an awkward defence to mount and has not been much used.

The sections of the 1996 Act creating the new defence were expected to come into effect in 1997. To avail himself of the defence, a defendant must make a written offer to make a suitable correction and apology, to publish the correction in a reasonable manner, and to pay the plaintiff suitable damages, although the precise terms on which this will be done may be left to be agreed at a later date.

The defence can only be used where the defendant did not know and had no reason to believe that the statement complained of referred to the plaintiff and was false and defamatory of him. The words are reminiscent of the 1952 Act, but there is an important difference. The plaintiff has the onus of showing that the publication was not 'innocent', whereas under the 1952 Act the onus was on the defendant to show it was.

Another difference compared with the 1952 Act is the requirement to pay damages.

If the offer of amends is not accepted, the defendant will have a defence to the action provided the court holds that he did not know and had no reason to believe that the words complained of were false and defamatory of the plaintiff.

## Other defences

Defences that may be available in certain circumstances are:

1 **That the plaintiff has died** The action for libel is a personal action. A dead person cannot be libelled (except in criminal libel, see chapter 21). Similarly, an action begun by a plaintiff cannot be continued by his heirs and executors if he dies before the case is decided. The action dies with him.

2 **That the plaintiff agreed to the publication** Short of obtaining a signed statement to that effect before publication, this might be extremely difficult to prove. It is no defence to say that you have shown the offending words to the plaintiff and he has had the chance to respond to the allegations.

3 **That proceedings were not started within the limitation period** This constitutes a complete defence, unless there is a new publication of offending material (as in a bygone days column, see preceding chapter). The period, formerly three years, was reduced to one year by a provision of the Defamation Act 1996 which came into effect in September 1996. Reporters should keep their notebooks carefully in case they are required to produce them in court.

4 **That the matter has already been adjudged** The court will not entertain a second action based on the same complaint against the same defendant, or against any other person jointly liable with him for that publication.

To sell copies of a publication containing the offending words after proceedings have begun, or the libel has been proved, would however constitute a separate publication, and could result in another action.

Note that this defence does not stop a plaintiff taking action against any number of defendants who are separately responsible for publishing the statement in different newspapers. See, for example, the case of Princess Bagaya mentioned in the previous chapter.

## Questions

1 Pick out the defamatory statements contained in your daily newspaper today, and explain how these might be defended in court.
2 To plead justification successfully, a newspaper must prove the truth not only of the words in their prima facie meaning, but also of any inference or innuendo behind the words. Give examples.

3  A defamation action may take several years after first publication to come to court. What difficulties does this present to the newspaper being sued?

4  Define the defence of fair comment.

5  Does a defendant in a libel action have to persuade the jury to agree with his views in order to succeed in a plea of fair comment? If not, in what way does he have to satisfy the jury?

6  What proposal has the Faulks Committee made on the naming of the defence 'fair comment'? Why has the committee taken this view?

7  In a women's page article which gave recipes for home-made stuffing, the writer suggested that a chef who advertised a branded packet of stuffing on television would not 'dream' of using the stuffing himself. What danger do you see in the statement?

8  What protection does absolute privilege give to a defamatory statement?

9  What protection is enjoyed by a newspaper report of a debate in Parliament?

10  What requirements does a newspaper report of court proceedings have to fulfil before it enjoys privilege?

11  A daily newspaper reporter is attending a trial. By his deadline time, only the prosecution case has been heard. Can his newspaper publish a report at this stage?

12  When a defendant in a magistrates court takes his place in the dock a man in the public gallery shouts, 'He is innocent. The policeman beat him up.' Can this comment be used safely?

13  Distinguish between the defences of absolute privilege and qualified privilege.

14  A councillor speaking at a council meeting makes allegations about a local builder, but the reporter does not hear him clearly. After the meeting the reporter approaches the councillor, who enlarges upon his allegations. Can the reporter use this matter safely?

15  Does the reporter have any protection for his report of a public meeting? What is meant by 'public meeting'?

16  At a council meeting a speaker makes an attack on a developer. His remarks are reported by a reporter representing a paid-for newspaper and another representing a free newspaper. The developer claims the remarks were defamatory and untrue. What redress, if any, does he have against the newspapers? (Your answer will differ depending upon whether the relevant provision of the Defamation Act 1996 is in effect.)

17  If a journalist is speaking with or writing to a person who alleges he has been defamed, how should he avoid prejudicing the outcome of any later legal proceedings?

18  What dangers do newspapers face in phrasing corrections?

19  Explain the defence of offer of amends.

20  How can a newspaper prove that a defamed person has agreed to the publication of the defamatory words?

21 Can a defamed person take action against four separate newspapers, each of which carries the same defamatory statement?
22 List the defences open to a newspaper sued for libel.

# 21 Criminal libel, slander, and malicious falsehoods

## Criminal libel

In the preceding chapters we have been looking at libel as a civil wrong for which damages are recoverable (ie a tort). It is also a criminal offence.

Criminal libel occurs in two forms: (a) defamatory libel, (b) blasphemous, seditious, and obscene libel. There are important differences between the two types, and we must deal with them separately.

### Criminal defamatory libel

Many defamatory statements might be dealt with either in the civil courts or in the criminal courts; indeed, the same publication could be the subject of proceedings in both places, and the defamer could be sent to prison *and* made to pay damages.

In 1975 the satirical magazine *Private Eye* published an article which Sir James Goldsmith, the financier, claimed was defamatory of him. He said the article meant that he was the ringleader in a conspiracy to obstruct the police in their search for Lord Lucan, who was wanted in connection with the murder of the family's nursemaid. Sir James also claimed that the magazine was conducting a campaign of vilification against him.

He sued *Private Eye* and its editor, and he also began a private prosecution for criminal libel against them.

As we saw in chapter 18, the civil law gives a remedy for defamation because an attack on a man's reputation may injure him as much as a physical attack, and he ought to be compensated for such an attack.

The reason behind criminal libel is different. The publication of a libel is a crime because it is an act which might lead to a breach of the peace.

Sir James Goldsmith told the magistrate hearing committal proceedings against *Private Eye* that after the magazine article there were bomb scares at the offices of his solicitors. He added, 'When a campaign of vilification takes place the repercussions can sometimes lead to a breach of the peace.'

But it seems that it is not essential for the prosecution to prove that the libel was likely to provoke a breach of the peace, a point accepted by the magistrates, as it had been earlier by the High Court judge who gave Sir James permission to begin his proceedings.

A prosecution may be brought where either the publication is likely to cause a breach of the peace, or the publication seriously affects the reputation of the person involved.

In practice, comparatively few cases of defamatory libel are heard in the criminal courts. Judges would be disinclined to jail a man if they felt that the payment of damages was sufficient to right the wrong that had been done.

Prosecutions are reserved for extreme cases where the libel is particularly monstrous or where it is persistently repeated, or where the defendant is impecunious and the complainant would otherwise be left with no redress.

The *Private Eye* case did not come to trial. Sir James withdrew the prosecution after the magazine withdrew its allegations about his involvement in the Lord Lucan affair, paid for an apology in a newspaper, and undertook not to pursue a vendetta against him.

But the law is still available to private prosecutors, and gives them advantages that would not be available under the civil law.

In 1977, a convicted sexual offender Roger Gleaves began a series of prosecutions against journalists. He had just left prison after serving a sentence for wounding and for committing homosexual offences at hostels he ran for homeless young people in London. At his trial, the judge had called him a 'cruel and wicked man with an evil influence on others'. Gleaves's activities had aroused considerable public concern and had been the subject of many articles.

He prosecuted among others the two authors of a paperback book *Johnny Go Home*, based on a TV programme by them which was screened in 1975, and three reporters of the *Sunday People*.

A magistrate committed all five to trial. She remanded the three newspaper reporters in custody to Brixton prison, because she said she felt they were likely to commit other offences, but they were released the following day by a judge in chambers.

Later the Director of Public Prosecutions took over the case against them and offered no evidence.

The television journalists were not so lucky. Their trial in 1980 lasted two and a half weeks. If they had been sued in a civil court, they could have brought evidence under the Civil Evidence Act 1968 that Gleaves had been convicted of the offences they had written about, and this would have been conclusive evidence that he had committed them. But this defence was not open to them in a criminal trial, and instead they had to prove Gleaves's offences again. They succeeded, and the jury acquitted them.

Legal aid is not available in a *civil* libel suit, but in this criminal libel case the entire cost of the action and the hearings leading to it, estimated at from £50,000 to more than £75,000, was paid from public funds because Gleaves had no money.

To sustain a prosecution for criminal libel the words must be written, or be in some permanent form, but there need be no publication to a third party: it is enough that they are addressed to the person injured by them. This is quite logical since it is the person defamed who is most likely to be angered to the point of hitting the man who insults him, and that would be a breach of the peace.

As we have seen, there can be no *civil* libel of the dead. But in criminal libel the position is different: words spoken of a dead person may be the subject of a prosecution, but only if it can be proved that they were used with the intention of provoking his living relatives to commit a breach of the peace, or that they had a tendency to do so.

In dealing with civil defamation, we saw that proving the truth of the offending words constituted a complete answer to an action.

This defence is available also in criminal proceedings for libel, but in addition the defendant has to satisfy the court that the words were published for the public benefit.

Failure to do so would result in a conviction.

The old saying 'The greater the truth the greater the libel' has no meaning in civil libel. In criminal libel it indicates that passions are more likely to be aroused and a breach of the peace more likely to occur if the allegation is true.

But even so the libeller has a defence if he has spoken out for the public benefit.

A further difference between criminal and civil libel is that it is a crime to libel a class of people, provided the object is to excite the hatred of the public against the class libelled. But a journalist guilty of such conduct is more likely to be prosecuted under the race relations legislation.

For publishing a defamatory libel a person may be sent to prison for up to a year, and/or fined. If it can be proved that he knew the libel to be untrue, the period of imprisonment may be doubled.

## Blasphemy, sedition, and obscenity

The publication of blasphemous, seditious, or obscene matter is a criminal offence whether it is published in writing or by word of mouth.

It is no defence to prove that the words complained of are true, or that they form part of a fair and accurate report of what was said on a privileged occasion. Only with obscene libel is it any defence to prove that publication of the words was for the public benefit.

Changes of fashion and outlook affect decisions about whether words are or are not criminal. Statements that in Victorian times might have been held to be blasphemous are freely made today. Sex, once almost taboo, is a subject for open discussion in speech and in the printed word today.

**Blasphemy**    Blasphemy consists in the use of language having a tendency to vilify the Christian religion or the Bible. As with criminal libel, the law is seeking to prevent words likely to cause a breach of the peace. It is therefore concerned with the form and expression of language used, and not the substance of the statements or the intention of the author.

Even fundamental tenets of the faith may be questioned without fear of a prosecution unless – and this is the important proviso – scurrilous and irreverent language is used.

The test is whether what is written is likely to shock and outrage the feelings of believers.

In 1977 *Gay News*, a newspaper for homosexuals, and its editor were convicted of blasphemous libel for publishing a poem written as if by a homosexual Roman centurion recalling his feelings towards Christ after the Crucifixion.

The poem stated that Christ had had homosexual relations with a number of men, and went on to describe homosexual acts by the centurion with the dead body. The defence claimed the poem was an expression of the ecstasy of loving God, but they were not allowed to bring evidence on the literary merits of the poem or the author's intentions.

*Gay News* was fined £1,000. The editor was fined £500 and given a suspended prison sentence of nine months. On appeal, the fines were upheld, but the suspended sentence was set aside.

The law of blasphemy applies only to words concerning the Christian religion, as the Queen's Bench Divisional Court confirmed in 1990 when refusing to allow the prosecution of Salman Rushdie for comments in his book *The Satanic Verses* which had offended Muslims.

**Sedition**    Any words which are likely to disturb the internal peace and government of the country constitute seditious libel.

The tests to apply to determine whether words constitute a seditious libel are these:
- Do they bring the sovereign or her family into hatred or contempt?
- Do they bring the government and constitution of the United Kingdom into hatred or contempt?
- Do they bring either House of Parliament, or the administration of justice, into hatred or contempt?

- Do they excite British subjects to attempt, *otherwise than by lawful means* (our italics), the alteration of any matter in Church or State by law established?
- Do they raise discontent or disaffection in British subjects?
- Do they promote feelings of ill-will and hostility between different classes?

From these tests, it seems that the law is very strict, but in fact the law will hesitate to interfere with an honest expression of opinion so long as it is couched in moderate terms. Thus criticisms of the monarchical and parliamentary *systems*, constructively advanced, would not be regarded as seditious.

Muslims tried to prosecute Salman Rushdie for sedition as well as blasphemy (see above) on the grounds that his words had created discontent among British subjects, had created hostility between classes, and had damaged relations between Britain and Islamic states.

But a magistrate rejected the attempt saying: 'The essential part of [the offence of seditious libel] is that any action should be directed against the state.'

The divisional court in 1990 agreed, saying the intention required to found a prosecution for seditious libel was an intention to incite to violence or to create public disturbance or disorder against the Queen or the institutions of government.

Not only had there to be proof of an incitement to violence, but it had to be violence or resistance or defiance for the purpose of disturbing constituted authority.

**Obscenity**    The test of obscene libel is whether the words or matter, if taken as a whole, would tend to deprave and corrupt those who are likely, having regard to all the circumstances, to read them.

The law used to be that, as with blasphemous libel, no evidence could be brought to show the literary merits of any work which was the subject of proceedings.

In 1928, for example, *The Well of Loneliness*, a literary work dealing with female homosexuality, was condemned as obscene. Evidence as to its literary merit was ruled inadmissible.

The Obscene Publications Act 1959 introduced a defence that the publication was 'for the public good…in the interests of science, literature, art, or learning, or of other objects of public concern'.

The publishers of D H Lawrence's *Lady Chatterley's Lover* were acquitted of obscenity as a result of this defence.

Before 1964, the law of obscene libel had caught only those who *published* obscene works. By the Obscene Publications Act of that year, it is an offence to *have* an obscene article for publication for gain.

In prosecutions brought under the Post Office Act of 1953, under which it is an offence to send 'indecent or obscene matter' through the post, the

test is simply whether ordinary people would be shocked or disgusted by
the material. There is no need for the prosecution to show that it tends to
deprave or corrupt.

## Slander

The most obvious difference between libel and slander is that, as we have
seen, libel is in some permanent form (eg written words, a drawing, or a
photograph), while slander is spoken or in some other transient form.

The exceptions are (i) a defamatory statement broadcast on radio or
television, or in a cable programme, which by the Broadcasting Act 1990
is treated as libel, (ii) a defamatory statement in a public performance of
a play, by virtue of the Theatres Act 1968.

In slander, as with libel, there must be publication to a third person for
a statement to become actionable.

There is one further difference between libel and slander. Whereas
actual damage will be presumed in a libel action, it must be proved
affirmatively by the plaintiff in a slander action, except in four cases.

A slander of this kind is said to be actionable *per se* (by itself). The four
cases are:
(a)  any imputation that an individual has committed a crime punishable
     by death or imprisonment;
(b)  any imputation that an individual is suffering from certain contagious
     or objectionable diseases, such as venereal disease or leprosy: the test
     is whether the nature of the disease would cause the person to be
     shunned or avoided;
(c)  any imputation of unchastity in a woman;
(d)  any statement calculated to disparage an individual in his office,
     profession, calling, trade, or business.

In these four instances, actual pecuniary loss does not have to be proved.

The journalist is less likely to become involved personally in a slander
action than in a libel action, but he must be aware of the danger of slander.

Let us suppose that X has said that Y, a member of a borough council,
has used his office to secure building contracts. This is clearly actionable
because it disparages him in his office of councillor. The reporter detailed
to check the story will have to interview a number of people to arrive at the
truth, and in these interviews he must be wary of laying himself open to a
writ.

In 1987 a cargo airline sought an injunction to prevent a freelance
journalist inquiring into the question of whether the airline had carried
armaments, an allegation it denied (*Seagreen Air Transport v George*).
The airline said that by simply asking the question the reporter was
slandering the firm.

The matter was not tested in court because the judge refused an injunction on the preliminary point that it was not defamatory to allege, even wrongly, that a cargo airline carried arms; the words did not, of themselves, carry any improper implications.

## Malicious falsehoods

Publication of a false statement, though it may cast no aspersions on the character of a man, or upon his fitness to hold a certain office or to follow a particular calling, may still be damaging to him.

For example, to say of a doctor that he has retired from practice would no doubt cause him pecuniary loss, if false. But it is clearly not defamatory.

Because it is not defamatory, a wronged man cannot bring an action for either libel or slander.

He may, however, be able to bring an action for malicious falsehood.

In such an action, the plaintiff must prove that the statement is untrue. Note the contrast with libel, where the court will *assume* that a defamatory statement is false.

The plaintiff in an action for malicious falsehood must also prove that the statement was published maliciously. If he fails to prove malice his action will fail.

As with libel, malice can mean not only spite or ill-will but also a dishonest or otherwise improper motive. A statement made by a man who knows that it is false is made maliciously; so also if he knows that the statement is likely to injure and makes the statement recklessly, not caring whether it is true or false. Negligence is not malice.

It used to be the case that, to establish malicious falsehood, the plaintiff had to prove he had suffered actual damage.

By the Defamation Act 1952, the rule no longer applies to words in permanent form, such as printed words, provided they are *likely* to cause financial damage.

Nor does it apply to words, whether spoken or written, that are likely to cause financial damage to the plaintiff *in his office, profession, calling, trade, or business.*

In 1990, when the television actor Gorden Kaye was in hospital seriously ill, his representative sued the *Sunday Sport* and its editor for malicious falsehood.

A journalist and a photographer had gained access to the hospital and taken photographs of Kaye, and in a proposed article the *Sunday Sport* planned to say Kaye had agreed to be interviewed and photographed.

The Court of Appeal said the words were false because Kaye was in no state to be interviewed or give any informed consent. Any publication would 'inevitably' be malicious because the reporter and photographer knew this.

As to damage, Kaye had a potentially valuable right to sell the story of his accident to other newspapers for 'large sums of money' and the value of that right would be seriously lessened if the *Sunday Sport* were allowed to publish.

The court made an order that until the matter came for trial the *Sunday Sport* should not publish anything that could convey to a reader that Kaye had voluntarily permitted the taking of photographs (see also references to the case in chapter 31, Privacy).

Another very important difference between libel and malicious falsehood is that a plaintiff cannot get legal aid for a libel action but may now be able to do so for malicious falsehood.

In 1992 a former lady's maid to the Princess Royal wished to sue *Today* newspaper over claims that she stole intimate letters to the Princess from Commander Tim Laurence, later her husband, but was too poor to do so. She was granted legal aid for an action in malicious falsehood and in a landmark decision the Court of Appeal ruled that her action was not an abuse of the process of the court. The following year she was paid out-of-court damages of about £25,000.

In the past another important difference between libel and malicious falsehood has been the 'limitation period'. A plaintiff had three years from the date of publication in which to sue for libel, but six years for malicious falsehood. The Defamation Act 1996, in a section that came into effect in September of that year, reduced the limitation period to one year for both actions.

Suppose an editor receives a solicitor's letter drawing attention to comments about a person or his goods which, the solicitor claims, are false and are likely to cause damage. The editor realises that his facts are wrong, but they were not defamatory and it was an honest mistake. The editor should act quickly to put the mistake right by means of an adequate correction to avoid any suggestion in subsequent legal action that he acted with malice.

Two types of malicious falsehoods are known as *slander of goods*, false and malicious statements disparaging the plaintiff's goods, and *slander of title*, false and malicious denial of the plaintiff's title to property.

The word slander is misleading in both cases. The damaging statement can be in permanent form or in spoken words.

## Questions

1 What is the function of the law of criminal defamatory libel?
2 State four differences between civil libel and criminal defamatory libel.

3    'The greater the truth the greater the libel.' Does this saying express the law accurately?

4    State the penalty for criminal defamatory libel.

5    Is it a defence to a charge of blasphemy to claim that the words were used without intention to vilify the Christian religion, or that they have literary merit?

6    What is the essence of the crime of seditious libel?

7    State the test for obscene libel. What defences, if any, are open to a person charged with obscene libel?

8    In what cases are slanderous statements actionable without proof of damage?

9    In what circumstances could a journalist be at risk of an action for slander?

10   What are the elements necessary to found an action for malicious falsehood? A journalist writes a news story saying that A has done a particularly generous deed. As the journalist knows, A's wealthy uncle is a miser and hates acts of generosity. A is cut out of the miser's will. The story was quite untrue. Can A take any action against the journalist?

11   Define slander of goods and slander of title.

12   A newspaper runs a feature on bathroom renovation in which it says the X Group sells taps only for bathrooms. Your reporter made this statement after making inquiries that led him to believe it to be true. A solicitor's letter says the X Group sells a successful range of fittings for kitchens also and the article has caused the firm serious losses. The letter demands an apology and substantial damages. What should the editor do?

# 22  Rehabilitation of Offenders Act

The Rehabilitation of Offenders Act 1974 is intended to allow people with comparatively minor convictions to live down their past. Such convictions become *spent* after a specified length of time known as the *rehabilitation period*. This period varies according to the severity of sentence.

The Act limits in two ways the defences available to a journalist who has mentioned a man's spent convictions and is being sued for libel as a result:

(a)  If the journalist pleads justification – that is, that the report of the plaintiff's previous convictions was true – the defence fails if the plaintiff can prove the journalist acted with malice.

(b)  If the journalist reports a reference made in court to a spent conviction, and that conviction was held to be inadmissible in evidence, he cannot plead privilege.

The Act breached for the first time the established principle of the civil law that truth is a complete answer to an action for defamation.

Investigative reporters often need to mention the previous convictions of villains whose activities they intend to expose. Suppose, for example, a journalist discovers that a person who is starting a youth club in his area has a large number of previous convictions for indecency and that these convictions have become spent.

The journalist can defend the defamatory statement that the man has previous convictions by pleading either qualified privilege or justification. His story also carries the defamatory inference that a man guilty of these offences is unfit to run such a club, and he can defend that allegation by pleading fair comment.

However, as we saw in chapter 20, if the plaintiff can show the journalist acted with malice, his defences of qualified privilege and fair comment fail. Under the 1974 Act, his defence of justification fails as well, if the plaintiff can prove malice.

It should be emphasised that if the journalist is not motivated by malice, he can still use justification, privilege, and fair comment to defend a reference to a spent conviction – except as to privilege in the situation mentioned under (b) above.

In 1977 the Labour Party presented a party political broadcast on television which took the form of a fierce attack on the right-wing party the National Front. The presenters wished to mention the spent convictions of John Tyndall, leader of the NF. Tyndall's most recent conviction was six months' imprisonment in 1966, 11 years previously, for having a loaded pistol without a licence. At the time he was a member of another right-wing party. The reference was deleted from the broadcast on the advice of the broadcasting authorities.

The lawyers were probably worried that, if the spent conviction had been mentioned and the case had come to court, Tyndall would have argued that the Labour Party's purpose was to speak out not in the public interest but for party political advantage, and that might amount to an improper motive – or malice as the law calls it.

Tyndall's convictions were published the following Sunday by the *News of the World* on its front page under the headline: 'We say you have the right to know the truth about such men as this.'

When a conviction has become spent it is as though, for all legal purposes, it has never occurred. If a person is giving evidence in any *civil* proceedings he should not be asked any questions about spent convictions and he is entitled to refuse to answer such questions unless the court tells him he must.

The Act does not apply to later *criminal* proceedings. If a rehabilitated person appears again before a criminal court after his conviction has become spent he can still be asked about it and the court can be told about it for the purpose of deciding sentence if he is found guilty.

Privilege applies to court reports of such references to spent convictions, unless ruled by the court to be inadmissible.

But the Lord Chief Justice has directed, in accordance with 'the general intention of Parliament', that spent convictions should never be referred to in criminal courts if such reference could be avoided and that no one should refer in open court to a spent conviction without the authority of the judge.

If a newspaper report contains any reference to spent convictions that were not referred to in open court, or that were referred to but held to be inadmissible, that part of the report will not be privileged.

Peter Carter-Ruck, a leading authority on libel, has said that in these circumstances 'it would still appear to leave available (provided there is no evidence of malice) the defence of justification, though publication in such circumstances might constitute a contempt of court'. This issue has not yet been tested in the courts.

The Act does not impose any criminal penalty on the journalist who mentions a spent conviction, but it is an offence for a public servant or someone involved in contracted out services to reveal details of spent convictions other than in the course of his official duties.

Obtaining information of spent convictions from official records by fraud, dishonesty, or bribery is also a criminal offence.


## Rehabilitation periods

Excluded from the provisions of the Act are sentences exceeding two and a half years of imprisonment, of youth custody, of detention in a young offender institution, or of corrective training: they can never become spent. Nor can a term of preventive detention.

The rehabilitation period varies between ten years (for a term of imprisonment exceeding six months) and six months (for an absolute discharge). But a further conviction during the rehabilitation period can have the effect of extending it.

There are *three* fixed rehabilitation periods that are reduced by half for offenders under 18.

* *Ten years* for prison sentence, detention in a young offender institution, youth custody, or corrective training for more than six months but not more than two and a half years; or for cashiering, or discharge with ignominy, or dismissal with disgrace from the armed services.
* *Seven years* for prison sentence or detention in a young offender institution or youth custody for six months or less; or dismissal from the armed services.
* *Five years* for fine, or some other sentence (such as community service order) for which the Act does not provide a different rehabilitation period, or for detention in the services.

There are *three* fixed rehabilitation periods relating to sentences that apply to young offenders.

* *Seven years* for borstal training or for armed services detention for more than six months.
* *Five years* for detention for more than six months but not more than two and a half years.
* *Three years* for detention or a custodial order for six months or less, or for a detention centre order.

For an absolute discharge the period is six months.

For probation the period is five years for an offender over 18, and until the order expires (with a minimum of two and a half years) for those under 18.

There are also *four* variable rehabilitation periods.

* *The period runs until the order expires (with a minimum of one year)* for conditional discharge, or binding over; and for fit person orders, supervision orders, or care orders under the Children Act 1989.

- *The period runs on for one year after the order expires* for custody in a remand home, attendance centre orders, or secure training orders.
- *The period runs on for two years after the order expires (with a minimum of five years from the date of the conviction)* for hospital orders under the Mental Health Acts.
- *The period lasts for the period of the disqualification* for disqualification and disabilities.

Suspended sentences are treated as if they were put into effect.

Journalists requiring further information about rehabilitation periods for particular sentences should consult *Stone's Justices' Manual*.

## Questions

1 What is meant by a *spent* conviction?
2 State the two ways in which the Rehabilitation of Offenders Act limits the defences available in a libel action.
3 Why, do you consider, did the broadcasting authorities prevent the Labour Party from mentioning John Tyndall's previous convictions in its party political broadcast? Would the same considerations apply to the publication in the *News of the World*?
4 You are writing an investigative story about a man who was sentenced to three years' imprisonment eleven years ago for an offence of dishonesty and is now starting a business in your locality. What limit, if any, does the Rehabilitation of Offenders Act place upon your ability to mention his previous conviction?

# 23  Breach of confidence

The law of confidentiality is being used increasingly in attempts to keep information out of the media, and this branch of the law is being developed and extended.

It is, said Lord Denning, a broad principle of equity that he who has obtained information in confidence should not take unfair advantage of it.

The main means used to enforce the law is the *injunction* – that is, an order of the court directing a party to refrain from doing something.

For many years judges have granted injunctions preventing the disclosure of facts which were imparted in circumstances imposing an obligation of confidence.

The law they developed had a useful role in protecting commercial and trade secrets; in a characteristic leading case the confidential information related to a blister treatment for horses.

The judges were using the discretionary powers available to them when dealing with equitable matters (see chapter 1, Sources of law). When they explained the legal concepts behind their decisions, individual judges put forward different ideas and sometimes reached apparently inconsistent conclusions. This is still a confusing characteristic of breach of confidence cases. The answers to many fundamental questions remain unclear.

A landmark in the development of the law of confidentiality was the declaration of the Lord Chief Justice in 1975 that the kind of secrets to be protected could include 'public secrets' – that is, information emanating from state or public business. Journalists consider their role includes the investigation of such secrets and, in appropriate cases, publication in the public interest.

As the *Times* newspaper declared during a confrontation with government in 1852: 'The first duty of the press is to obtain the earliest and most correct intelligence of the events of the time, and instantly, by disclosing them, to make them the common property of the nation.'

In the 1980s, the law of confidentiality was used for the first time by local authorities against local newspapers. As each councillor 'leaking' stories to the press is, on the face of it, breaking his duty of confidence to the council, there is ample scope for further extension of the law in this direction.

In the late 1980s, the law of confidentiality was used by the British Government in an attempt to silence former members of the security services (in particular Peter Wright, author of *Spycatcher*) and journalists trying to report their disclosures. Previously, such disclosures in this country would have resulted in prosecution under the Official Secrets Act, but juries had shown themselves unwilling to convict and the Act had become unworkable (see chapter 30).

Applications for injunctions on the ground of breach of confidence come before judges sitting without juries and if granted are enforceable under the law of contempt – again by judges sitting without juries; and the judges have generally shown themselves more amenable to government claims of national security.

In 1988, however, the House of Lords refused to grant a permanent injunction restraining newspapers from publishing information contained in *Spycatcher*.

More effective official secrets legislation was introduced in 1990, but the Government said it would continue to use the law of confidentiality to prevent disclosure it believed would damage the public interest.

## Injunction against one is against all

In 1987, in a decision of great importance for the press, the Court of Appeal held that when an injunction is in force preventing a newspaper from publishing confidential information, other newspapers which know of the injunction can be guilty of contempt of court if they publish that information, even if they are not named in the injunction.

The court said papers committed a serious offence against justice itself by taking action which destroyed the confidentiality that the court was seeking to protect and so rendered the due process of law ineffectual. In 1989 two papers were fined £50,000 each for publishing extracts from *Spycatcher* because at the time of publication they knew that interim injunctions were in force against the *Observer* and the *Guardian* preventing them from publishing this material.

The fines were later discharged, but the convictions were upheld and the ruling on the law was confirmed by the House of Lords in 1991.

The implications of the 1987 decision quickly became clear when officials of the Department of Trade and Industry telephoned all national newspapers to warn them that an injunction existed against the *Observer* preventing it from publishing details of a leaked Department of Trade and

Industry report on the takeover of House of Fraser; the other papers were unable to publish details from the report in case they committed contempt.

This legal device for silencing the press is all the more effective because the injunction is sometimes phrased in such a way that journalists are forbidden even to mention the existence of the proceedings.

In 1992, when Paddy Ashdown, leader of the Liberal Democrats, was attempting to prevent the media from revealing an affair with a former secretary, he was granted an injunction against News Group Newspapers that forbade publication not only of information concerning any sexual relationship between the two but also of 'any information as to the existence of these proceedings'.

The newspaper proprietor Robert Maxwell, wishing to conceal his misdeeds, also used the device. He obtained an injunction to prevent the publication of confidential material, then persuaded the judge the media must not be allowed to publish the fact that the injunction had been issued.

## Breach of confidence and privacy

In the 1990s, breach of confidence was increasingly being used in attempts to protect *privacy* rights, but with only limited success. In 1994 Camelot, organisers of the National Lottery, failed to get a permanent ban preventing the media from identifying the winner of the first major jackpot.

In 1995 the Princess of Wales sued Mirror Group Newspapers for publishing a photograph of her exercising in a gymnasium, taken with a concealed camera; her lawyers claimed the resulting out-of-court settlement as a victory, but it is far from clear what the result would have been had the case gone to court. Both cases are discussed below.

## The journalist's dilemma

The law of confidentiality regularly presents journalists with a difficult dilemma. Suppose a reporter learns about some newsworthy misconduct from a source who has received his information confidentially. The journalist is impelled, both by his instinct for fair play and by his respect for the law of libel, to approach the person against whom the misconduct is alleged to get his side of the story.

If he does, however, he faces the risk that the culprit will immediately obtain an injunction preventing the use of the information and thus killing the story.

In 1977 the *Daily Mail* obtained a copy of a letter from the National Enterprise Board to British Leyland, the nationalised car manufacturer, that appeared to show BL was paying bribes and conspiring to defraud foreign governments to win overseas orders. It published the story under the headline 'World-wide bribery web by Leyland'.

No doubt the journalists assumed that if they checked the story with BL the firm would immediately get an injunction preventing them from publishing. In fact the letter turned out to be a forgery and the paper had to pay substantial libel damages.

By contrast, in several of the cases mentioned below – eg the Bill Goodwin case – the journalist attempted to check the story with the source and was then prevented by injunction from using it until it was no longer news.

You should certainly check the story if it is defamatory, but in doing so you must phrase your questions in such a way that you do not reveal that you have written material in your possession, thus laying yourself open to an injunction. It is better to use the information at your disposal to try to get the facts from a different, non-confidential, route. You can then return to the original source of the information to check.

Bear in mind that the court can order you to 'deliver up' confidential material, and this can result in the identification of your source. In the Bill Goodwin case the reporter refused to hand over his notes and was heavily fined (see below).

In a case brought under the Official Secrets Act the *Guardian* was forced to hand over confidential material that revealed the identity of its source, who was jailed (see chapter 30). If you wish to avoid the risk of having your source identified, you should destroy the documents after writing the story.

But note that Lord Denning said: 'It is contempt deliberately to mutilate a document which is likely to be called for in a pending action.'


## How the media are affected

*Injunctions*

The law of confidentiality affects the media because a person who passes information to a journalist may have received it confidentially. If the person to whom the confidence belongs discovers, before the paper is published or the programme is broadcast, that the information is to be disclosed, he can try to get an interim (temporary) injunction prohibiting publication of the confidential material.

His lawyer applies to a High Court judge. He has to persuade the judge that he has a real prospect of succeeding in his claim for a permanent injunction when the matter comes to trial – that is, that his case is not frivolous.

The application may be *ex parte*, meaning 'from one side'; only one party is represented, and the newspaper may learn about the proceedings only when it is told that an injunction has been granted.

At this stage, the newspaper may be printed and ready to go on sale, or the programme may be ready for broadcasting and such an injunction may cause great inconvenience and expense, but defiance of the order would be a serious contempt of court.

On many occasions, interim injunctions which appear to be harsh and wide-ranging in their terms are lifted when the newspaper's case is heard. This does not mean that the judges made a mistake, legally speaking, the first time. The purpose of an interim injunction is to 'hold the ring' (in the words of Lord Donaldson, Master of the Rolls), until the matter can be fully argued at trial.

When deciding whether to grant such an injunction, the judges, following the rules of equity (see chapter one), have to consider the 'balance of convenience'. They argue that if they do grant an injunction which is later lifted little harm will have been done because the defendant newspaper can then publish the material, but that if they do not grant an injunction, irreparable damage will have been done because the confidential information will be published and cease to be secret.

But it is in the nature of news that once it is delayed it ceases to be news. The trial may not take place for a year or more, so the granting of an interim injunction can have serious repercussions.

**Local papers**   The following two examples show the effect of injunctions on local newspapers.

In 1982, the *Watford Observer* planned to publish a story based on a document which showed that Robert Maxwell's printing operation, Sun Printers, was losing money, and he wanted to reduce the workforce.

The day before press day, a reporter telephoned the company asking for comments. At midday on press day, Maxwell telephoned the paper's editor and asked for an assurance that the material would not be published, on the grounds that it was confidential and that negotiations with the trade unions were at a delicate stage. When the editor declined, Sun Printers' lawyers applied to the High Court for an injunction and telephoned the paper at 4.30 pm to say an injunction had been granted. By this time all editorial and typesetting work on the paper would normally have been completed.

Fortunately, the paper, alerted by the call from Maxwell, had prepared alternative material for use in its pages. The injunction was later lifted (see this chapter).

In 1984, Medina Borough Council, on the Isle of Wight, got an injunction preventing the *Southern Evening Echo*, of Southampton, from publishing details of a consultant's report on plans for development in Newport, the island's capital.

As the papers were unloaded from the hydrofoil taking them from the mainland, an officer of the Newport county court stood on the quayside with the injunction. The papers could not be distributed, and another edition had to be sent to the island.

**The *Spycatcher* affair**   This affair arose out of attempts by the British Government to prevent publication of information acquired by Peter Wright, a former senior officer of MI5, Britain's internal security service. The Government acted against Wright and a number of newspapers in many courts in several countries. Only a brief summary is given below. Those wishing to study the cases in detail should refer to *The Spycatcher Cases* (European Law Centre) by Michael Fysh QC.

In 1985 the British Attorney-General began proceedings against Wright in New South Wales, Australia. Wright was living in Tasmania.

Wright's book recounted his experiences in MI5; among other allegations, it said that MI5 officers had plotted to destabilise the government led by the Labour Prime Minister Harold Wilson in the mid-1970s, and that officers of the security services had plotted to assassinate President Nasser of Egypt.

The Attorney-General sought an injunction or an account of profits (see below, Account of profits), arguing that former members of the security services had an absolute and lifelong duty not to reveal any details of their employment.

In June 1986 the *Observer* and *Guardian* newspapers both carried stories reporting the forthcoming hearing in Australia. The stories contained brief accounts of some of the allegations. An English court granted the Attorney-General interim injunctions against both newspapers preventing them from disclosing any information obtained by Wright in his capacity as a member of the British security service.

The following year, as mentioned earlier in this chapter, other newspapers published information from *Spycatcher*, believing they were not prevented by the injunctions, but the courts held they were guilty of contempt of court.

In 1988, after many legal actions involving the Government and a number of newspapers, the House of Lords held, among other things, that the articles in the *Observer* and *Guardian* in 1986 were not in breach of confidence; that the Government was not entitled to an injunction preventing the two papers from further comment on the book and use of extracts from it; and that the Government was not entitled to a general injunction restraining the media from future publication of information derived from Wright or other members or former members of the security service. By the time the two papers were free to publish the material legally, the story was history rather than news.

**Security service cases**   While the Spycatcher cases were dragging on the Government became committed to taking legal action whenever members and former members of the security services breached what the Government saw as their lifelong duty of confidence, and many actions followed.

A characteristic of the injunctions imposed by courts was their very wide scope. For example, in the *Zircon* affair (see chapter 30) the Government was granted an injunction against journalist Duncan Campbell preventing him from publishing anything about the GCHQ spy centre at Cheltenham which might have been given to Campbell by serving or former officials there, *whether previously published or not.*

The Government was granted an injunction preventing BBC Radio 4 from broadcasting a series of programmes 'My country: right or wrong'. The injunction was at first in terms that prevented the BBC from broadcasting all information of whatever kind about the security services from former members, or even naming former members of the security services.

**The Bill Goodwin case**   In 1989 an engineering company, Tetra Ltd, obtained injunctions against the magazine the *Engineer* and Bill Goodwin, a trainee reporter. The company, which was in financial difficulties, had prepared a business plan for the purpose of negotiating a substantial bank loan.

A copy of the draft plan 'disappeared' from the company's offices and the next day an unidentified source telephoned Goodwin and gave him information about the companies, including the amount of the projected loan and the company's forecast results.

Goodwin phoned the company and its bankers to check the information. The company obtained an *ex parte* injunction restraining the magazine from publishing information derived from the draft plan and later obtained an order requiring Goodwin and the *Engineer* to hand over notes that would disclose the source of the information. Goodwin refused to comply with the order and was fined £5,000. In 1996 the European Court of Human Rights held that the court order and the fine violated his right to freedom of expression under Article 10 of the European Convention on Human Rights (see 'Sources of law', chapter 1; 'Tainted information' below; and 'The journalist's sources', chapter 24).

**The National Lottery winner**   In 1994, in the early days of the National Lottery, Camelot, the lottery's organiser, obtained an injunction preventing the *Sun* and the *Daily Mirror* – and hence the whole media – from identifying the winner of the jackpot, an unprecedented £17.8 m. The injunction was granted *ex parte* by a judge sitting late at night. The injunction was successfully challenged the following day (see below).

**Princess in the gym**   In 1993 the *Sunday Mirror* published on its front page a picture of Princess Diana, the Princess of Wales, dressed in a leotard and working out on an exercise machine in a gymnasium, under the headline 'World exclusive: Di spy sensation'. The picture was one of a series taken by the owner of the gymnasium, Bryce Taylor, with a camera concealed in the ceiling. The following day the *Daily Mirror* printed more pictures.

The princess gained an interim injunction preventing further publication of photographs of her and sued Taylor and Mirror Group Newspapers (MGN).

In 1995 the princess reached an out-of-court settlement with Taylor and MGN. It is unclear what would have been the outcome of the princess's case against the newspaper, had the case gone to court, for reasons referred to below.

Many people regarded the publication as a gross invasion of the princess's privacy, and the affair illustrated the inadequacy of breach of confidence as a cure for such intrusion.

**Cost of injunctions**  As a condition for the granting of an interim injunction the person seeking the injunction has to give a cross-undertaking in damages – that is, an undertaking that he will pay any damages to the defendant if, at the trial, it is held that the interim injunction should not have been granted.

The defendant may also get costs. In the National Lottery case mentioned above, the newspapers that succeeded in having the injunction lifted were awarded costs, estimated at £5,000, against Camelot.

Even so, the cost to a newspaper that decides to challenge an injunction may be considerable. The *News of the World* claimed in 1987 that it had spent £200,000 in an unsuccessful attempt to defeat an injunction granted to a health authority preventing the paper using information from personal medical records supplied by one or more of the authority's employees. The records showed that two practising doctors employed by the authority had the HIV virus.

*Fines*

Disobeying an injunction can result in an action for contempt of court. The *News of the World* was fined £10,000 for publishing a story headlined 'Scandal of Docs with AIDS' after the granting of the injunction mentioned above.

*Order to reveal source*

A court can order a journalist to reveal the name of his informant, as happened in the Bill Goodwin case (see next chapter, The journalist's sources).

## Delivery up

A court can order that confidential matter be 'delivered up' or destroyed.

## Account of profits

A person misusing confidential information must account for the profits to the person who confided the information.

## Damages

If confidential matter is published, the person whose confidences have been breached may be able to claim damages.

## Elements of a breach

There are three essential elements of a breach of confidence:
(a) the information must have 'the necessary quality of confidence';
(b) the information must have been imparted in circumstances imposing an obligation to confidence; *and*
(c) there must be an unauthorised use of that information to the detriment of the party communicating it.

## The quality of confidence

**Quality of confidence**   The law of breach of confidence safeguards ideas and information. In general, information is not confidential if it is in the public domain – that is, if it is public knowledge.

In the *Watford Observer* case, mentioned above (Local papers), the injunction was discharged by the Court of Appeal because, among other reasons, the document upon which the story was based could not properly be regarded as confidential. It had started life as a highly confidential document, with a limited distribution. It was distributed personally, and the recipients were told it was confidential. Later, however, the report was circulated on a wider and wider basis throughout the company to management and trade union officials, so that all concerned could discuss it. It had thus lost the quality of confidentiality.

In the *Spycatcher* case, the Government finally lost largely because, in the words of one of the many judges who considered the issue, the cat had been let out of the bag. Mr Justice Scott said that the book and its contents had been disseminated on a world-wide scale. In Britain, anyone who wanted a copy could obtain one.

In the National Lottery case, the two papers involved, together with the *Daily Express*, successfully challenged the injunction the following day on the ground that the identity of the jackpot winner was widely known in his home town, by his workmates and neighbours.

In the Princess in the gym case, had the case gone to court the newspapers would have claimed the exercise machine the princess was using was visible, through a window, to people outside the gymnasium.

But information in the public domain cannot always be used with impunity. In 1981, the Court of Appeal confirmed an injunction restraining Thames Television Ltd from showing a programme, 'The Primodos Affair', about a pregnancy-testing drug because the TV producer got the idea for the programme while doing private consultancy work for the company concerned, Schering Chemicals Ltd, even though Thames said the programme would contain no material not freely available from other sources.

The information, though in the public domain, had been gleaned originally by diligent work, and the conduct leading to the injunction was, in the court's view, reprehensible.

**Public secrets**    The kind of secrets to be protected can include 'public secrets'. In 1975, the Attorney-General tried to prevent the publication of the diaries of the former Cabinet minister Richard Crossman by the publishers Jonathan Cape and by the *Sunday Times*. He said the diaries contained confidential information relating to Cabinet discussions and that publication would be contrary to the public interest.

The court said the law of confidentiality could be applied to prevent the publication of 'public secrets' as well as private or domestic ones. Cabinet ministers owed an obligation of confidence to the Queen. (In this case, the injunction was not in fact granted, on the grounds that the confidential information had become stale with the lapse of time.)

## Obligation of confidence

An obligation of confidence can arise in a variety of ways.

**Contractual relationship**    The most frequent is a contractual obligation. People working for others may have signed a contract to say that they will not reveal their employer's secrets, but even if they have not there is an implied term in every contract of employment that the employee will not act in a way detrimental to his employer's interests.

**Membership of security services**    Members have no contract of employment with the crown, but in the *Spycatcher* cases the courts accepted the view that they had a duty of confidence that resulted from the nature of their employment and the requirements of national security and which lasted for life.

**Discovery**   Under the process of 'discovery' in legal proceedings, parties have to disclose relevant documents to the other side. This information has an absolute protection.

**Domestic relationship**   In 1967 the Duchess of Argyll prevented the *People* newspaper, and her former husband, from publishing marital secrets. By the 1980s the courts were willing to extend the protection to prevent the publication of kiss-and-tell stories originating from less formal relationships. In 1988 a woman was given leave to sue the *Mail on Sunday* for damages for a story about her love affair with another woman.

**Other circumstances**   In the *Spycatcher* case in the House of Lords a judge expressed the obligation of confidence in very wide terms. Lord Goff of Chieveley said a duty of confidence arose when the information came to the knowledge of a person who knew the information was confidential, in circumstances where it would be just that he should be prevented from disclosing it to other people.

Lord Goff said he had expressed the duty in wide terms to include the situation where an obviously confidential document was wafted by an electric fan out of a window into a crowded street, or when an obviously confidential document such as a diary was dropped in a public place and then picked up by a passer-by.

Fortunately the judge's view is not universally accepted. In 1993, 'Infringement of Privacy', a consultation paper issued by the Lord Chancellor's Department, commented: 'It may be that the law of breach of confidence will develop in accordance with the wider view of breach of confidence put forward by Lord Goff ... At present, however, the generally held view is that the obligation of confidence will only be implied where there is a recognised relationship between the parties, such as that of doctor and patient or employer and employee.'

**Third parties – such as a journalist**   The information may have been obtained *indirectly* from the confider. A third party, such as a journalist, who comes into possession of confidential information and realises it is confidential may come under a legal duty to respect the confidence.

For example, in the *Primodos* case, mentioned above, the chemical company supplied the TV producer with the information about the drug for the purpose of public relations work he was doing for the company. Thames TV, the third party, was prevented by injunction from using the information for a television film.

But in what circumstances does this duty arise?

The question is of considerable practical importance for journalists. Suppose an editor is brought a bundle of highly confidential documents that have been found in a public place in circumstances that make it clear they have been left there by accident. Can he safely contact the owners of the documents to check the facts, or will he find his use of the information restrained by an injunction because he is held to have a duty of confidence towards the source of the information? Unfortunately no clear answer is available; Lord Goff's comments above suggest the answer is yes, the comment in the Infringement of Privacy paper suggests no.

If there is no obligation of confidence, no permanent injunction can be granted. In the National Lottery case, Camelot, the lottery's organiser, had a duty of confidence towards the winner imposed by statute, but there was no suggestion that anyone from Camelot had divulged that information to the papers.

In the Princess in the gym case, had the case come to court the princess would have argued that the gymnasium owner owed her an obligation of confidence through contract, but the *Daily Mirror* claimed it had published the photographs only after being told by the gymnasium owner he was free to take and sell them.

**Tainted information**    Suppose you, as a reporter, overhear confidential information when you are eavesdropping. Or suppose you use a hidden microphone, with the same result. Or suppose you persuade someone to give you confidential information by deceit, pretending to that person you have authority to receive it.

Does that information become impressed with an obligation of confidence 'by reason only of the reprehensible means by which it has been acquired'?

In 1981, the Law Commission put that question in a report to Parliament, and it went on to say that the decided cases provided no clear answer.

In the Bill Goodwin case, the court was told a copy of the confidential report 'disappeared' after it was left in an unattended, unlocked room at the company's premises.

In the House of Lords Lord Bridge said Goodwin's source had been involved in a 'gross breach of confidentiality'.

## Detriment

The detriment suffered by the confider does not have to be a financial loss. In the *Spycatcher* case in the Lords, Lord Keith of Kinkel said it would be a sufficient detriment to an individual that information he gave in confidence was to be disclosed to people he would prefer not to know of it.

That applied even if the information to be disclosed was to the person's credit.

But a government was in a different position from an individual. It had to show that publication would be harmful to the public interest.

In the *Spycatcher* case, he said, the book's contents had been disseminated world-wide, and general publication in this country would not bring about any significant damage to the public interest beyond what had already been done.

In 1994 a judge refused to order journalist Neil Hyde to reveal the source of a story derived from a confidential report on the escape from Broadmoor Hospital of two convicted killers. The judge, Sir Peter Pain, said a health authority was 'an emanation of the state' and therefore could not obtain an order requiring a journalist to reveal his source unless it could show that it was in the public interest that such an order should be granted.

## The party communicating

By 'the party communicating it' in (c) is meant the person communicating the information originally, the person to whom the confidence is owed. This person may be several stages removed from the one who eventually passes on the information to, say, a journalist.

## Disclosure in the public interest

A newspaper defending a breach of confidence can argue that disclosure was in the public interest.

It is established law that there is 'no confidence as to the disclosure of iniquity'.

In 1984, Mr Justice Scott in the High Court varied an earlier injunction to enable the *Daily Express* to use material that supported allegations of miscarriages of justice and police corruption. The allegations were related to 'Operation Snowball' and concerned the smuggling of cocaine into Britain.

But the defence is now a good deal wider than that.

In the *Watford Observer* case, referred to above (Local papers), Lord Denning said that when considering applications for an injunction on grounds of confidentiality, courts had to hold the balance between two competing interests. On the one hand there was the public interest in preserving confidence. On the other was the public interest in making known to people matters of public concern.

In this case, he said, the balance came down in favour of publishing the matters in the report. They were of great interest to all the many people in the Watford area who were concerned with printing. They were fit to be discussed, not only with the immediate workers in the Sun Printers' works, but also those outside connected with the printing industry or interested in it.

Mr Justice Scott in one of the *Spycatcher* hearings also adopted the idea of a balance between two interests. Referring to the articles in the *Observer* and the *Guardian* about the forthcoming court hearing in Australia he said the public interest in the freedom of the press to report the court action outweighed the damage, if any, to the national security that the articles might cause.

He added:

> The ability of the press freely to report allegations of scandals in government is one of the bulwarks of our democratic society. It could not happen in totalitarian countries. If the price that has to be paid is the exposure of the government of the day to pressure or embarrassment when mischievous and false allegations are made then, in my opinion, that price must be paid.

However, the Appeal Court and later the House of Lords attached little significance to the defence and the case, as mentioned, was determined on other issues.

In the Bill Goodwin case in 1990 the breach of confidence involved leaking Tetra's business plan. Geoffrey Robertson QC, representing Goodwin, argued that the company's previous published results had shown it as a prosperous expanding concern and the public was entitled to know it was experiencing difficulties.

But Lord Donaldson in the Court of Appeal said the proposed story was in reality a piece of 'wholly unjustified intrusion'.

In 1994 the *Liverpool Echo* successfully challenged an injunction granted to the accountants KPMG Peat Marwick preventing the reporting of the findings of the firm's inquiry into Liverpool City Council's involvement in a controversial cable television contract which had lost millions of pounds.

The judge said the public interest in having published the findings of the report outweighed the private interests of the accountants who had been called in by the council. The public had a right to know.


## People in the public eye

Public interest may give a defence for matters concerning people in the public eye. In 1977 Tom Jones and other well known singers tried unsuccessfully to get an injunction to prevent publication in the *Daily Mirror* of articles in which their former press agent gave details of their private lives.

The court held that the pop singers, who had sought and welcomed publicity of every kind, were not entitled to an injunction pending the trial of a court action. Lord Denning said that if there were another side to their image it was in the public interest that this should be made known.

The same principle was applied by a court in 1993 when the *Daily Mirror* published material from *The Downing Street Years*, memoirs of

Lady Thatcher, the former Prime Minister. *The Sunday Times*, which had bought exclusive rights to the book, was planning to run lengthy extracts but the *Daily Mirror* obtained a leaked copy and published first, leading on the story three days running. The *Sunday Times* tried to obtain an injunction.

The Conservative Party conference was in progress when the *Mirror* published its first splash 'What she said about him' (referring to John Major, her successor). 'Intellectually he drifted with the tide.' On the following day the paper's headline was 'What she says about them' (leading members of the Party). 'Thatcher sticks the knife in Major's men.'

The judge rejected the application for an injunction. He said that because the Conservative Party was making a public show of unity in Blackpool, the publication of the *Mirror*'s claims could be in the public interest. The Court of Appeal agreed.

In the case of the Princess in the gym, it was thought that had the case gone ahead the princess would have been required to go into the witness box where she would have been subjected to rigorous cross-examination on her relations with the media by counsel attempting to show the 'other side to the image'.

**Disclosure to whom?**    Even if the publication does indicate iniquity, it does not necessarily follow that there is a public interest in disclosing that iniquity in the press. The answer to this question depends upon the circumstances.

In the *Operation Snowball* case (see above, Disclosure in the public interest), the judge said it had been suggested that disclosure should be made not to the public at large, but to certain holders of high office, such as the Commissioner of Police. However, the allegation concerned the administration of justice. Such corruption was properly a matter of public interest as opposed to a matter which should be taken up and dealt with by the authorities.

The *Daily Mirror* was not so fortunate when it wanted to publish information, obtained from tapes made illegally, that revealed alleged breaches of Jockey Club regulations and possibly the commission of criminal offences. The newspaper's lawyers argued that the paper would use the tapes to expose iniquity. But the judges rejected the argument, saying the best thing would be for the paper to tell the police or the Jockey Club. Publication would serve the newspaper's interests rather than any public interest.

# Questions

1    What is the main means used to enforce the law of confidentiality, and how are the media affected by it?

2    What are the three essential elements of a breach of confidence?

3    You learn from Councillor Brown that the chairman of the council has told him in confidence that he is about to leave his wife to set up home with an 18-year-old council clerk. Councillor Brown now tells you that if you try to publish the story he will get an injunction preventing you because of breach of confidence. Will he be successful?

4    Can matter be protected from publication by the law of confidentiality if the matter is public knowledge?

5    You learn confidentially from the private secretary of the general manager of your local engineering company that the firm is about to discharge 2,000 employees. You approach the firm for confirmation, but the general manager says he will seek an injunction because of the breach of confidence. Can your paper defeat such a move on the grounds that the matter is one of public interest?

# 24 The journalist's sources

It is a matter of professional principle that a reporter does not reveal his source of confidential information.

The journalist's job is to discover and record news. Wherever he looks he will find people with vested interests trying to prevent him from doing so.

For this reason, to get his story he must often rely on information passed to him by people who would be injured if it became known that they had done so.

The journalist will sometimes be asked, 'Where did you get that story?' Sometimes the person asking will be a judge. Like any other citizen, the journalist is under an obligation to answer questions properly put to him in a court of law. Failure to answer may constitute contempt of court. That can lead to a fine or even prison, but it may be that the journalist will feel impelled to preserve the anonymity of his source even at the risk of his personal liberty.

In 1989, Bill Goodwin, a trainee reporter on the *Engineer*, was ordered by a judge to reveal the source of information he had been given in a telephone call that an engineering company was in financial difficulties and seeking a large loan. He refused to do so and was fined £5,000 for contempt of court. In 1996 the European Court of Human Rights said the order and the fine violated his rights to freedom of expression (see below, Contempt of court; chapter 1, Sources of law, and chapter 23, The Bill Goodwin case).

Sometimes the person asking the journalist for his source will be a tribunal chairman or an official. Increasingly in recent years Parliament has given authorities the power to demand information on specific issues and provide penalties under these Acts.

In 1963 two journalists appearing before a tribunal of inquiry were jailed for refusing to identify sources of information in stories in the *Vassall* case. Vassall had been convicted of spying. A number of newspapers suggested he was a known homosexual, a fact considered to make it inadvisable that he should be employed on secret work because it rendered him susceptible to blackmail. The tribunal had been set up under an Act which gave tribunals wide powers to send for and examine witnesses.

In 1988, Jeremy Warner, of the *Independent* newspaper, was fined £20,000 and ordered to pay costs estimated at £100,000 after refusing to disclose to government inspectors his sources for articles on takeover bids which involved insider dealing, a criminal offence (see Statutes giving disclosure powers, below).

Sometimes the person asking the journalist for his source will be a police officer. Like other citizens, the journalist has no legal duty to provide information to the police for their inquiries, except in the special circumstances mentioned below. This would seem an elementary item of civic knowledge, but in 1990 a journalist who declined to tell a police inspector his source for a story about the leak of a council document was threatened with prosecution for obstructing the police in their duties.

If the police need to obtain 'journalistic material' to assist their investigations they normally have to apply to a judge first. They also generally need the consent of a judge before searching a journalist's premises for such material. These provisions are contained in the Police and Criminal Evidence Act 1984 (see section on the Act, below).

The Act does not apply in Northern Ireland, where the police have wide powers under regulations concerned with the prevention of terrorism. In 1992 Channel 4 and the independent production company Box Productions were fined £75,000 for contempt of court after refusing to comply with an order requiring them to disclose the identity of a source used in a television programme 'The Committee', part of the Dispatches series (see Prevention of terrorism, below).

The opportunities for police officers lawfully to gain access to confidential information held by citizens, including journalists, were increased by the Police Act 1997.

Traditionally, the prior consent of a judge has been necessary before any intrusion by authority into private property: 'an Englishman's home is his castle'. Under the Act, however, a chief police officer can authorise entry upon property, and the placing of surveillance devices ('bugging and burgling'). In 'sensitive' cases authorisation is subject to prior approval by a government-appointed commissioner, unless the matter is urgent (see the Police Act, below).

Under the Security Service Act 1996 the security service, which now has police functions, also is enabled to enter on and interfere with property if it is investigating serious crime in the United Kingdom, but curiously in this case a warrant from the Home Secretary is required.

Police wishing to tap a journalist's phone (or anybody else's), an activity that does not require entry into the property, also need to obtain a warrant signed by the Home Secretary.

As stated above, the Police and Criminal Evidence Act 1984 requires the police to make a formal application before a judge to obtain journalistic material they want to help with their investigations. In several of the cases brought under the Act the application has concerned photographs or film taken in public places where disturbances were taking place.

Most editors take the view that they should hand over such material only after careful consideration and generally only after a court order. Their argument is that if it becomes routine for the police to obtain unpublished photographs or untransmitted film journalists will be seen as an arm of the police.

They will thus lose credibility as impartial observers and, in practical terms, will be subjected to violence. Journalistic no-go areas will be created during disturbances. In this way, they will be prevented from fulfilling their role as the 'eyes and ears of the general public' (see Lord Donaldson's comments, chapter 1).

A judge may reject the application if, among other things, he does not consider it in the public interest to grant it. In court, media lawyers have argued that it is not in the public interest that the media should be prevented from doing its job. But in nearly every case that has come to court judges have considered that argument outweighed by the police's need for evidence to convict.

For example, a judge rejected the media's argument in November 1994 when the police were successful in obtaining film and photographs by the major press and broadcasting organisations after a demonstration against the Bill that became the Criminal Justice and Public Order Act 1994 even though counsel pointed out that at the demonstration 'class war' leaflets were distributed that showed the media were being branded 'agents of the police'.

The provision was intended to provide a new protection for journalistic material, but in practice has led to accelerating demands for the handing over of such material.

## Contempt of court

Courts claim to recognise that there is a public interest in journalists being able to protect their sources, but have ordered disclosure when they considered it necessary.

In 1980, a court ordered Granada Television to reveal the identity of a 'mole' who had passed on confidential documents belonging to the British

Steel Corporation. The documents, which were used for a current affairs programme, revealed mismanagement at the corporation, which was then making huge losses. Fortunately for Granada, the mole himself came forward and revealed his identity.

The following year, the Contempt of Court Act gave statutory form to the courts' recognition of the public interest in allowing journalists to protect their sources.

Section 10 says:

> No court may require a person to disclose, nor is any person guilty of contempt of court for refusing to disclose, the source of information contained in a publication for which he is responsible, unless it is established to the satisfaction of the court that disclosure is necessary in the interests of justice or national security, or for the prevention of disorder or crime.

Three cases have illustrated that the protection given to the journalist by the section, as interpreted by the courts, is not as great as many had hoped (and probably not as great as Parliament had intended).

The first case showed the scope of the phrase 'national security'. In 1983 the *Guardian* newspaper was ordered to return to the Government a leaked photostatic copy of a Ministry of Defence document revealing the strategy for handling the arrival in Britain of Cruise missiles.

The *Guardian* did not know the identity of its informant, but realised the identity might be revealed by examination of the document, and claimed that as a result of section 10 it did not have to hand it over.

But the House of Lords said the interests of national security required that the identity of the informant must be revealed; publication of the particular document posed no threat to national security, but there was a risk that the person who leaked that document might leak another, with much more serious consequences for national security.

The *Guardian* handed over the document and the informant, a Foreign Office clerk, Sarah Tisdall, was convicted under the Official Secrets Act and jailed for six months.

Journalists should note that had the *Guardian* destroyed the document after it was used to prepare the article but before its handing over was ordered, the paper would have escaped the painful necessity of having to reveal the identity of its source.

The case involving Jeremy Warner showed what the courts understood by the word 'necessary' and the phrase 'prevention of crime'.

Inspectors investigating insider dealing asked for a court order compelling Warner to reveal his sources. Action was taken under the Financial Services Act (see Statutes giving disclosure powers, below). The Act provides that if a person has no reasonable excuse he shall be punished as if he had committed contempt of court, and the court therefore considered whether he would have had a defence under section 10 of the Contempt of Court Act.

The House of Lords rejected the idea that disclosure was 'necessary' only if it was the only means of preventing further insider dealing, and that it was the 'key to the puzzle'. Lord Griffiths said 'necessary' had a meaning which lay somewhere between 'indispensable' on the one hand and 'useful' or 'expedient' on the other.

And Lord Griffiths rejected Warner's argument that 'prevention of crime' was limited to the situation in which identification of the source would allow steps to be taken to prevent the commission of 'a particular identifiable future crime'.

He said it was not the job of inspectors to take immediate action to frustrate a particular crime. Their task was to probe into and lay bare the whole dishonest web of suspected insider dealing so that measures could be taken to deter and contain it. Warner's evidence was 'really needed' by the inspectors for the purpose of their inquiry, the aim of which was the prevention of crime.

In the case involving William Goodwin and the *Engineer*, the House of Lords in 1990 considered the phrase 'interests of justice'. Earlier, in the 1984 case against the *Guardian*, the distinguished judge Lord Diplock said this phrase meant 'the administration of justice in the course of legal proceedings in a court of law'.

But there was no suggestion of immediate legal proceedings in the *Engineer* case, and Lord Bridge said the phrase could simply refer to the wish of a private company to discipline a disloyal employee 'notwithstanding that no legal proceedings might be necessary to achieve this end'.

Some commentators suggested this wide interpretation of the words of the section made its protection for journalists' sources illusory but it may be that the House of Lords' decision in Goodwin's case marked a low-point in the protection offered by the section.

Goodwin appealed to the European Court of Human Rights, where the matter was first considered by the European Commission, which in 1994 found that the order forcing him to name his source violated his human rights.

The Commission said:

> Protection of the sources from which journalists derive information is an essential means of enabling the press to perform its important function of 'public watchdog' in a democratic society. If journalists could be compelled to reveal their sources, this would make it much more difficult for them to obtain information and, as a consequence, to inform the public about matters of public interest.

Any compulsion must be limited to exceptional circumstances where vital public or individual interests were at stake.

The Commission added that the continuing injunction prevented newspapers and journalists from publishing information which was of a type commonly found in the business press. While it may have derived from a breach of confidence, so did much of the information provided by the press.

In 1996 the European Court itself reached the same conclusion. It said an order of source disclosure could not be compatible with Article 10 of the Convention (see chapter 1, Sources of law) unless it was justified by an overriding requirement in the public interest.

The views of the European authorities were beginning to influence the decisions of English judges. In 1994, a court declined to require Neil Hyde, head of the news agency INS News Group, to reveal the source of a leaked confidential report because this was not 'necessary'.

The top-security Broadmoor Hospital wanted Hyde to reveal the source of a report on the escape of two convicted killers while on trips out of the hospital.

But the judge said the hospital authorities had failed to make any attempt themselves to find out who leaked the documents and had instead relied on the court application.

In 1996 two chief constables failed to have a journalist, Daniella Garavelli, jailed over her refusal to reveal the sources of a story to a police disciplinary tribunal. The reporter refused to say who supplied her with information for a front-page exclusive in the *Newcastle Journal* over allegations that Northumbria police crime figures had been massaged.

A High Court judge said Garavelli 'put before the public, fully and fairly, a question which had been raised of considerable public importance'. The police had failed to show that the 'interests of justice' outweighed her right not to disclose her source.


## Statutes giving disclosure powers

As stated above, increasingly statutes give authorities the power to demand information on *specific* issues and provide penalties under these Acts. The Vassall tribunal, which led to the jailing of two journalists, had been set up under the Tribunals of Inquiry (Evidence) Act 1921, which gives tribunals wide powers to send for and examine witnesses.

Another example is the Criminal Justice Act 1987, which empowers the director of the Serious Fraud Office to summon before him any person he believes has information relevant to an investigation and the person must answer questions or give information about any relevant matter. If he fails to do so he faces a maximum prison sentence of six months or a fine.

The director is also empowered to demand from any person documents relating to his investigation. The obligation to hand over information contains no public interest defence similar to that contained in the Police and Criminal Evidence Act (below).

In 1996 Westcountry Television journalists were forced to hand over video footage and documents to the SFO, which was investigating the collapse of a local computer firm.

The Financial Services Act 1986, which was used to prosecute Jeremy Warner (see above), was enacted after newspaper disclosures of criminal misconduct in the City. It made it an offence for a person without reasonable excuse to refuse to comply with a request to attend before inspectors of the Department of Trade and Industry, or to assist them or to answer any question put by them about any matter relevant to their inquiries.

The Prevention of Terrorism (Temporary Provisions) Act 1989, section 18, gives the police power to demand information from a person who has information that he knows or believes might be of material assistance in preventing the commission of an act of terrorism or in securing the arrest of a person for such an offence. The person who fails to give such information is liable on conviction on indictment to imprisonment for up to five years, or a fine, or both.

The Criminal Justice Act 1993 inserted a new section 18A into the 1989 Act, creating the offence of failing to disclose knowledge or suspicion of financial assistance for terrorism. The section is applicable to persons acting in the course of their trade, profession, business or employment unless they have reasonable excuse for failing to disclose their information (see also Prevention of terrorism, below).

The 1993 Act also created offences of failing to disclose suspicion or knowledge concerning money laundering and insider dealing. There is a defence of 'reasonable excuse'. The Home Office Minister assured the Guild of Editors the legislation on insider dealing would not criminalise the conduct of a financial journalist preparing editorial analysis and news items.

## Police and Criminal Evidence Act 1984

Special protection is given to 'journalistic material' in the sections of the Police and Criminal Evidence Act 1984 which lay down the procedure whereby the police may search premises for evidence of serious arrestable offences.

Journalistic material is defined as 'material acquired or created for the purposes of journalism'.

## Special procedure material

The police have to apply to a circuit judge if they want to obtain journalistic material under the 'special procedure'.

The application will normally be *inter partes,* which means that the holder of the evidence is present to argue against disclosure if he wishes.

Before the judge makes an order he has to be satisfied that there are reasonable grounds for believing that a serious arrestable offence has been committed; that the evidence would be admissible at a trial for that offence and of substantial value to that investigation; that other methods of obtaining it have been tried without success, or not tried because it appears they are bound to fail; and that its disclosure would be in the public interest.

The Act therefore appeared to give useful protection to journalists. However, judges have interpreted the Act in such a way that (as with section 10 of the Contempt of Court Act) the protection is not as valuable as had been hoped.

In 1986, after a police operation in Bristol led to disturbances, the *Bristol Evening Post*, the *Western Daily Press*, and a freelance picture agency were asked by the police to hand over unpublished pictures and refused to do so.

The police applied to the court and the judge ordered that the pictures be produced.

The judge did not require the police to specify the offence which had been committed, nor the value and relevance of the material, nor the *particular material* which was sought; they asked for all the pictures taken between two specific times, and 264 pictures and negatives had to be handed over.

The 1990 applications for the handing over of pictures relating to the anti-poll tax riot, referred to above, illustrated again the way in which the courts would apply the test that material must be admissible at trial and of substantial value to the investigation.

At the second hearing the news organisations' counsel said the applications were premature because the police had not yet examined all the material handed over by the other 25 organisations. But the judge said that until the police had seen the material they could not say if it was relevant or not.

## Excluded material

Excluded material is exempt altogether from compulsory disclosure. It includes journalistic material which a person holds in confidence and which consists of documents or records.

The protection is not limited to professional journalists, but extends to any material acquired or created for the purposes of journalism.

Evidence which was already liable to search and seizure under the previous law is not protected. For example, if a journalist acquired a stolen document, even on a confidential basis, it would not be excluded material because such documents are already liable to seizure under a warrant issued under the Theft Act 1968.

If the journalist is ordered to produce either special procedure material or excluded material on the ground that a warrant for its seizure would have been available under another statute, and if he fails to do so, the police can apply for a search warrant (see below).

## Search warrants

*Police and Criminal Evidence Act*   Instead of asking for an order that a newspaper shall produce material, the police can apply to a circuit judge for a search warrant under the Police and Criminal Evidence Act to obtain either non-confidential or confidential material. The newspaper does not have to be told of the application, and does not have the right to be heard by the judge.

Before the judge grants a warrant, he must be satisfied that the criteria for ordering the production of the material (see above) are satisfied, and that one of the following four circumstances applies:
(a)  It is not practicable to communicate with anyone entitled to grant entry to the premises.
(b)  It is not practicable to communicate with anyone entitled to grant access to the material.
(c)  The material contains information which is subject to an obligation of secrecy or a restriction on disclosure imposed by statute (for example, material subject to the Official Secrets Act) and is likely to be disclosed in breach of that obligation if a warrant is not issued, *or*
(d)  That to serve notice of an order to produce may seriously prejudice the investigation.

In the *Zircon* case (see Security service cases, previous chapter), police used a warrant under these provisions to raid the offices of the *New Statesman* and the journalist Duncan Campbell (see chapter 30). Although material was 'excluded', it was not protected because a warrant could previously have been issued under the Official Secrets Act (see below).

Once inside a newspaper office, lawfully executing their search warrant, the police have powers under the Police and Criminal Evidence Act to remove additional journalistic material without getting a new production order or warrant.

*Official Secrets Act*   Section 9 of the Official Secrets Act 1911 gives the police wide powers to carry out searches. A magistrate may grant a warrant authorising the police to enter at any time any premises named in the warrant, if necessary by force, and to search the premises and every person found there; and to seize any material which is evidence of an offence under the Act. If a police superintendent considers the case one of great emergency, he can give a written order which has the same effect as a warrant.

This was the section used to carry out the raids on the offices of BBC Scotland in the *Zircon* case. (The search provisions of the 1984 Act do not apply to Scotland.)

See also the information on search powers given in chapters 25 and 32.

## Police Act 1997

The Police Act 1997 gives the police the power to authorise themselves to break into premises and place bugs provided they believe this action will help them to investigate serious crime. Under section 89 of the Bill, entry to or interference with property or with 'wireless telegraphy' is lawful when a chief constable or, in urgent cases, an assistant chief constable, 'thinks it necessary ... on the ground that it is likely to be of substantial value in the prevention or detection of serious crime'.

The authorising officer must be satisfied that what the action seeks to achieve cannot reasonably be achieved by other means.

Police and customs officers had been carrying out similar operations for years against major criminals without any statutory permission, on the authority of chief constables, under guidelines laid down by the Home Secretary in 1984. But they had no legal right to do so and technically could have been sued for trespass if 'caught in the act'.

Under the Act, the Government appoints a small number of commissioners, existing or former High Court judges, and the police have to get the prior approval of a commissioner for the bugging of homes, offices, and hotel bedrooms, and in respect of doctors, lawyers, and 'confidential journalistic material'. Prior approval is not necessary in urgent cases, but the chief officer has to apply for approval as soon as reasonably practicable and specify why he could not do so before.

A commissioner approves the operation if he is satisfied that there are reasonable grounds for believing that the action is likely to be of substantial value in the prevention or detection of serious crime and that what the action seeks to achieve cannot reasonably be achieved by other means.

A commissioner can order that an operation be abandoned if he regards it as 'blatantly unreasonable'. Authorisation lasts for three months.

Serious crime is defined very broadly. It covers offences which involve 'the use of violence, results in substantial financial gain, or is conduct by a large number of persons in pursuit of a common purpose'. Those opposing the measure as it went through Parliament said the 'common purpose' clause could embrace groups such as environmentalists protesting at road developments, and the Act contains no exemption to protect journalists pursuing their inquiries.

## Official secrets

The Official Secrets Act 1920, as amended by the Official Secrets Act 1939, operates where a chief officer of police is satisfied that there is reasonable ground for suspecting that an offence under section 1 of the Act, which is concerned with espionage, has been committed and for believing that any person is able to furnish information about the offence.

The officer may apply to the Home Secretary for permission to authorise a senior police officer to require the person to divulge that information. Anyone who fails to comply with any such requirement or knowingly gives false information is guilty of an offence.

Where a chief officer of police has reasonable grounds to believe that the case is one of great emergency and that in the interests of the state immediate action is necessary, he may demand the information without the consent of the Home Secretary.

## Prevention of terrorism

The Police and Criminal Evidence Act does not apply in Northern Ireland, and Channel 4 and Box Productions were prosecuted for their programme 'The Committee' under the Prevention of Terrorism (Temporary Provisions) Act 1989, an Act described by Lord Justice Woolf in the divisional court as 'draconian'.

Schedule 7 (paragraph 3) of the Act enables a constable for the purpose of a terrorist investigation to apply to a circuit judge for an order to produce material that includes excluded material or special material (see above for definition).

The judge has to be satisfied that the following conditions are met:
(a) that a terrorist investigation is being carried out and that there are reasonable grounds for believing that the material is likely to be of substantial value ... to the investigation
(b) that there are reasonable grounds for believing that it is in the public interest, having regard
   (i) to the benefit likely to accrue to the investigation if the material is obtained; and
   (ii) to the circumstances under which the person in possession of the material holds it,

that the material should be produced.

In the case of 'The Committee' what the authorities wanted was information rather than material. Why then was the prosecution brought under Schedule 7 rather than section 18 (see Statutes giving disclosure powers, above)?

Notice that the schedule specifically allows for an order relating to excluded material and special material. The source's identity was information held by the researcher in confidence, and would otherwise arguably have been protected as excluded material.

Notice also that the more severe penalties under section 18 follow a trial on indictment – that is, before a jury. Defying an order made under Schedule 7 leads to contempt of court, triable by a judge. As noted in chapter 1, juries are unpredictable in this kind of case. They will sometimes acquit where they believe the defendant has acted in the public interest, even if that decision is not in strict accordance with the law.

Also, there is no right of appeal against an order under Schedule 7.

## Subpoenas

Occasionally reporters may be asked to supply evidence of what they themselves have seen, rather than to say where their information came from.

For example, in 1992 a *Wales on Sunday* photographer was asked to give evidence against eight defendants allegedly involved in riots. Cuttings from the paper had been produced in court, and the photographer's byline appeared on the pictures.

In this situation, most journalists will wish to retain their reputation for neutrality and will agree to give evidence only after receiving a subpoena or witness summons.

Then if the journalist does not attend the hearing and give evidence, he will be in contempt of court.

Sometimes journalists accompany police officers on raids. Where such a raid leads to an arrest, the defendant's lawyers can demand that the prosecution produces all the material gathered in the investigation. For this reason the journalists are required to sign an indemnification agreement in which they acknowledge that any recording or film may be liable to be used as evidence.

## Questions

1   Under the Contempt of Court Act, a person is not forced to disclose the source of information contained in a publication for which he is responsible. There are four exceptions to this rule. What are they?

2   Suppose a judge is asked to make an order under the 'special procedure' of the Police and Criminal Evidence Act 1984 requiring a newspaper to hand over journalistic material. He has to satisfy himself on four points. What are they? What limits to this protection to the press have emerged since the passage of the Act?

3   Police officers want to search a journalist's home for stolen documents. Is there any special protection for this material under the Police and Criminal Evidence Act?

4   A police officer demands, under the Official Secrets Act, the name of a journalist's source for a story about corruption in the handling of council contracts. Is he acting within his powers?

# 25  Race relations

The law that may affect a journalist when he is reporting matters involving race is contained in the Public Order Act 1986.

It is an offence for any person to display, publish, or distribute written material that is threatening, abusive, or insulting if he intends thereby to stir up racial hatred or if, having regard to all the circumstances, racial hatred is likely to be stirred up thereby.

Notice that the offence can be committed without any *intent* to stir up racial hatred. As a result, a newspaper and its staff reporting an inflammatory speech or election manifesto (such as that of an extremist politician), or other expression of anti-immigrant propaganda is as liable to prosecution as the person who originally made the statement.

An editor must decide in the light of all the circumstances if hatred and not just ill-will is likely to be stirred up, and whether the words of an election candidate or other speaker should be paraphrased instead of being reported directly.

How does a paraphrase help? The words have to be 'threatening, abusive, or insulting'. The tone of the language must be objectionable for an offence to be committed. The expression of views in a moderate or reasoned, non-threatening manner is not caught by the Act.

'Racial hatred' is defined as being 'hatred against a group of persons in Great Britain defined by reference to colour, race, nationality (including citizenship), or ethnic or national origins'. Religion as such is not covered, but frequently a reference to a particular religion will also embrace a particular racial or ethnic group, such as Jews or Sikhs.

The phrase 'having regard to all the circumstances' was inserted into the Act at the insistence of the Guild of Editors, because its inclusion in earlier legislation had been seen as a protection for bona fide news reports of, for example, a racist rally, because it required the court to consider the publication in its context.

The Attorney-General has to give his consent to any prosecution, and in 1987 the Attorney-General said that in making a decision to allow the prosecution of a newspaper he would probably take into account the nature of the publication, its circulation, and the market at which it was aimed, as well as any special sensitivity prevailing at the time of publication which might influence the effect on those who read the material.

Handling readers' letters calls for particular care. During the passage of the Bill leading to the 1986 Act, the Home Office wrote to the Guild saying it was wrong to suppose newspapers could publish inflammatory letters provided they juxtaposed them with other letters or editorial comment putting a contrary view. A single letter written in inflammatory language which was likely to stir up racial hatred would contravene the Act and could not be saved by countervailing comments elsewhere. But in deciding *whether* racial hatred was likely to be stirred up, the courts would not look at the letter in isolation, but would consider all the surrounding circumstances, which would include the context of the publication in which it was printed.

It is also an offence under the Act for a person to have in his possession written material which is threatening, abusive, or insulting, with a view to its being displayed, published, distributed, broadcast, or included in a cable programme service, if he intends racial hatred to be stirred up thereby or if, having regard to all the circumstances, racial hatred is likely to be stirred up thereby.

Editors who receive unsolicited racialist material do not commit an offence, even if such material is kept for background information, provided they do not intend to publish the material itself.

The police can get a warrant from a justice of the peace to enter and search premises where they suspect a person has possession of racialist material. The protections contained in the Police and Criminal Evidence Act do not apply.

Penalties for any of the offences mentioned are up to six months' imprisonment or a fine, or both, on summary conviction and up to two years' imprisonment or a fine, or both, on conviction on indictment.

The Act does not apply to fair and accurate reports of proceedings in Parliament or to fair, accurate, and contemporaneous reports of public proceedings in courts or tribunals.

## Question

1    In what circumstances could a newspaper be prosecuted for publishing a story on racial matters? What is the test applied by the Public Order Act 1986?

# 26   Election law

Special rules on the reporting of elections that apply to broadcasters and not to print journalists are covered in chapter 33. But print journalists should be aware of some dangers they share with the broadcasters while elections are pending, whether municipal, parliamentary, or European.

Anyone who, before or during an election campaign, makes or publishes a false statement of fact in relation to the personal character or conduct of a candidate for the purpose of affecting his return is guilty of an illegal practice and is liable on summary conviction to a fine and disqualification as an elector for five years. Where a company (eg the owners of a newspaper) is guilty of the offence, the directors are liable to the fine and disqualification.

Note that the falsity must be contained in a statement of fact, not an expression of opinion.

Note also that the false statement must relate to the personal as opposed to the political character or conduct of the candidate. A statement that a candidate supports a political splinter group, for example, would not come within the section.

It is a defence to this charge if the person accused can show that he had reasonable grounds for believing that the statements made by him were true. This law is contained in the Representation of the People Act 1983.

The publisher of such a false statement might also be liable in defamation.

It is also an offence under the 1983 Act to publish, in order to promote or procure the election of a candidate, a false statement that another candidate has withdrawn from an election.

Only the candidate himself or his agent may incur any expenses for, among other things, publishing an advertisement. It is an offence for anyone else unless he is authorised in writing by the election agent to do so. This precludes well-wishers from seeking to insert advertisements in a newspaper on behalf of a candidate without his express authority. But the Act states that this rule does not restrict publication of editorial matter relating to the election.

The law of libel is, however, a serious restriction at election times.

Journalists should remember that there is no particular privilege for the publication of election material, although a good deal of cover is given by the privilege for fair and accurate reports of public meetings. There is no privilege for statements made by candidates or agents at press conferences or during interviews.

Remember also that there is no privilege for remarks, even when made at a public meeting, which are not 'of public concern and the publication of which is not for the public benefit' (see chapter 20, Qualified privilege). Nor is the defence of fair comment available for personal attacks which impute base motives (see chapter 20, Fair comment).

Be careful of associating members of such parties as the Labour and Conservative parties with extremist parties of the left or right wing. In particular, be careful of the terms 'fascist', 'communist', and 'racist'.

When reporting speeches by extremist candidates, remember that such reports are subject to the provisions of the Public Order Act 1986 relating to inciting racial hatred (see chapter 25).

Do photographers have a right to be present at election counts? Admission is at the discretion of the returning officer and there is no national policy.

According to advice to the Newspaper Society and the Guild of Editors, the position is different if television cameras are present. In that case the Newspaper Society has established precedents whereby the press has an equal right to have cameramen present and pass film out of the count.

## Question

1    What legal restriction, or restrictions, prevent the publication of false statements about candidates at elections?

# 27  Gambling

The law has traditionally strictly controlled gambling in this country, and still forbids certain advertising relating to gambling. The object of such restrictions was that people should not be encouraged to squander money they could ill afford to lose. A Home Office consultation paper on casinos and bingo clubs issued in February 1996 said: 'Restrictions are desirable to discourage socially damaging excesses and to protect the vulnerable.'

Curiously, these protective and paternalistic laws remain in place though the Government now actually encourages people to spend money on the National Lottery and premium bonds. (The latter, instead of paying interest, provide the opportunity for bondholders to win a prize decided by lottery.) The promoters of the National Lottery have been allowed to engage in a huge publicity drive.

As this edition of *McNae* went to press, welcome attempts were being made to impose some sort of logic on the hotchpotch of legislation covering the advertising of gambling and various proposals for change are mentioned below.

The young reporter should at least be aware of the restrictions because it is possible that an editorial report might be regarded as an advertisement, under the legislation, even if it was not paid for.

In 1972, the *Evening Standard*, London, published a diary piece under the headline 'High stakes'. It said:

For the big money gamblers, there is now a chance to win nearly £20,000 on a single turn of the wheel at the roulette table. This is at the Palm Beach Casino Club in the Mayfair Hotel. The club believes that the maximum stakes now accepted at the club are the highest for any roulette game in Britain.

The paper was prosecuted but was cleared both by the magistrates and on appeal because:

(a) the intention and main effect of the paragraphs was to interest and/or amuse the readers with items of gossip and news (such as they were accustomed to in the diary) and not to promote the services of the casino; *and*

(b) the information about the gaming facilities was only incidental to the purpose and main effect of the paragraphs, and therefore they were not advertisements within the meaning of the legislation.

Prosecutions of journalists have been rare, but Gaming Board inspectors have continued to take an interest in the editorial columns of newspapers. In 1987 an inspector wrote to the editor of the *Western Daily Press* complaining about a picture of the proprietor of a bingo club and the accompanying article. The headline was 'Clickety-cluck! Peter hatches egg bingo idea' and the story was that the man had numbered 90 eggs and would be basing a bingo game on the order in which the chicks emerged.

The inspector told the editor the incident highlighted 'the jeopardy which any person might find himself in when what is intended to be purely a news item takes on the forbidden aspect of advertising gaming.'

The law is complex. If you want to run a story about a bingo club or a casino, say, and are worried that your report may be unlawful you can telephone the Gaming Board (0171 306 6200) or one of its regional officers to check the law.

## Lotteries

A lottery is a distribution of prizes by lot or chance, where participants pay for their chances. The law relating to lotteries is contained in the Lotteries and Amusements Act 1976 and the National Lottery Act 1993, but these Acts give no specific answers to some of the questions confronting journalists.

All lotteries are unlawful except:

(a) *the National Lottery*

(b) *local lotteries*, promoted by a local authority and registered with the Gaming Board.

(c) *societies' lotteries*, conducted generally for charitable, sporting, or cultural purposes, other than for private gain. If the total value of tickets to be sold is £20,000, or if more than £250,000 is raised during the course of a year, the lottery must be registered with the Gaming Board. If the figures are less, it is sufficient to register the lottery with the local authority.

(d) *private lotteries*, such as a sweepstake conducted within a club or in a block of flats.

(e) *small lotteries*, which are incidental to certain entertainment – eg a raffle for a cake at a bazaar.

Save in the case of the excepted lotteries (a), (c), and (e) mentioned above, it is an offence to publish any advertisement of a lottery, or any list of prizewinners or winning tickets in a lottery or any matter calculated to act as an inducement to people to take part in a lottery.

It is lawful to advertise a *local lottery* and a *society's lottery*. Advertisements must specify the name of the authority or society, the name and address of the promoter, and the date of the lottery.

A *private lottery* can be advertised on the premises of the society for whose members it is being promoted, but must not be advertised in a newspaper.

It is considered safe to give a 'passing reference', in advance, to a *small lottery*, provided the advertisement or news item relates principally to the entertainment of which it is a part. After the event, the reporter can mention that the lottery was held, and give the amount raised and the winner – provided the results have already been declared on the premises or during the progress of the entertainment.

Newspapers often refer to such lotteries as 'competitions', presumably to avoid drawing attention to a possible breach of the legislation.

The advertising code of practice issued by the Camelot group, which runs the National Lottery, makes specific provision in respect of young people and to guard against 'excessive gambling'. In particular:

(a)  no advertising should be designed to or be likely to lead to under 16-year-olds persuading or pressuring their parents to participate in the National Lottery;

(b)  no advertising (whether in terms of style, tone, content, medium, location, or any other factors) should be directed at or likely to appeal primarily to under 16-year-olds;

(c)  all advertising must clearly set out the under age-16 restriction;

(d)  advertising should not encourage excessive or reckless playing or feature large individual ticket purchases;

(e)  advertising should not exaggerate or otherwise misrepresent the chance of winning in any National Lottery game.

It is a condition of Camelot's licence from the regulatory body OFLOT that lottery winners remain anonymous if they wish, but there is no similar restriction on the press (see chapter 31, Privacy).

Premium Savings Bonds, a government-sponsored lottery, do not come within the scope of the legislation.

## Gaming

Gaming means the playing of games of chance for money, and includes bingo. The law is contained in the Gaming Act 1968, the Lotteries and Amusements Act 1976, and the Bingo Act 1992.

When a licence is granted for gaming, an advertisement announcing this, in a form approved by the licensing authority, may be published within 14 days or within such a time limit as may be set by the licensing authority. No further advertisement, such as one naming premises in which gaming takes place, is permitted.

But gaming taking place under the following circumstances can be advertised:

(a) gaming with machines, for amusement, with prizes, at bazaars, sales of work, fetes, dinners, dances, sporting or athletic events, other than for private gain;

(b) gaming, other than with machines, on premises not licensed under the 1968 Act, being entertainment other than for private gain. (This may include working men's club premises, provided the club is not licensed or registered for gaming under the Act.);

(c) gaming, with machines, wholly or mainly for amusement, and for which a permit is in force. (This relates to 'prize bingo' at amusement arcades, where, again, the prizes and stakes are limited.);

(d) gaming at any travelling showman's fair.

Advertisements for bingo conducted as a commercial undertaking are therefore generally illegal, but this prohibition does not extend to 'prize bingo' played at amusement arcades and to bingo sessions at sports clubs and working men's clubs, in the circumstances set out above.

Under the 1992 Act, national newspapers can now carry general advertisements about bingo prizes.

Regional and local newspapers can now carry advertisements for specific bingo clubs, identifying the premises and inviting the public to play, provided the advertisement does not contain any 'inducement' to join – defined as a promise or offer of a gift or information about the value of prizes that can be won.

Suppose a newspaper carries a story saying that a bingo enthusiast, after playing two or three times a week for 30 years at the local bingo club, which is named, has scooped the £25,000 jackpot. The story gives details of her plans for the money.

It seems unlikely the story would be considered an advertisement containing an inducement to join.

In 1996 the Government announced proposals that bingo operators should be allowed to advertise their facilities and prizes on television, radio, and cinema. It laid before Parliament the draft Deregulation (Betting and Gaming Advertising) Order 1997, which was expected to come into effect later that year.

In November 1996 the Home Office published a second consultation paper on casinos, which proposed that operators should be able to advertise the name, address, and telephone number of the casino, and give limited factual information about the facilities available. Subject to the consultation, a draft deregulation paper on casinos was expected in 1997.

## Betting

Advertisements identifying particular premises as a licensed cash betting office, or publicising its facilities, are prohibited. In 1996 the Government proposed that betting shops should be allowed to advertise their facilities in print – but not broadcast – media. Advertising of fruit machines would be allowed inside premises. The changes are covered in the draft deregulation order laid before Parliament in 1996, referred to above.

## Questions

1   Name the five types of lawful lotteries.
2   Can the premises of a licensed cash betting shop be lawfully identified in a newspaper?

*NB*. The Deregulation (Betting and Gaming Advertising) Order 1997, referred to above in two sections, Gaming and Betting, was made on 22 March and came in to force on 19 April.

# 28 Information from government

As pointed out in chapter 1, for democracy to work, citizens must have access to information so that they can reach valid decisions.

But there is no general right of access to information about the work of government in the United Kingdom.

There is indeed a strong tradition of secrecy in government arising historically from the wish of authoritarian regimes to govern with as little interference as possible. King James I said: 'None shall presume ... to meddle with anything concerning our government or deep matters of state.'

It remains true today that the job of governing is easier without 'meddling' by well informed citizens. It can be argued it is also more efficient. The advice on open government proffered in the television comedy series Yes Minister by the senior civil servant Sir Humphrey to his assistant has a ring of truth: 'My dear boy, it's a contradiction in terms. You can be open, or you can have government.'

A White Paper on Open Government published in 1993 said: 'Open government is part of an effective democracy. Citizens must have adequate access to the information and analysis on which government business is based.'

The White Paper was followed in 1994 by a Code of Practice on Access to Government Information, but it in fact gave no rights of access. It was later recognised as an advance on the previous position because it gave an opportunity to challenge government secrecy by complaint to an ombudsman but this procedure was not being used much by journalists (see below).

Information from government can conveniently be considered under three headings, central government, local government, and quangos.

The situation in the United Kingdom today is summed up by Patrick Birkinshaw in his book *Freedom of Information*:

'Local government is local, elected and increasingly under statutory obligations to be open to the public and the press. Where central government gives information, it is invariably as an act of grace and favour or instrumental necessity. In the world of quasi-government, there is no elected representation, no public voting and no political accountability, and very rarely are there duties to inform the public in even the most exiguous of terms of what is being carried out on the public's behalf.'

## Central government

With certain rare exceptions, press and public have no rights to know about the workings of central government. Without that information it is difficult to judge the real effects of government policies on, for example, unemployment, the council tax, the crime rate, the health service, and education.

If policies are not working a government is in a good position to conceal the facts if it wishes to.

In addition, citizens have no rights to know about most of the activities for which central government is responsible. For example, they have no rights to know about the hygiene of their food or any side-effects of the medicines they may be prescribed.

In substantial areas of life the handful of people who know the facts face criminal prosecution if they tell the journalist about them and the journalist faces criminal prosecution if he publishes them (see Official secrets, chapter 30).

In 1984 Sarah Tisdall, a foreign office clerk, was jailed for six months for giving the *Guardian* details of government plans to deploy Cruise missiles. The *Guardian* published information from a memo dealing with the public relations aspect of the deployment.

Clive Ponting, a senior Ministry of Defence official, was prosecuted for revealing to a Member of Parliament in 1985 that ministers had misled Parliament over the sinking of the Argentinian cruiser the *Belgrano* during the Falklands war and was acquitted only because of the obstinacy of the jury trying him, who disregarded the ruling of the judge.

The White Paper on Open Government lists some 200 items of legislation prohibiting the disclosure of information held by public authorities. It adds that the associated criminal sanctions have proved an effective protection against disclosure of confidential and private information held by the state.

Governments can also use the civil law of breach of confidence to prevent the media from publishing information (see Breach of confidence, chapter 23).

Of more day-to-day significance is the fact that, whatever the situation at criminal or civil law, the unauthorised disclosure of information by a civil servant is a sacking offence.

The situation is very different in America and most of the western nations because they have freedom of information acts – that is, acts that require governments to make information available except in certain circumstances.

There have been many efforts in recent years, all unavailing, to change this situation in the United Kingdom by introducing freedom of information legislation placing the onus on government to provide information unless there is some good reason not to.

At the general election in 1992 the Conservatives declared themselves in favour of open government and promised action to reduce official secrecy, but not a freedom of information Act.

After they won, a cabinet minister was given responsibility for implementing the open government policy. The White Paper was published and the Code of Practice introduced.

Its purpose was to support 'the Government's policy under the Citizen's Charter of extending access to official information, and responding to reasonable requests for information, except where disclosure would not be in the public interest…'

It includes five commitments:

1   to give facts and analysis with major policy decisions;
2   to open up internal guidelines about departments' dealings with the public;
3   to give reasons with administrative decisions;
4   to provide information under the Citizen's Charter about public services, what they cost, targets, performance, complaints, and redress; and
5   to answer requests for information.

But the code has no statutory basis and provides civil servants with so many reasons for not providing information that it was not at first expected to bring about a large change in the Whitehall culture. Many requests for information were met by the objection that the information was 'commercially sensitive'.

Complaints about the way the code is being implemented may be made to the parliamentary ombudsman, through an MP. He was seen to be adopting a robust attitude to government departments who withheld information without good reason. Though his findings are not binding on the Government, departments were said usually to accept his recommendations.

Journalists, however, seemed reluctant to make complaints, partly no doubt because they are reluctant to be 'in hock' to an MP in seeking information they believe should be freely available and also because the process is so slow: investigations by the ombudsman take a year on average. The procedure had been in place for two years in 1996 before the first press complaint by the *Economist*, which had decided to test the procedure.

In February of that year the magazine wrote to an MP saying the public should know how much publicly owned assets were being sold for. It pointed out that many of the businesses whose sale prices the Government was refusing to disclose, such as the Red Star freight business, had nothing in common with the businesses remaining to be sold: thus the information about those sales would not affect future ones. Three months later the ombudsman issued an initial finding in the magazine's favour. The Department of Transport had agreed to release the sale prices of four of the smaller businesses that had been privatised. The Department later published the sale prices of some of the other businesses in a parliamentary answer and said it would publish the rest soon.

The magazine commented: 'Contrary to our expectations, the ombudsman's intervention did work. We got the information we wanted. Still it took him more that five months to prise the information out of Whitehall. Without his intervention, it would still not be available. Whitehall has not yet hung up its cloak [of secrecy].'

However, even if the procedure itself proves unattractive to journalists, it may be that the prospect of a complaint to the ombudsman will jolt a department into releasing information it would otherwise refuse. The journalist has to be persistent.

The few examples of a public right to know, outside the field of local government, include measures on environmental issues. The Environmental Protection Act 1990 requires the pollution inspectorate and local authorities to keep registers with considerable detail of pollution standards applying to individual firms, monitoring data relating to those firms, applications by them to release more pollution, and other useful data. The Environmental Information Regulations 1992 create a general right of access to environmental information held by public bodies, subject to broad exemptions.

These regulations are, however, enforceable only by judicial review.

Authorities responsible for four safety and environment Acts must keep a register of notices they have served on occupiers of premises. Under the Environment and Safety Information Act 1988, registers must be open to public inspection free of charge, showing details of enforcement notices under the Fire Precautions Act 1971, the Health and Safety at Work Act 1974, the Safety of Sports Grounds Act 1975, and the Food and Environment Protection Act 1987.

## Local government

Ministers in Whitehall, slow to give access to information about their own activities, have often urged local councillors to co-operate with the press in order to achieve open local government, arguing that council-tax payers have a right to know what is done in their name.

Electors, it has been said, should be able to find out not only what action these bodies are taking, but the reasons for it and the attitude on these issues of those they have elected to represent them. Some councils accept that it is only through newspapers that informed electors get a chance to influence council policy, by reading committee proposals before the council puts the final stamp on them.

Rights to report meetings are laid down in the Local Government (Access to Information) Act 1985 (for county and district councils) and the Public Bodies (Admission to Meetings) Act 1960 (for parish councils, parish meetings, and meetings of health authorities).

## Local Government (Access to Information) Act 1985

The Local Government (Access to Information) Act 1985 says that all meetings of county councils, district councils, their committees, and sub-committees must be open to the public on the same basis.

The position regarding working parties and advisory or study groups, which may in effect act as sub-committees without the name, is unclear. It is possible that a court would take into account whether the meeting was that of a genuine working party or merely a device for decisions to be taken without the use of the name sub-committee.

Another view is that a local authority can delegate the exercise of power, or the fulfilment of a duty, only to a committee or sub-committee, and a working party acting in this way is thus a sub-committee.

In a case in 1988 involving a member of Eden District Council in Cumbria, Lord Justice Croom-Johnson said officers of the council were present at a working party as members (and not as advisers) and this was inconsistent with its being a sub-committee. It was not therefore covered by the 1985 Act.

County and district councils, their committees and sub-committees *must* exclude the public when confidential information is likely to be disclosed. Confidential information is defined as information supplied to the authority by government in confidence or information that cannot be disclosed because of an Act of Parliament or a court order.

A local authority *may*, by passing a resolution, exclude the public when it is likely that exempt information would be disclosed. The resolution must state to what part of the meeting the exclusion applies and must describe the category in the schedule of the exempt information.

Occasionally attempts are made to exclude the press when the matter to be discussed does not fall under any of the categories.

Exempt information under the Act may be summarised as:

1   information relating to a particular employee, job applicant, or office holder of the council, or an employee, applicant, or official of the magistrates courts or the probationary committee;
2   information relating to a particular council tenant or a particular applicant for council services or grants;
3   information relating to the care, adoption, or fostering of a particular child;
4   information relating to a particular person's financial or business affairs;
5   information relating to the supply of goods or services to or the acquisition of property by the council, if to disclose the information would place a particular person in a more favourable bargaining position or otherwise prejudice negotiations;
6   labour relations matters between the council and its employees, if and so long as to disclose the information would prejudice negotiations or discussions;
7   instruction to and advice from counsel;
8   information relating to the investigation and prosecution of offenders, if to disclose the information would enable the wrongdoer to evade notice being served on him.

While the meeting is open to the public, 'duly accredited representatives' of newspapers or news agencies reporting the meeting must, under section 5(6c) of the Act, be afforded reasonable facilities for taking their report and for telephoning it, at their own expense, unless the premises are not on the telephone.

A newspaper or news agency must on request (and on payment of postage or other transmission charge) be supplied with (a) agendas, (b) further particulars necessary to indicate the nature of the items on the agenda, and (c) if the 'proper officer' thinks fit, copies of any other documents supplied to council members. The 'proper officer' may exclude from what he sends out any report, or part of a report, relating to items not likely to be taken in public.

Late items, reports and supplementary information can be admitted at the meeting only if the chairman regards the matter as urgent and specifies the reason for the urgency. Oral reports will be admissible only if reference to them is on the agenda or is covered by the urgency procedure.

Copies of agendas and of any report for a meeting of a council must be open to public inspection at least three clear working days before the meeting (except for items not likely to be taken in public). Where a meeting is called at shorter notice they must be open to inspection from the time the meeting is convened.

Copies of minutes and reports and summaries of business taken in private must be open to public inspection for six years (except for confidential or exempt information).

A list of background papers and a copy of each background paper must be open to public inspection for four years. Background papers are those on which a report for a meeting is based and which have been relied upon to a material extent in preparing the report.

Publication of a fair and accurate copy or extract made in this way is subject to qualified privilege.

Any person who intentionally obstructs the right of any person to inspect agendas, minutes, and reports is liable to a fine on summary conviction. The Act contains no sanction, however, to enforce access to background papers or to ensure that meetings are held in public, and the general law covering these rights would have to be enforced by a civil action.

The only redress a journalist or newspaper might have at law would be to take the authority to the Queen's Bench Divisional Court and apply for an order of mandamus directing the authority to adhere to the law.

The Act applies also to combined police or fire authorities, to meetings of joint consultative committees of health and local authorities, and to some joint boards.

The Act does *not* apply to parish and community councils. The Public Bodies (Admission to Meetings) Act 1960 still applies to these councils.


## Public Bodies (Admission to Meetings) Act 1960

The 1960 Act says that these bodies must admit the public to their meetings and to meetings of their committees consisting of all the members of the body.

The Act says, however, that such a body or committee can exclude the public for the whole or part of a meeting, 'whenever publicity would be prejudicial to the public interest because of the confidential nature of the business to be transacted or for other special reasons stated in the resolution and arising from the nature of that business or of the proceedings'.

It says that public notice of the time and place of the meeting must be given by posting it at the offices at least three days before the meeting, or if the meeting is convened at shorter notice, then at the time it is convened.

On request and on payment of postage, if demanded, the body must supply to any newspaper, news or broadcasting agency, a copy of the agenda as supplied to members of the body, but excluding if thought fit any item to be discussed when the meeting is not likely to be open to the public, 'together with such further statements or particulars, if any, as are necessary to indicate the nature of the items included', and copies of reports and other documents, if thought fit. The Act gives no indication *when* the copies have to be supplied.

The 1960 Act says that, so far as it is practicable, reporters shall be afforded reasonable facilities for taking their report and, unless the meeting is held in premises not belonging to the body or not having a telephone, for telephoning a report at the reporter's expense.

Rights to admission and to reporting facilities, agendas, and telephones under the terms of the 1960 Act also apply to:
(a) parish meetings of rural parishes where there are fewer than 200 electors;
(b) a number of bodies set up under the Water Act 1989. These are: regional and local flood defence committees, regional rivers advisory committees, salmon and freshwater fisheries advisory committees, and customer service committees.

## Council meetings held in private

If after a local authority meeting held in private under the Local Government (Access to Information) Act 1985 or the Public Bodies (Admission to Meetings) Act 1960, an official statement was issued to the press, a report of such a statement would be privileged under the Schedules to the Defamation Acts of 1952 or 1996 (see chapter 20).

Information about such meetings, held when the press is excluded, and obtained from an unofficial source would not be so privileged under the Acts should it be defamatory.

Minutes of the proceedings of a parish or community council must, under the Local Government Act 1972 as amended by the 1985 Act, be open to inspection by a local government elector for the area who may make a copy or extract. Publication of a fair and accurate copy or extract from such minutes is protected by qualified privilege.

## Access to council accounts

Many journalists miss the chances to dig out local authority stories provided by the provisions of the Local Government Finance Act 1982. 'Local authorities' includes police and fire and civil defence authorities.

Under section 17(1) of the Act, 'any persons interested' may inspect a local authority's accounts and 'all books, deeds, contracts, bills, vouchers and receipts related thereto', and make copies. The Accounts and Audit Regulations 1983 say each authority must make these accounts and documents available for public inspection for 15 full working days before a date appointed by the auditor. An advertisement about this right must be published in at least one newspaper 14 days before the date the accounts and documents become available, but the best way to find out is to ask the authority directly.

Lawyers differ as to whether 'any persons interested' include reporters as such, but if the reporter is also a local elector there is no problem.

The *Express and Star*, Wolverhampton, has used the Act to great effect in many stories. It revealed, for example, the details of a Birmingham City car pool equipped with expensive chauffeur-driven cars which were readily available to those in the know. The pool cost about £350,000 a year.

Jonathan Leake, a journalist formerly with the *Express and Star*, points out that the sheer volume of the 'treasure trove' made available by the Act is a problem. He recommends alternative approaches.

First is going in knowing what you are looking for. If you suspect some dubious deals have been struck, ask for all the original documents relating to them, and go through the ledger to check. Get the original invoices and tenders, and don't be palmed off with ledger entries or computer print-outs.

Or go to a particular department equipped for a general trawl. Demand access to the files containing original invoices and receipts and go through them one by one.

Your reception from the council officers may not be welcoming, so you may need to insist on your rights. In 1994 the Kent Messenger Group had to employ a solicitor before forcing Kent County Council to provide a copy of a document containing details of an agreement between the council and a developer expected to create 10,000 jobs.

In that case the document was described as confidential, but the duty of disclosure under the Act overrides such claims.

A council officer refusing a proper demand for a copy or obstructing a person entitled to inspect one of these documents is in fact committing a criminal offence. The London Borough of Haringey was prosecuted and fined in 1996 for refusing to disclose documents relating to the audit which had been requested by a resident.

An exception to the general rule is that there is no right to examine documents relating to personal expenses incurred by officers of the council.

A full explanation of the Act is contained in 'Local government audit law' by Reginald Jones, published by HMSO.

The Local Government (Allowances) Regulations 1974 enable electors at any time of the year to demand to see a breakdown of allowances and expenses paid to councillors.

Under the Local Government Finance (Publicity for Auditors' Reports) Act 1991 a council must make available any report produced by the auditors immediately on a matter of particular concern.

## Health authorities

Admission to meetings of regional and district health authorities and family health services authorities, and rights to their agendas, are subject to the Public Bodies (Admission to Meetings) Act 1960.

Department of Health guidance to these authorities in 1990 said although authorities could exclude press and public in the public interest under the terms of the 1960 Act, they were expected to conduct their business in public in as open a manner as possible.

Authorities should seek to keep the public informed about their work, aims, and objectives. The circular envisaged that authorities might wish to exclude press and public when discussing patients and staff, labour relations, contracts, and legal action.

Under the 1960 Act, the same rights of admission are given to any committee of a health authority consisting of all members of the authority.

These obligations do not apply to hospital trusts (see section on Quangos, below).

Community health councils are subject to the provisions of the Local Government (Admission to Meetings) Act 1985. Minutes, agendas, and reports are open to public inspection for only three years and background papers for only two years. Added to the list of exempt information for these councils is information on (a) a person providing or applying to provide NHS services (b) an employee of such person or (c) information relating to a person's health.

Health authorities are required to publish details each year about maximum waiting times for beds in each speciality, about the number of complaints received and how long it has taken to deal with them, and how successful the authority has been in relation to national and local standards under the Government's patients' charter.

There is a Code of Practice on Openness in the NHS which is similar to the central government code, but is supervised by the Health Service Ombudsman. It applies to health authorities, trusts, and individual practitioners, such as general practitioners.

## Police authorities

The Police and Magistrates' Courts Act 1994 gave added power to central government over policing and the workings of magistrates courts. The Act changes the membership of police authorities and empowers the Home Secretary by order to determine objectives for them.

The authorities have to draw up local policing plans that acknowledge the objectives set by the Home Secretary. Publication of the plans is arranged by the authorities in such manner as appears to them to be appropriate. The plan must state the authority's priorities for the year, the financial resources available and its objectives.

The authority must also issue an annual report as soon as possible after the end of the financial year and arrange its publication. The report must include an assessment of the extent to which the local policing plan has been carried out.

*Magistrates courts committees*

The public must be admitted to a meeting of the magistrates courts committee at least once a year. The minutes of every meeting must be open to public inspection at the committee's office, except that confidential information can be excluded: in that case, the committee must state its reason. For a fee, copies must be made available.

The Lord Chancellor can require a committee to submit reports and plans and make these available to the public for a reasonable fee.

*Schools*

Under the Education (Schools) Act 1992, the Education Secretary is empowered to require both state and independent schools to provide information on examination results, truancy rates, rates of pupils staying on after 16, and employment or training undertaken by school leavers. The Education Secretary is also empowered to require the information to be made available to newspapers.

Governing bodies of every county, controlled, and maintained school must, under the Education (No 2) Act 1986, keep written statements of their conclusions on policy matters. Regulations require the head teacher to make the statement available at all reasonable times to persons wishing to inspect it.

Governing bodies of grant-maintained schools are required to make an annual report available for inspection at all reasonable times.

**Quangos**

Many of the day-to-day services to the public that used to be administered by bodies on which representatives of the public served have been hived off or are being hived off to independent agencies on the ground that they will become more efficient when exposed to the disciplines of the market. The managing bodies are staffed by appointees rather than representatives.

The term quango (quasi-autonomous non-governmental organisation) is conveniently used to describe non-elected public bodies that operate outside the civil service and that are funded by the taxpayer.

They include NHS trusts, grant-maintained schools, further education colleges, urban development corporations, training and enterprise councils, and a wide variety of other bodies.

Government prefers to use the term non-departmental public bodies (NDPBs), which includes only public bodies in the formal sense. It does not cover bodies that in legal terms are private enterprises, even if they are spending public money. Another term used by government is appointed executive bodies.

As a result of this difference in definition, estimates of the number of quangos in existence in the 1990s vary from 2,000 to 5,000 and estimates of the amount of money spent annually also varies widely. A report published in 1994 claimed they now exercise more power and influence than the entire structure of local government (*Ego trip: Extra-governmental Organisations in the UK*, edited by Stuart Weir and Wendy Hall).

The Government reported in 1994 that the amount of state funding to appointed executive bodies had doubled in real terms since 1979 to £15 billion annually. That figure does not include NHS trusts and other large spending agencies such as training and enterprise councils, and the Labour Party claimed £54.4 billion was spent by 'the unelected state'.

Before this development occurred, it was generally accepted that the bodies that then had corresponding duties were accountable to the public and should provide information about their activities to the public. Many of them – for example, the old water authorities but not the new water authorities – were required to admit the press to their meetings. They were generally required to provide documentation. In most cases, fair and accurate reports of their meetings and statements were covered by qualified privilege.

The argument on accountability no longer applies in the same way. Demands for information can be countered by the argument that the body cannot operate in market conditions when the details of its operations are known to its competitors. Public access to information would therefore work against normal commercial confidentiality.

The minister in charge of the water authorities justified the clamp-down on public access by saying these authorities were no longer operating like public corporations but more like private companies under the Companies Act, with executive and business responsibilities.

In general, there is no right of access to the meetings of quangos and no right to documents, and reports of their activities do not enjoy qualified privilege (see chapter 20, Privilege).

The scale of this development and the variety of institutions is too great to allow coverage in any detail in this chapter. As an example, we consider the hospital trusts that are increasingly running the hospitals.

A government publication *NHS Trusts: A Working Guide* says that 'Trusts should be as open as possible in their management.' However, there is no right of access to the regular meetings. The Department of Health explains that 'much of their business will relate to confidential contractual issues.'

Each trust is required to hold an annual public meeting. At this meeting the trust presents its summary business plan and annual report, audited annual accounts and any report made on those accounts by the auditor. An additional public meeting must be called if the auditor issues a report in the public interest other than at the end of the financial year.

A trust also has to issue a strategic plan every three years.

Service agreements between health authorities and trusts are open to public scrutiny. The Department of Health comments: 'It has been decided that contracts for health services with both public and private providers should be publicly available once they are signed.' These contracts (service agreements) can be obtained from the district health authority.

All substantial trusts now have their own PR (public relations) organisations and the open meetings tend to be PR set pieces, contrasting sharply with the meetings of the health authorities, which include elected representatives. The financial statements tend to contain no detailed breakdowns of the figures such as used to be available from the district health authorities. The summary business plan is indeed a summary.

One result of the lack of information from official sources in the trusts is said to be that employees are leaking more. So, for journalists, not only is there a greater need for digging, but perhaps there are greater opportunities for digging. But remember that your sources are probably risking their jobs, and watch out for injunctions (see Breach of confidence, chapter 23).

Urban development corporations have now taken on many of the planning functions of local authorities but are not subject to the Local Government (Access to Information) Act 1985.

## Questions

1   You are having difficulty extracting from a government department information that you believe should be available to you in accordance with the provisions of the Code of Practice. To whom can you complain?

2   What does the law require a county or district council to do before it excludes press and public from its meetings? What is the position at committee and sub-committee meetings of these councils?

3   How can a journalist find out what decision has been taken by a local authority after excluding the press? Discuss the practical difficulties.

4   Discuss the difficulty of a newspaper seeking to compel a local authority to obey the Local Government (Access to Information) Act 1985.

5   What are the rights of press and public to attend meetings of parish councils?

6   How can the journalist use the provisions of the Local Government Finance Act 1982 to find council stories?

7   Outline the rights of press and public to attend meetings of health authorities and of community health councils.

8   What are the rights of the press and public to attend meetings of NHS hospital trusts?

# 29   Copyright

A journalist needs to know the basic rules of the law of copyright if he is to determine how much of other people's words, artistry, or photographs he can use in his paper.

## What is protected

Copyright is a branch of intellectual property law – that is to say, it protects the products of people's skill, creativity, labour, or time.

Under the Copyright, Designs and Patents Act 1988, copyright protects any literary, dramatic, artistic or musical work, sound recording, film, broadcast, or typographical arrangement. Artistic works include photographs and graphics. Typographical arrangements cover the way the page is set out. Copyright does not have to be registered.

A judge once said: 'Anything worth copying is worth protecting.' Reproduction of a substantial part of a copyright work may constitute infringement.

However, for a work to be protected by copyright it must satisfy the test of originality. Some work or effort must have gone into it. Brief slogans and catchphrases have been ruled to be too trivial to be protected by copyright.

There is no copyright in facts, news, ideas, or information. Copyright exists in the form in which information is expressed and the selection and arrangement of the material — all of which involves skill and labour.

Sir Nicolas Browne-Wilkinson, Vice Chancellor (later Lord Browne-Wilkinson), said in the Chancery Division in February 1990 that it was very improbable that the courts would hold there was copyright in a news story, *as opposed to the actual words used*.

He said the law as to copyright in a verbatim report of the spoken words of another was settled in a case in 1910 which established that the mere reporting of the words of another gave rise to copyright, so long as skill, labour, and judgement had been employed in the composition of the report. That case, he said, was still good law.

On the other hand, persistent lifting of facts from another paper, even if there is rewriting each time, may still be an infringement because of the skill, labour, and judgement that went into research on the stories. In an 1892 case, a judge made the distinction between lifting from another paper now and again at long intervals, and not likely to be repeated, and deliberate, persistent abstraction from the first paper.

The defence of fair dealing for reporting current events will however often allow some quoting from another paper (see later, this chapter).

Literary work is protected by copyright as soon as it is recorded in writing or otherwise and it includes newspapers and the writing that goes into them.

Copyright in material supplied to newspapers by outside contributors, whether paid or not, will normally be owned by the contributor. A person sending a reader's letter for publication will by implication have licensed the newspaper to use his or her copyright work free on one occasion, while still retaining the copyright. On the other hand an editor who uses a freelance writer's article sent in without first negotiating the fee may be in difficulty.

An official of a sporting or trade association may find it part of his duty to make material available to the paper free of charge but the copyright is still the association's and it can withdraw the facility, or start to make a charge, or prevent another journal from copying it.

This applies to much material available to newspapers — TV and radio programmes, sporting fixtures, lists of events, and tide tables. The company whose employee compiled the material owns the copyright.

The Football League many years ago established in a test case against Littlewoods Pools that the league owned the copyright in the fixture lists and could control copying. The league is thus able to charge pools promoters for the use of the fixtures while allowing newspapers to use them free.

Under the Broadcasting Act 1990, those who provide a broadcast service (and own the copyright in the programme listings) must make information about the programmes available to any newspaper or magazine publisher wishing to use it, through a licensing scheme. In case of dispute as to the charge to be made by the broadcasting organisation for the use of the information, the matter is decided by the Copyright Tribunal.

### Copyright in speeches

Under the 1988 Act, copyright is conferred for the first time on spoken words, even if they are not delivered from a script, as soon as they are recorded, with or without the speaker's permission. This raises many questions on the reporting of meetings, etc, some of which will not be answered until there is a test case.

The speaker, as the author of a literary work, will own the copyright in his words, unless he is speaking in the course of his employment.

Under Section 58 of the Act, it is not infringement to use the record of the words for reporting current events, subject to four conditions:

(a) The record is a direct record and not taken from a previous record or broadcast.

(b) The speaker did not prohibit the making of the record and it did not infringe any existing copyright.

(c) The use being made of the record, or material taken from it, was not of a kind prohibited by the speaker or copyright owner before the record was made.

(d) The use being made of the record is with the authority of the person who is lawfully in possession of it.

Could a speaker have second thoughts about his remarks and prohibit the reporting of them afterwards? It seems not. He must have prohibited the note or tape being taken or, before the speech, have said he did not want them to be used in a certain way, for example in a newspaper.

What will be the position in copyright law if reporters attend a meeting which they would normally wish to report but they are barred from taking notes?

One of the difficulties in this situation would be knowing how much of the speech could be reproduced before it would constitute a substantial part in law. In recent years, courts have been ruling that a substantial part may not necessarily be of great length. Substantial part can, in any case, refer to the quality or importance of the material reproduced as well as to the quantity or length.

There is, as we have already seen, no copyright in facts conveyed in the speaker's words and it is possible that the courts would take the view that if the actual words were not used and the arrangement of the facts was altered, there had been no reproduction of a substantial part. It is also possible that limited use of a speaker's words might be covered by fair dealing (see later, this chapter).

Another problem in section 58 is in defining current events and how far back they stretch.

It seems however that surreptitious recording of a speaker's words is not a breach of copyright in itself. Once the words have been recorded however, there is copyright in them and it will be owned by the speaker. In many cases, there will be a separate copyright in the record because of the skill involved in making it. In certain circumstances there might be an action available for breach of confidence (see chapter 23).

Copyright in the speaker's words is not infringed in reporting parliamentary or judicial proceedings.

Apart from any copyright in the spoken word, there is a copyright in the manuscript from which a speaker reads.

In this way, Buckingham Palace made legal history in 1993 when it used copyright law to take legal action for breach of an embargo. The *Sun*, together with other newspapers, had been sent copies of the Queen's 1992 Christmas Day message, embargoed until after it had been broadcast. The *Sun* published the message on 23 December under the headline 'Our difficult days, by the Queen'. After Buckingham Palace started proceedings for a breach of the Queen's copyright, the *Sun* agreed to pay a large sum to a charity nominated by her. The owner of copyright material has the right to enforce his or her own terms for the use of it and can take action if those terms are breached. In this case Buckingham Palace had by implication licensed reproduction of the Queen's speech, but only after the broadcast.

## Who owns the copyright

The first owner of a copyright work created after 31 July 1989 (when the 1988 Act came into force) is the author but in the case of work done in the course of employment the employer is the owner, subject to any agreement to the contrary. Thus in the absence of any contrary agreement the employer can sell the work of an employee to whom he wishes.

There is no automatic right on the part of a newspaper or magazine or periodical to the copyright of work done by non-members of the staff, even if the work has been ordered.

The copyright can be assigned to the newspaper, or magazine, or periodical but an assignment is not effective unless in writing signed by the copyright owner. He can license the publisher to use his work but if it is an exclusive licence this also must be in writing.

Where a photograph is commissioned from a freelance or commercial photographer today, the copyright is owned by the photographer (or his employer) unless there is an agreement to the contrary. If the photograph was taken before the 1988 Act came into force, however, the copyright will be owned by the person or company who commissioned it, even though the photographer or his employer will own the negatives or film.

A person who commissions a photograph for private and domestic purposes is protected by one of the 1988 Act's moral rights — the right not to have copies of the photograph issued to the public even if he does not own the copyright.

This has implications for the reporter who borrows a photograph, say of a wedding, when the bride or bridegroom comes into the news months or years afterwards. The relative who lends the photograph to the reporter is unlikely to own the copyright and may not have commissioned the taking of it in the first place.

If the paper were to publish the photograph (provided it was taken after 31 July 1989) two rights may be said to have been infringed — that of the photographer (who owned the copyright unless there was an agreement to the contrary) and that of the bridegroom who commissioned it and has the right not to have it made available to the public.

The photographer may be glad to accept a fee for publication of his copyright picture but the response of the bridegroom may raise problems under the 1988 Act.


## Moral rights

The 1988 Act, to meet the needs of the Berne Convention on copyright, gave moral rights to authors of copyright work.

These gave the author the right to be identified, not to have his work subject to derogatory treatment, and not to have a work falsely attributed to him.

The rights to be identified and not to have the work subject to derogatory treatment do not apply to any copyright work created for publication in a newspaper, magazine, or periodical or to any work made available for such publication with the consent of the author.

The right not to have a work falsely attributed to a person does not have these exceptions. If a person gives an interview and the newspaper publishes an article purporting to have been written by the person himself and that person has not consented, he may have an action for false attribution.


## Fair dealing

Fair dealing with a copyright work (apart from a photograph) for the purpose of reporting current events will not constitute infringement provided it is accompanied by sufficient acknowledgement of the work and its author. Fair dealing with a copyright work (including a photograph) for the purposes of criticism or review of that work or of another will also not be treated as infringement, subject again to sufficient acknowledgement.

This allows for reporting which quotes from books, plays, films, other publications, and so on, when writing a criticism, story, or feature.

If the copyright work is obtained by unfair means this may be outside the scope of fair dealing, as would use of quotations from the work merely to avoid having to pay.

Copying which prevented the copyright owner from gaining financial benefit from the sale of rights to his work would also be ruled to be not fair dealing.

It is also not an infringement of copyright to extract or copy an abstract of a scientific or technical article which is published with the article, for example a blurb or standfirst used with a feature.

If more of the work is quoted than is necessary to make the point in reporting current events or in criticism or review, this may not be fair dealing. It is difficult to put a figure to the proportion of a copyright work that can be used. Authors and publishers tend to think in terms of low percentages.

In 1991, Mr Justice Scott dismissed a copyright action brought by the BBC against British Satellite Broadcasting over the use on the satellite company's sports programme of highlights from BBC coverage of the World Cup finals. The BBC had bought exclusive rights. He held that the use of short clips varying from 14 to 37 seconds, with a BBC credit line, up to four times in 24 hours was protected by the defence of fair dealing. The managing director of BBC Television had said anarchy would result if the case went against the BBC but the judge said that was the frequent cry of those who saw a monopoly they had enjoyed being threatened, and was often shown by later events to have been exaggerated.

There is no copyright infringement in reporting Parliament, the courts, or public inquiries, but this does not permit copying of a published report. There is normally no copyright infringement in copying material which must be open to public inspection by Act of Parliament.

## Public interest defence

The 1988 Act recognises the common law defence of public interest against any action for breach of copyright but does not attempt to define it.

In 1984, in the *Intoximeter* case, the *Daily Express* was successful in asking the Court of Appeal to lift injunctions granted to restrain breach of confidence and infringement of copyright. The court said it was well established that there was a defence of public interest to actions in both copyright and confidentiality if it could be shown there was a public interest to publish the information. The court stressed the need to differentiate between what is interesting to the public (which is not covered by the defence) and what is in the public interest to be made known (where the defence might be available). Professor Gerald Dworkin and Richard D Taylor, joint editors of *Blackstone's Guide* to the 1988 Act, say: 'The precise limits of the defence still await definitive demarcation, a task which Parliament prefers to leave to the courts.'

In 1994, the Department of Trade turned down a suggestion that the Act should be amended to allow a clear statutory defence to copyright infringement for newspapers which publish private photographs issued to them by the police, usually in order to trace persons wanted for serious crime or as witnesses. The Department took the view that a public interest defence would be upheld by the courts.

Publication without permission of a photograph of the whole or a substantial part of a television image is an infringement under section 17 of the Copyright Act.

## Length of copyright

The Government extended the length of copyright in 1995 from 50 years to 70 years from the end of the year of the author's death, to conform with a European Union directive. Copyright in a broadcast is retained at 50 years.

In 1996, under the Copyright and Related Rights Regulations, a person publishing for the first time a previously unpublished photograph which has gone out of copyright establishes a publication right for 25 years from the end of the year of that first publication.

## Remedies for breach of copyright

*Civil action* The owner of the copyright can obtain an injunction in the High Court or county court to restrain a person from infringing his copyright. He can also seek damages and an order for the possession of infringing copies of the work and of material used in the infringement.

*Criminal law* Under the 1988 Act a person guilty of infringement can be prosecuted.

## Innocent infringement

If the infringer did not know and had no reason to believe the work was subject to copyright, for example if he genuinely believed the copyright had run out, the copyright owner is entitled to an account of profits but not to damages.

## Acquiescence

If the owner of a copyright work has encouraged or allowed another to make use of that work without complaint, this may destroy a claim for infringement of copyright.

Mr Justice Carnwath held in the Chancery Division in 1996 that the owner of copright who was aware of a breach of that copyright, but did not complain or take any action to stop it, had acquiesced and was therefore not entitled to claim. In a case before him involving the use of adult films, the company owning the copyright became aware in early 1993 that use, beyond what was permitted in a licence it had granted, was being made of its films. The judge said that the defence of acquiescence was made out at least from the middle of 1993. (*The Times*, 2 December 1996.)

## Questions

1   What copyright extends to facts, ideas, and information? May a newspaper regularly lift stories from another paper if it changes the introduction and changes the text?

2   What is the position in the law of copyright of a reader who sends a letter to a newspaper with a view to publication?

3   Could a speaker at the end of a meeting decide to use the law of copyright to prevent his speech from being reported?

4   If the secretary of a county football league sends in a fixture list to a newspaper with his compliments, what is his position and the newspaper's in copyright law? May another newspaper copy it in its next issue?

5   What conditions are imposed by the Copyright Act 1988 on a newspaper which wants to use a speaker's words for reporting current events?

6   Subject to any overriding claim in his contract, what is the journalist's position in the law of copyright for work done in the course of employment?

7   Discuss the copyright position of a newspaper in quoting from a book in a review.

8   What would be the copyright position of a newspaper publishing a picture made available to it by a commercial photographer?

9   Suppose a person orders a wedding photograph from a commercial photographer. What right does that person have to stop a newspaper using the photograph if it has acquired a copy of it without his permission?

# 30  Official secrets

Journalists eager to obtain news, either from their own observations or through information supplied by others, should be aware of the dangers involved in contravening the provisions of the Official Secrets Acts.

The Official Secrets Act 1911, as amended, contains provisions about spying, but journalists need to know about them. The Official Secrets Act 1989 is concerned with the wrongful communication of state secrets and with breaches of official trust. Prosecutions under both Acts can be brought only by or with the consent of the Attorney-General, except in cases where the secret concerns crime or special investigation powers, when the consent of the Director of Public Prosecutions is required.

The 1989 Act replaced section 2 of the 1911 Act. This section became known as the 'catch-all section' because of the wide range of information covered. Under the section, no crown servant or government contractor could lawfully make an unauthorised disclosure of any information which he had learnt in the course of his job.

The section made it a crime to report, for example, the number of cups of tea drunk each week in a government department or the details of a new carpet in a minister's room. Similarly, under the section it was an offence for a person to receive such information. This was the part of the Act used most frequently against journalists.

In cases in the 1970s and 1980s, mentioned below, the Attorney-General failed to persuade juries to convict defendants prosecuted under section 2. The new Act abolished the section. It restricted the range of information covered to six areas. It made *disclosing* information in those areas an offence. It ended the offence of *receiving* information – though if a journalist actively procures a damaging disclosure of information he is likely to be guilty of aiding and abetting the offence of disclosure.

The 1989 Act removed an important protection that had been available previously; it did not renew the provision under section 2 that no offence was committed if a person disclosed the information to someone to whom it was his duty to communicate it 'in the interests of the state'. This was sometimes referred to loosely as the public interest defence.

However, in most cases the prosecution must prove that the disclosure by a journalist was 'damaging' and the journalist knew or had reasonable cause to believe that it would be damaging; and lawyer David Hooper, author of *Official Secrets*, tells the editors of *McNae* he believes this may let in public interest 'by the back door'.

Suppose the journalist exposes a scandal. A jury may take a subjective view and take into account the public interest in deciding whether the journalist knew the disclosure would be damaging.

In some cases the law assumes that *any* disclosure of *any* information is damaging.

There is no defence of prior publication – that is, that the information is not secret because it was published previously.

Penalties for the offence of deliberate disclosure are a maximum of two years' imprisonment or a fine or both. If the case is tried summarily (by the magistrates) the maximum is six months or a fine or both.

A revised code was introduced to discipline civil servants who disclose information in areas not now covered by the Act and who would previously have been prosecuted. In some cases new offences were created to fill the gaps: for example, the Finance Act 1989 made it an offence for a civil servant to disclose a taxpayer's returns.

Section 2 caused journalists many headaches but because it was so comprehensive it was at least comparatively easy to understand. By contrast the 1989 Act is extremely complicated. In effect it creates more than a dozen different offences. Journalists who wish to check whether disclosure of particular information would be an offence should consult the table at the end of this chapter.

As a result of the Government's failures in its attempts to use the Official Secrets Act to persuade the courts to punish people involved in the leaking of official information, in the 1980s it began to make extensive use of the civil remedy of breach of confidence (see chapter 23). This branch of the law enabled it to obtain injunctions without the matter coming before a jury.

Cases under the 1989 Act still have to come before a jury. In 1988 the Home Secretary, Douglas Hurd, said the Government would continue to use the civil law to prevent disclosures which it believed would damage the public interest. The new criminal law would be used if the Government failed to prevent publication.

People concerned with civil liberties criticise the standpoint represented by the Act. They say that in a democracy all official information should be available to the public except that which is restricted for special reasons.

They continue to press for legislation giving rights of access to information on the lines of laws in the United States and other Western nations (see chapter 28).

The Criminal Justice and Public Order Act 1994 created new offences of collecting or recording any information likely to be useful to terrorists in planning or carrying out any act of terrorism; or possessing any record or document containing any such information.

'Reasonable excuse' provides a defence, and the Home Office has told the Guild of Editors that an accused person involved in legitimate newsgathering should have little difficulty in demonstrating the existence of a reasonable excuse.

## The 1911 Act

### A 'purpose prejudicial'

Under section 1 of the 1911 Act it is an arrestable offence, carrying a penalty of up to 14 years' imprisonment, to do any of the following 'for any purpose prejudicial to the safety or interests of the state':
(a)  approach, inspect, pass over, be in the neighbourhood of, or enter any prohibited place;
(b)  make any sketch, plan, model, or note that might be or is intended to be useful to an enemy;
(c)  obtain, collect, record, or communicate to any person any information that might be or is intended to be useful to an enemy.

Offences under (c) are most relevant for journalists – that is, offences concerned with obtaining or communicating information.

The report of the Government-appointed Franks Committee, published in 1972, said section 1 was concerned only with spying, and it pointed out that actions punishable under the section must be for a 'purpose prejudicial' and that the subject matter must be of possible use to the enemy.

However, in 1978, in a case that became known as the ABC trial after the initials of the three defendants, a judge said the Act was not restricted in that way. Two journalists and a former soldier were tried at the Old Bailey charged with a total of five offences connected with the section. A freelance journalist, Duncan Campbell, was accused of collecting information concerning the Government's electronic surveillance systems, and obtaining material from John Berry, the former soldier.

Berry was accused of communicating information to Campbell.

Crispin Aubrey, a reporter on *Time Out* magazine, who had arranged the interview between the two, was accused of aiding and abetting Campbell to commit a section 1 offence, and also of doing an act preparatory to the commission of such an offence. The last two offences, under section 7 of the Act, also carry maximum sentences of 14 years.

The prosecution claimed that a person need not be a conventional spy to commit an act which could be directly or indirectly useful to an enemy. Sincere in intent though a person might be, he could still be doing the work of the enemy.

All the section 1 charges were dropped after the judge said they were 'oppressive': there was no suggestion, he said, that any of the defendants intended to use the information to assist an enemy. He added, however, 'I find it impossible to say that section 1 can only be applied to cases of spying or sabotage.' As described below, the three men were found guilty on other charges.

## Prohibited place

Section 3 of the 1911 Act gives a lengthy definition of a prohibited place. It includes 'any work or defence, arsenal, naval or air force establishment or station, factory, dockyard, mine, minefield, camp, ship, or aircraft' and 'any telegraph, telephone, wireless or signal station, or office' used by the state.

The reporter or press photographer who wishes to avoid prosecution under the Act must ensure that he is not gathering information or obtaining photographs at or near a 'prohibited place'.

## Duty to name sources

Section 6 enables a chief officer of police to require a person to divulge information when he believes an offence under section 1 has been committed (see chapter 24, section on Official secrets). The section used to apply to section 2 offences also, but the law was changed in 1939 after a journalist was convicted for failing to reveal the source of police information published in his paper.

## The 1989 Act

### The journalist's position

**Section 5** of the Act says a journalist or other member of the public commits an offence if he discloses information, without lawful authority, knowing or having reasonable cause to believe that it is protected against disclosure by the provisions of the 1989 Act.

He must have received the information from a crown servant or government contractor (a) without lawful authority, or (b) in confidence.

Or the journalist or an informant must have received it from someone who received it in confidence from a crown servant or government contractor.

And the journalist must know or have reasonable cause to believe that he received the information under these circumstances.

'In confidence' means either that the journalist has been told the information is being given to him in confidence or the circumstances are such that the discloser could reasonably suppose the information would be held in confidence.

In cases concerning four of the classes of information mentioned below the prosecution in a case against a journalist has to prove that the disclosure is damaging, and the test of what is damaging differs according to the class of information, as the table shows.

The prosecution also has to prove that the journalist made the disclosure knowing, or having reasonable cause to believe, that it would be damaging.

In most cases (but see table) the journalist does not commit an offence if the person from whom he received the information, although a government contractor or a person to whom it was entrusted in confidence, was not a British citizen or the disclosure did not take place in the United Kingdom, the Channel Islands, the Isle of Man, or a British colony.

It is also an offence under the section to disclose any information which the discloser knows or has reasonable cause to believe came into his possession as a result of a contravention of section 1 of the 1911 Act.

**Section 6** of the Act deals with the disclosure of information communicated in confidence to other states or international organisations, and there are no requirements that the information must have been disclosed originally by crown servants or government contractors.

The journalist or other member of the public commits the offence if he discloses such information when it relates to security or intelligence, defence, or international relations.

The information must have come into his possession as a result of being disclosed, whether to him or another, without the authority of the state or organisation – or, in the case of an organisation, of a member of it.

The journalist must know, or have reasonable cause to believe, that the information is of the type covered by the section, and has come into his possession in the way mentioned, and that its disclosure would be damaging.

**Section 8** makes it an offence for a person to fail to comply with an 'official' order to return a document, where it would be an offence under the Act if he disclosed that document.

## The six classes

The six classes of information covered by the 1989 Act are:

1   security and intelligence (section 1 of the Act);
2   defence (section 2);
3   international relations (section 3);
4   crime (section 4);
5   information on government phone-tapping, interception of letters or other communications (section 4 also);
6   information entrusted in confidence to other states or international organisations (section 6)

For convenience, we shall refer to these as Classes 1 to 6, in accordance with the numbers to the left of the classes, above. In parentheses we have given the section of the Act that covers a particular class.

## The damage test

Though the Act can catch journalists and other members of the public, it is directed particularly at members of the security services, crown servants and government contractors who make disclosures without lawful authority.

The degree of damage necessary for conviction under the Act varies according to the class of information and the category of person accused. In most cases, but not all, the prosecution has to show that a disclosure made by a journalist was damaging, and he made it knowing, or having reasonable cause to believe, it would be damaging (see table). Consider these examples:

1   Suppose a journalist writes a story based on information received from a policeman that the telephone of a senior opposition MP is being tapped under warrant but for dubious reasons (Class 5 information). A policeman is a crown servant under the Act. The prosecution does not have to prove damage because damage is assumed, and the journalist and his informant cannot plead that disclosure was in the public interest because it disclosed iniquity.
2   A journalist writes a story based on information received from a member of the security services that members of the services have been involved in illegal activities (Class 1 information). Again, the Act assumes that any disclosure about security by a member of the security services is damaging, and he cannot defend himself on the ground that the disclosure was not damaging. On the other hand, if a crown servant or government contractor makes a disclosure on the same subject, *he* is guilty only if the disclosure is proved to be damaging. The Act states that in this context a disclosure is damaging if:
    (a)   it causes damage to the work of, or of any part of, the security and intelligence services; *or*
    (b)   it is of information which is such that its unauthorised disclosure would be likely to cause such damage or which falls within a class or description of information the unauthorised disclosure of which would be likely to have that effect.

If a journalist is accused of making a disclosure about security the prosecution has to prove damage and the test is the same as for a crown servant, whether the journalist got the information from a crown servant or a member of the security services.

3    In defence matters (Class 2 information), the prosecution always has to prove the disclosure was damaging. See the table for what makes a disclosure on a defence matter damaging. Note that it is again sufficient to show that the information was 'such that' its unauthorised disclosure would be likely to be damaging, but there is no 'class' test as in the previous example. The same test of damage would be applied to a crown servant making a disclosure or a journalist writing a story based upon it.

Even where the prosecution has to prove disclosure is damaging, the test is expressed in every case in very wide terms. In all cases where a definition of damage is given it includes the 'such that' formula.

## The onus of proof

Journalists standing trial under the Act will take a keen interest in who has to prove what. As with the *test* of damage, the onus of proof in the matter of damage also varies according to the class of information and the category of the person accused. Consider an example:

If a member of the security services makes a disclosure about his work the court will assume damage and no proof is necessary. If a crown servant or government contractor makes a disclosure about security the prosecution has to prove the disclosure was damaging but the crown servant has a defence if *he* can show that he did not know or had no reasonable cause to believe the disclosure would be damaging. In the case of a journalist making a disclosure about security, *the prosecution* must prove not only that the disclosure was damaging but also that the journalist knew or had reasonable cause to believe that it would be damaging; that is, the onus of proof is on the prosecution.

(Where, in the following table, knowledge of the damaging nature of the information is part of the offence, and the onus is on the prosecution to prove it, this is included in column 3. Where lack of knowledge is a defence, which the defendant had to establish, this is included in column 5.)

## Effects of the Act

Suppose a journalist reports information he received from a crown servant about Cabinet papers, advice to ministers, or economic information. This is not an offence provided the matters are not included in the six protected categories. (This is, however, just the sort of case where the Government might seek an injunction on grounds of breach of confidence if it learnt about the intended story before publication, or an order for delivery up of any leaked papers. See chapter 23.)

A defence correspondent writes a story revealing crime, fraud, abuse of authority, neglect in the performance of official duty, or other misconduct which would otherwise continue unchecked. The prosecution must prove the disclosure was damaging for one of the reasons listed in the table and the correspondent knew, or had reasonable cause to believe, the information would be damaging. He cannot defend himself on the basis that the disclosures were in the public interest.

A reporter working on a local newspaper in an area dominated by the fishing industry writes a story about two boats that have got their nets entangled with a submarine and have sunk, with the loss of several lives. The reporter gives the location of the submarine, information he received from a friendly coastguards officer. If he is prosecuted, the prosecution will have to show the information was 'such that' its unauthorised disclosure would be likely to damage the capability of the navy to carry out its tasks, and also that he knew, or had reasonable cause to believe, the information would be damaging.

An environment correspondent writes a story about infractions of EEC regulations on water pollution and inadequate safeguards operated by Britain. He uses an EEC letter marked 'Confidential' and leaked to him by a civil servant. The document is covered by the Act because it is 'confidential information … obtained from … an international organisation'. The prosecution would have to prove disclosure was damaging (see table), eg by showing that the document was 'such that' its disclosure would be likely to damage the interests of the United Kingdom abroad.

The Government's confidential reply to the EEC document is leaked in Brussels by a foreign civil servant in the Commission and published in a Belgian newspaper. A British newspaper reprints the information. The information is presumably covered by the Act because it relates to international relations and was 'communicated in confidence by the United Kingdom to an international organisation'. The prosecution would have to show the disclosure was damaging and the test would be the same as in the previous example.

A reporter hears from a friendly policeman that responses to 999 calls in a particular area are slow. The question for the court would be whether the disclosure would encourage criminals to operate in that area and therefore would be 'likely' to result in the commission of an offence. In that case, damage would be assumed.

In the remainder of this section an attempt is made to suggest the effects of the Act by applying its provisions to some earlier cases. Readers may like to use the table to reach their own conclusions before reading the comments in italic.

In 1932 a journalist was sent to prison for two months after he received information about wills from a clerk in the Principal Probate Registry. The information was published in a daily paper a few hours before it was to be officially published.

*Under the 1989 Act no offence would have been committed because the information disclosed does not come within any of the six classes of protected information.*

In 1948 a journalist was fined for receiving information about police activities which was passed to him by a telephone operator.

*There is no offence of receiving information under the 1989 Act, but the journalist might be guilty of aiding and abetting the offence.*

In 1970 the *Sunday Telegraph* published a confidential assessment of the situation in Nigeria – then involved in the Biafran civil war – written by the defence adviser at the British High Commission in Lagos. The report showed that ministers had been misleading the House of Commons about the amount of arms being supplied to the federal government. Those charged included Jonathan Aitken, then a freelance journalist, later a minister in John Major's Government; the newspaper; and its editor, Brian Roberts. Defence counsel argued that it was 'in the interests of the state' for the public to be aware that ministers had made misleading statements to Parliament. Aitken said also he believed the general from whom he had received the report was lawfully in possession of it and that he was entitled to use it provided he did not disclose its source. The judge told the jury the prosecution had to prove that when the journalist received the report he had reasonable grounds to believe it had been passed to him in contravention of the Act. The jury acquitted all the defendants.

*Under the 1989 Act the subject matter would still be protected because it relates to international relations. The prosecution would have to prove the disclosure was unauthorised and damaging and it would do so by showing that it 'endangered the interests of the United Kingdom abroad' – in fact, the British official who had written the report was expelled from Nigeria after the story was published. The journalists could no longer defend themselves on the ground that the disclosure was in the interests of the state. Aitken's view, in a letter to the editors of McNae, is that 'the public interest defence and the arguments and evidence which could be introduced under it were crucial in securing our acquittal.'*

In the ABC case, mentioned above, the three defendants were charged with section 2 offences as well as section 1 offences. The defence claimed that every fact contained in the files was available or deducible from published sources. But the judge said it was not necessary to prove the information communicated by Berry was secret, or that Campbell and Aubrey knew it was secret. All three men were found guilty.

*Under the 1989 Act the information would still be protected because it relates to the intelligence services. There would still be no defence that the information was not secret because it had all been published before; the Government refused to include in the Act a defence of prior publication. The prosecution would have to prove disclosure was damaging either because it caused damage to the work of the intelligence services (which would be difficult on the facts of the case) or because it fell within a 'class or description' of information the unauthorised disclosure of which would be likely to have that effect (which might be much easier). The three men would have a defence if they could show that they did not know and had no reasonable cause to believe that disclosure would be damaging.*

In 1984 Sarah Tisdall, a clerk in the private office of the Foreign Secretary, was jailed for six months for photocopying memoranda written by the Defence Secretary, Michael Heseltine, and sending them to the *Guardian*, which used one of them as the basis for an article. As reported in chapter 24, the House of Lords said publication of the particular document posed no threat to national security, but there was a risk that the person who leaked that document might leak another, with much more serious consequences for national security.

*Under the 1989 Act the prosecution would have to prove disclosure was damaging, a hurdle the prosecution did not have in the Tisdall case. It could do so by proving the memoranda concerned defence and were 'such that' their unauthorised disclosure would be likely to be damaging. In the light of the judicial view expressed above this might seem a simple task, but the decision would have to be taken by a jury.*

In 1985 a civil servant, Clive Ponting, was accused of an offence under section 2 for passing papers on the sinking of the Argentinian warship the *General Belgrano* to an MP. He claimed his action was lawful because he had disclosed the information to 'a person to whom it is in the interest of the state his duty to communicate it'. The jury acquitted Ponting.

*The Government strongly opposed the inclusion of the 'interest of the state' protection in the new Act, and it is not included.*

In 1987 the Act was used against those involved in producing a BBC television programme dealing with the intelligence-gathering satellite Zircon and publishing the substance of the programme in the *New Statesman* magazine. The programme claimed that the Government had deceived Parliament by failing to acknowledge that it was spending £500 million on the project. The programme was one of a six-part series called 'The Secret Society', presented and scripted by Duncan Campbell, the journalist involved earlier in the *ABC* case, and produced by BBC Scotland. The Attorney-General initiated a police investigation into possible offences under the Official Secrets Act. Special Branch detectives with warrants under the Police and Criminal Evidence Act searched the offices of the *New Statesman* and Campbell's home, taking away documents. Detectives with a warrant under the Official Secrets Act searched the Glasgow offices of BBC Scotland and removed material (see Search warrants in chapter 24).

*Under the 1989 Act the information would still be protected and the rights of arrest and search contained in the 1911 Act have been extended to most parts of the 1989 Act.*

In 1987 also, a reporter, John Lee of the *Croydon Post*, was arrested after 'highly confidential' police documents about a rapist were found in a hotel bar and handed to the police. His counsel argued there was no evidence that the documents were given to Mr Lee in contravention of the Act and Mr Lee had not known the papers were covered by the Act. Mr Lee was acquitted.

*Under the 1989 Act the prosecution would have to show that disclosure of the documents would have one of a number of specific effects (such as impeding the prosecution of a suspected offender), in which case the reporter could say that he did not know and had no reasonable cause to believe that disclosure would have that effect. Or the prosecution could prove that the documents were 'such that' their unauthorised disclosure would be likely to have such effects, and in this case the journalist could say he did not know and had no reasonable cause to believe that the documents were ones to which the Act applied.*

## Defence Advisory Notices

*The system*

Guidance on national security is made available to the media by the Defence Press and Broadcasting Advisory Committee by means of Defence Advisory (DA) Notices. The system is advisory and voluntary and has no legal authority. Editors do not have to seek advice, nor do they have to take any advice that may be offered. In effect, the system is a code of self-censorship by the press in matters of national security.

The committee is composed of senior officials of the Ministry of Defence, the Home Office, and the Foreign Office, and nominees from newspapers, periodicals, news agencies, and broadcasting organisations. The chairman is the Permanent Under-Secretary of State for Defence. The press and broadcasting members select one of their number as chairman of their side of the committee. He acts as their spokesman at meetings of the committee and provides a point of day-to-day contact for the permanent secretary of the committee (the DA Notice secretary), who is normally a retired senior officer from the armed forces.

There are six standing DA Notices. They are written in general terms and describe the broad areas where the government and media members of the committee have agreed that guidance is required to avoid damage to national security. Machinery exists to issue DA Notices to protect specific pieces of information, but the machinery had not been used for many years as this book went to press. In 1991 the media widely reported, inaccurately, that a D Notice (as the notices were then known) had been issued after a computer containing Gulf War plans was stolen from an officer's car. In reality guidance to editors was given in accordance with an existing Notice.

Notices are distributed to the editors of national and provincial newspapers, radio and television organisations, and some publishers of periodicals, and books on defence and related subjects, who are invited to seek advice before publishing information that falls within the broad area of the DA Notices.

The DA Notice secretary is available at all times to give advice. His telephone number is 0171 218 2206. Editors, defence correspondents, other journalists, and authors frequently consult the secretary to check whether information considered for publication comes within a sensitive area. When the secretary learns of media interest in any of the DA Notice areas, he contacts the editor, publisher or programme maker.

As a result of consulting the secretary, editors sometimes feel able to get information into the paper that they might otherwise leave out. On the other hand, the secretary may advise editors not to publish information which is covered by a DA Notice but which has already appeared elsewhere. The secretary says that terrorists or other 'hostile organisations' get their information from a variety of sources and by piecing it together can build up a composite picture of a subject.

Suppose an editor consults the DA Notice secretary, who consults other civil servants; will the government not be tempted to seek an injunction preventing the editor from using the information? The secretary told the editors of *McNae* in 1995 that if a journalist who consulted him was injuncted, that would be the death knell of the system. But the secretary's conversations with officials were 'ring-fenced' and they would not initiate legal action as a result of an approach from him.

The committee has no statutory powers of enforcement and the final decision whether or not to publish always rests with the editor. The system has no direct link with the Official Secrets Acts, but an editor who publishes information which is the subject of a DA Notice knows that the Government regards that information as sensitive and realises, therefore, that he is risking action under the Acts.

On the other hand, an editor who complies with a DA Notice does not necessarily escape such action. As noted above, the DA Notice system is concerned only with national security matters but the Official Secrets Acts have much wider concerns, including, for example, breach of trust. The secretary will not advise on whether any publication will breach the Act – only whether it is a danger to the country's security.

In 1987 the integrity of the system was called into question after the Government was granted an injunction preventing the BBC from broadcasting the programme 'My Country: Right or Wrong' (see chapter 23). The BBC had followed DA Notice procedures and was confident the programme did not endanger national security. However, the Attorney-General learnt from a newspaper gossip column (as he told the House of

Commons) that a number of former members of the security services were to take part and on the eve of the programme obtained an injunction.

## The Notices

The six DA Notices in force since 1993 cover the following subjects:
1    operations, plans, and capabilities;
2    non-nuclear weapons and operational equipment;
3    nuclear weapons and equipment;
4    cyphers and secure communications;
5    identification of specific installations;
6    United Kingdom security and intelligence services..
    Each Notice describes what it is seeking to protect and why. DA Notice No 1 is given below as an example.

Operations, plans and capabilities

1 It is requested that disclosure or publication of highly classified information of the kind listed below should not be made without first seeking advice:
a.    details of present or future operations, methods, tactics, and contingency planning, to meet particular hostile situations and to counter threats of terrorist attacks;
b.    details of the state of readiness and operational capability of individual units or formations whose involvement in such operations is current or may be imminent;
c.    operational movements of such individual units or formations (as distinct from routine movements unconnected with operations);
d.    particulars of current or projected tactics, trials, techniques and training (including anti-interrogation training and operational techniques and tactics used to counter terrorism);
e.    details of defensive or counter-terrorist measures taken by individual installations, units or formations.
    2 *Rationale.* It is important not to publish information which could be damaging to national security by giving a potential enemy important strategic or operational advantages; which could be exploited by terrorists to devise counter-measures with the consequence that attacks which might otherwise have been frustrated could prove successful; or which could compromise counter-terrorist operations, endanger lives, or put sources at risk.

Before 1993, the Notices were issued to editors marked 'Private and confidential' (for reasons that are difficult to understand) but though they

are still issued direct to editors the public can obtain copies from the
Secretary, DPBAC, Room 2235, Ministry of Defence, Main Building,
Whitehall, London SW1A 2HB.

## The reporter's duty

The reporter's duty is to report. It is particularly important to remember
this in cases where the nature of the report is such that consideration at a
high executive level in the office will obviously be required before
publication is decided upon.

The uttering of defamatory statements or the disclosure of state secrets
is not an occasion when the reporter puts down his pencil.

It is tempting to government departments to use the Official Secrets Act
to prevent the publication of information merely because it is embarrassing.
But, as defence counsel in the *ABC* case said, it is the task of a vigorous
press 'to examine, probe, question, and find out if there are mistakes and
abuses and to embarrass governments, of whatever complexion, and not
just accept handouts from people in high places and churn out what they
are told to say'.

Responsibility for what goes into the paper is the editor's and a note on
the copy calling attention to the need for vetting is all that is called for. In
making his decisions the editor requires to have the fullest report of the
circumstances.

## Questions

1   State the provisions of section 1 of the Official Secrets Act 1911.
2   What is meant by a 'prohibited place' in the Official Secrets Act 1911?
3   What classes of information are covered by the Official Secrets Act
    1989?
4   A reporter on a local newspaper writes a story, based on information
    he has received indirectly from a member of the security services, that
    officers given a warrant to search a house under the Security Services
    Act 1989 have broken into the wrong one. What defence does the
    reporter have?
5   A finance reporter on a national newspaper writes a story revealing a
    change to be made in tomorrow's Budget. The story originates from
    a Treasury leak. Has the journalist committed an offence under the
    Act? Any other legal problems?
6   What legal force, if any, does a DA Notice have?
7   List the subjects covered by the DA Notices.

| Class of information | Who does it apply to? | The offence | Disclosure damaging if | Defences |
|---|---|---|---|---|
| *Information resulting from unauthorised disclosures or entrusted in confidence (section 5)* | A person into whose possession the information protected under Classes 1 to 5 has come, as a result of having been (a) disclosed (whether to him or another) by a crown servant or government contractor without lawful authority; *or* (b) entrusted to him by a crown servant or government contractor on terms requiring it to be held in confidence or in circumstances in which the crown servant or government contractor could reasonably expect that it would be so held; *or* (c) disclosed (whether to him or another) without lawful authority by a person to whom it was entrusted as above | Guilty if he discloses it without lawful authority knowing, or having reasonable cause to believe, that it is protected against disclosure by the provisions of the Act and that it came into his possession as stated  The offence in respect of Classes 1, 2, and 3 is not committed unless (a) the disclosure is damaging; *and* (b) the person makes the disclosure knowing, or having reasonable cause to believe, that it would be damaging  The offence is not committed if the information was disclosed as mentioned in (a) or (c) in column 2 but the person making the disclosure was not a | Same test as with crown servant or government contractor in Classes 1, 2, and 3. Damage is assumed in Classes 4 and 5 | |

| Class of information | Who does it apply to? | The offence | Disclosure damaging if | Defences |
|---|---|---|---|---|
| *Information resulting from unauthorised disclosures or entrusted in confidence (section 5) continued* | | British citizen or the disclosure did not take place in the United Kingdom, Channel Islands, Isle of Man, or a colony | | |
| *Class 1 Security and intelligence (section 1). Defined as: The work of, or in support of, the security and intelligence services or any part of them, and references to information relating to security or intelligence include references to information held or transmitted by those services or by persons in support of, or any part of them* | A person who is or has been: (a) a member of the security and intelligence services; *or* (b) a person notified that he is subject to the provisions of this subsection | Guilty if without lawful authority he discloses any information, document, or other article relating to security or intelligence which came into his possession because of his work as a member of any of those services or in the course of his work while the notification is or was in force | No proof of damage required | At the time of the alleged offence the defendant did not know, and had no reasonable cause to believe, that the information related to security or intelligence |

| Class of information | Who does it apply to? | The offence | Disclosure damaging if | Defences |
|---|---|---|---|---|
| *Class 1 continued* | A person who is or has been a crown servant or government contractor | Guilty if without lawful authority he makes a damaging disclosure of any information etc. relating to security or intelligence which came into his possession because of his work | (a) it causes damage to the work of, or of any part of, the security and intelligence services; *or* (b) it is of information etc. which is such that its unauthorised disclosure would be likely to cause such damage or which falls within a class or description of information etc. the unauthorised disclosure of which would be likely to have that effect | At the time of the alleged offence the defendant (a) did not know, and had no reasonable cause to believe, that the information related to security or intelligence *or* (b) that disclosure would be damaging |

| Class of information | Who does it apply to? | The offence | Disclosure damaging if | Defences |
|---|---|---|---|---|
| *Class 2 Defence (section 2) Defined as:* (a) *the size, shape, organisation, logistics, order of battle, deployment, operations, state of readiness and training of the armed forces of the Crown;* (b) *the weapons, stores or other equipment of those forces and the invention, development, production and operation of such equipment and research relating to it;* (c) *defence policy and strategy and military planning and intelligence;* (d) *plans and measures for the maintenance of essential supplies and services that are or would be needed in time of war* | A person who is or has been a crown servant or government contractor | Guilty if without lawful authority he makes a damaging disclosure of any information relating to defence which is or has been in his possession by virtue of his work | (a) it damages the capability of, or of any part of, the armed forces of the Crown to carry out their tasks or leads to loss of life or injury to members of those forces or serious damage to the equipment or installations of those forces; *or* (b) it endangers the interests of the United Kingdom abroad, seriously obstructs the promotion or protection by the United Kingdom of those interests, or endangers the safety of British citizens abroad; *or* (c) it is of information etc. which is such that its unauthorised disclosure would be likely to have any of those effects | At the time of the alleged offence the defendant (a) did not know, and had no reasonable cause to believe, that the information etc related to defence; *or* (b) that its disclosure would be damaging |

| Class of information | Who does it apply to? | The offence | Disclosure damaging if | Defences |
|---|---|---|---|---|
| *Class 3  International relations (section 3). Defined as:  The relations between states, between international organisations or between one or more states and one or more such organisations and includes any matter relating to a state other than the United Kingdom or to an international organisation which is capable of affecting the relations of the United Kingdom with another state or with an international organisation* | A person who is or has been a crown servant or government contractor | Guilty if without lawful authority he makes a damaging disclosure of (a) any information etc relating to international relations; or (b) any confidential information etc which was obtained from a state other than the United Kingdom or an international organisation where such information has come into his possession because of his work | (a) it endangers the interests of the United Kingdom abroad, seriously obstructs the promotion or protection by the United Kingdom of those interests, or endangers the safety of British citizens abroad; *or* (b) it is of information which is such that its unauthorised disclosure would be likely to have any of those effects. In the case of information under (b) in column 3, its nature or contents may be sufficient to establish that the information was 'such that' etc. | At the time of the alleged offence the defendant did not know, and had no reasonable cause to believe, that the information was such as is mentioned in column 3 or that its disclosure would be damaging |

| Class of information | Who does it apply to? | The offence | Disclosure damaging if | Defences |
| --- | --- | --- | --- | --- |
| *Class 4. Crime (section 4). Not defined* | A person who is or has been a crown servant or government contractor | Guilty if without lawful authority he discloses any information etc to which this section applies and which came into his possession because of his work This section applies to any information, document, or other article (a) the disclosure of which (i) results in the commission of an offence; *or* (ii) facilitates an escape from legal custody or the doing of any other act prejudicial to the safekeeping of persons in legal custody; *or* (iii) impedes the prevention or detection of offences or the apprehension or prosecution of suspected offenders; or (b) which is such that its unauthorised disclosure would be | No proof of damage required | At the time of an alleged offence under (a) the defendant did not know, and had no reasonable cause to believe, that the disclosure would have any of the effects mentioned At the time of any alleged offence under (b), the defendant did not know, and had no reasonable cause to believe, that the information was information to which this section applies |

| Class of information | Who does it apply to? | The offence | Disclosure damaging if | Defences |
|---|---|---|---|---|
| *Class 4 continued* | | likely to have any of those effects | | |
| *Class 5 Special investigation powers (section 4 also). Not defined* | A person who is or has been a crown servant or government contractor | Guilty if without lawful authority he discloses any information to which this section applies and which came into his possession through his work<br><br>This section applies to any information obtained by execution of a warrant permitting phone-tapping or other surveillance or searches by the police or security services; or to information relating to the obtaining of information by such means; or to any document 'which is or has been used or held for use in' any interception | No proof of damage required | At the time of the alleged offence, the defendant did not know, and had no reasonable cause to believe, that the information was information to which this section applies |

| Class of information | Who does it apply to? | The offence | Disclosure damaging if | Defences |
|---|---|---|---|---|
| Class 6 *Information entrusted in confidence to other states or international organisations (section 6)* | A person into whose possession information has come and that information (i) relates to security or intelligence, defence, or international relations; *and* (ii) has been communicated in confidence by or on behalf of the United Kingdom to another state or to an international organisation and has come into the person's possession as a result of having been disclosed (whether to him or another) without the authority of that state or organisation or, in the case of an organisation, of a state which is a member of it | Guilty if he makes a damaging disclosure of the information knowing, or having reasonable cause to believe, that it is such as is mentioned in column 2, that it has come into his possession as mentioned, and that its disclosure would be damaging The offence does not occur if the information is disclosed with lawful authority or has previously been made available to the public with the authority of the state or organisation concerned or, in the case of an organisation, of a state which is a member of it | Same test as for crown servant disclosing information on security, intelligence, defence, or international relations | |

| Class of information | Who does it apply to? | The offence | Disclosure damaging if | Defences |
|---|---|---|---|---|
| *Official Secrets Act 1911* | A person who has information in his possession which he knows or has reasonable cause to believe has come into his possession as a result of a contravention of Section 1 of the Official Secrets Act 1911 | Guilty if without lawful authority he discloses the information | | |

# 31  Privacy

Privacy is the right of the individual to be protected against intrusion into his personal life or affairs, or those of his family, by direct physical means or by publication of information. This was the definition adopted 'for working purposes' by the Calcutt Committee on Privacy and Related Matters, which reported in 1990 (see Proposals for new laws, below).

But if there is such a right, it is not one that is protected by the law of England. For example, a journalist can lawfully name a person involved in a news event without getting permission, however embarrassing that may be to the person concerned. In 1994 Camelot, organiser of the National Lottery, was unable to prevent newspapers from publishing the name of the winner of a £17.8 million jackpot.

Similarly, a photographer can lawfully take a picture of anyone and a newspaper can print it without getting permission. Thus the Duchess of York had no remedy against British newspapers that published pictures of her topless with a friend while on holiday in France, though she won damages for infringement of privacy against a French newspaper in a French court. The photographs were taken with a long-range camera.

There is no law, apart from trespass and breach of confidence (see below), preventing the placing of a concealed transmitter (a bug) or recorder on private property.

There is no law of privacy to prevent the interception of mobile phone messages, except in the circumstances outlawed by the Wireless Telegraphy Act 1949 (see below) or breach of confidence (see chapter 23). In 1992 recorded conversations between the Prince of Wales and a married woman, Camilla Parker Bowles (the Camilla tapes), revealed that the two were intimate, but there was no evidence that wireless apparatus had been used 'with intent' to obtain information, as the Act requires.

Nor does the law catch the tapping of landline phones, except in the circumstances outlawed by the Interception of Telecommunications Act 1985 (see below) or breach of confidence (see chapter 23). Thus David Mellor, then National Heritage Secretary, had no remedy when his private conversations with an actress, Antonia de Sancha, were recorded and published.

The absence of any law of privacy was graphically illustrated in 1990 in the Gorden Kaye case. The television star was in hospital with severe injuries to the head and brain when a reporter and a photographer from *Sunday Sport* got into his room, ignoring notices.

There they 'interviewed' him, using a tape recorder, and used a flash to take pictures of him showing his scars. 'Interviewed' is in quotation marks because the evidence was that he was in no fit state to be interviewed and a quarter-of-an-hour later had no recollection of the incident. Nurses tried in vain to persuade the journalists to leave and they were finally ejected by security staff.

When the case came to court Lord Justice Bingham, one of the judges (later Lord Chief Justice), said: 'The defendants' conduct towards the plaintiff was a monstrous invasion of his privacy … If ever a person has a right to be let alone by strangers with no public interest to pursue, it must surely be when he lies in hospital recovering from brain surgery and in no more than partial command of his faculties.'

Yet however gross this invasion of his privacy it did not entitle him to a remedy in English law, said the judge.

Unjustified infringement of privacy is prohibited by various *ethical codes*. For example, the Press Complaints Commission code, framed by the newspaper and periodical industry, declares: 'Intrusions and inquiries into an individual's private life without his or her consent are not generally acceptable and publication can only be justified in the public interest.'

But this code, applying to the conduct of print journalists, cannot be enforced by legal sanctions. In the case of broadcasters, however, legal sanctions can result from infringing various codes.

From a case in 1994 where Granada, a television company, challenged the Broadcasting Complaints Commission, a regulatory authority, it appears that if there were a law of privacy the courts would take the view that it would be infringed if private matters were published even though they had once been in the public domain (see chapter 33, section on Privacy).

A series of news stories in the 1980s and 1990s led to a demand by politicians and others that there should be greater protection for privacy, and a number of suggestions have been put forward.

Most journalists have opposed these suggestions strongly because they believe laws intended to protect the privacy of private individuals would in fact be used to prevent the media from revealing matters in the public interest, such as the misdeeds of wealthy and powerful people.

Though there is no specific protection for privacy, a number of laws may give limited protection. These include trespass and harassment in addition to other laws already mentioned, the most important being defamation, criminal libel, breach of confidence, copyright, laws regulating press reports of court proceedings, the Wireless Telegraphy Act 1949, and the Interception of Communications Act 1985. See also the Data Protection Act 1984 (next chapter).

The Protection from Harassment Act 1997 aims to provide protection to the victims of stalkers, disruptive neighbours, and racial abusers, but journalists claimed it is also capable of providing protection for villains from the attentions of investigative reporters (see below).

## Trespass

Trespass is a direct injury to land, to goods, or to the person. At first sight it would appear to impose significant restrictions on journalists' conduct, but the impression is largely illusory.

*Trespass to land* is a wrongful interference with the possession of 'land', which includes a building such as a house.

It is a tort – a *civil* wrong, and the occupier of the land can sue for damages or get an injunction to stop it. No one else can.

In the case mentioned above involving the TV actor Gorden Kaye, Kaye could not sue for trespass because, as a hospital patient, he was not legally the occupier of the land. The hospital authority was.

The person who sues must show *unauthorised* physical entry upon the land. In 1977 Lord Bernstein, chairman of Granada Television, failed to get damages from a firm of aerial photographers who, he said, had trespassed in the airspace above his property and invaded his right to privacy by taking photographs of his house. The court found that, even if the aeroplane had flown over Lord Bernstein's property, no trespass was committed.

As a result of this need for the occupier of the land to show unauthorised entry, a journalist cannot be sued for trespass for using binoculars to watch another person on his own land, or photographing that person on his own land, provided the journalist did not enter the land – although he might be sued if he were on a highway that remained in the possession of the adjoining occupiers.

Note that a journalist's entry is unauthorised if he has obtained permission to enter by fraud – for example, by pretending to be a doctor. And even if his entry is legal, he may be trespassing if he takes advantage of his admission to do things, such as carrying out a search of the property, not covered by his permission to enter.

Even if damages are awarded, they are not likely to be substantial. After all, how much actual damage to land is done, for example, by fixing a microphone to a bed?

But if the trespass has taken some particularly outrageous form the court may award heavy damages, known as exemplary or punitive damages. It may be that a journalist who forced his way into a house to get a story would be liable to pay substantial damages, even though he had done little or no damage to the house.

In addition to seeking damages, the occupier of the land can use reasonable force to eject the trespasser. The police may lawfully assist, though they have no duty to do so and when doing so are not protected by the special powers and privileges of constables.

So there is a civil action for trespass but there is no general *criminal* offence. After an intruder was found in the Queen's bedroom in Buckingham Palace in 1982, consideration was given to the creation of an offence of trespassing on residential property in a manner likely to cause the occupier alarm and distress, but no such law has been made.

The changes proposed by the Calcutt Committee would, if enacted, in effect create a law of criminal trespass for journalists.

It is convenient to mention here provisions relating to trespass in the Criminal Justice and Public Order Act 1994, though these provisions are related to public order rather than privacy.

The Act created an offence of aggravated trespass, but this involves trespassing on land in the open air and doing anything intended to intimidate, obstruct, or disrupt some lawful activity. The law is aimed primarily at hunt saboteurs and those protesting about road developments, such as the M11. It carries a penalty of up to three months' imprisonment.

What is the position of the journalist covering this type of activity? A senior police officer can direct anyone to leave if he reasonably believes the person is committing, has committed, or intends to commit an offence. Failure to leave can be punished by imprisonment or a fine or both. The journalist may have a defence that he had a reasonable excuse.

The first journalists charged under the Act had the cases against them thrown out by Leeds magistrates in 1996.

The Act gives the police new powers to deal with raves and with trespassory assemblies. They can direct those organising or attending to leave and they can stop and redirect any one on the way to such an event. Failure to comply with such a direction can lead to a fine.

*Trespass to goods* . If a journalist visiting a contact picks up and reads a letter on the contact's desk, while the latter has been called out of the room, the journalist commits a trespass to the goods and is liable. Only the person in possession of the letter can bring an action – even if someone else is injured by the information disclosed. The journalist cannot be sued for reading the letter while it is lying on the desk.

*Trespass to the person* involves actual physical interference with a person, or threats of it. Such action, however, would probably lead to a criminal prosecution rather than a civil action.

## Harassment

In 1996 Diana, Princess of Wales, obtained an injunction against a freelance photographer whom she accused of persistent harassment. She was relying on the precedent of a case in the Court of Appeal in the previous year, when a man was consistently pestering a woman and the court stated that it would restrain conduct which might not be unlawful if it was necessary to protect 'legitimate interests'.

Until recently it was doubted that the English law recognised a tort of harassment, but in the 1995 case referred to Sir Thomas Bingham, Master of the Rolls, said: ' ... in the light of later authority ... the view [cannot] be upheld that there is no tort of harassment.'

Under the Protection from Harassment Act 1997 harassers can be arrested and imprisoned. The Act declares that a person must not pursue 'a course of conduct' that amounts to harassment of another and which he knows or ought to know amounts to harassment. The Act does not define harassment, but says it includes 'alarming the person or causing the person distress'.

The Act introduces two new criminal offences and a civil measure. A high level offence, not expected to affect the work of journalists, is intended to catch the most serious cases of harassment, where, on more than one occasion, the conduct is so threatening that victims fear for their safety. This carries a maximum penalty of five years in prison, or an unlimited fine, or both.

A lower level offence catches harassment which may not cause the victim to fear that violence will be used. The action has to have occurred at least twice. This carries a maximum penalty of six months in prison, or a £5,000 fine, or both.

For these offences to have been committed, there does not have to be an *intention* on the part of the harasser to cause the victim to fear violence or feel harassed. The prosecution has to prove only that the conduct occurred in circumstances where a reasonable person would have realised that this would be the effect.

Both offences are immediately arrestable, without a warrant, and the police are able to search the harasser's property.

The courts would also have the power to make a restraining order immediately after convicting a person of either of the two offences. A breach of this order is a criminal offence with a maximum penalty of five years in prison, or an unlimited fine, or both.

There is also a civil remedy. Victims are able to take action themselves to stop the behaviour described in the low level offence by obtaining an injunction. For example, a journalist might be banned from telephoning the 'victim'. A breach of the injunction would be a criminal offence, carrying the power of arrest, with a maximum penalty of five years in prison, or an unlimited fine, or both.

The Home Secretary said the law would not prevent people going about their lawful activity, and the legitimate work of the police, the security service, journalists, and others would be protected. He was referring to section 1(3)(c), which says that the course of conduct will not amount to an offence if 'in the particular circumstances' it is reasonable.

But journalists feared that the legislation could be exploited by those who wanted to gag the press or stop an investigation by a particular journalist. The media could effectively be restrained by police powers of arrest and by applications for injunctions by those who believe they might be subject to media harassment, even if no prosecution is brought, and even if the journalist can successfully defend his conduct as reasonable in particular circumstances.

There have been complaints that journalists in pursuit of a story have harassed people reluctant to be interviewed by massing on the pavement outside their homes.

An Act of 1875 makes it a criminal offence, among other things, to besiege people's homes or workplaces with a view to forcing them to do something against their will. But there is no record of this Act being used against journalists.

The police normally move the press aside to allow people to pass, using powers under the Highways Act 1980 to prevent 'wilful' obstruction of the free passage along a highway. These powers include arrest.

Photographers are sometimes arrested and charged under the Public Order Act 1986, which makes it an offence to use 'threatening, abusive, or insulting words or behaviour' or disorderly behaviour ... within the hearing or sight of a person likely to be caused harassment, alarm or distress'.

Problems generally occur when photographers are covering demonstrations or marches and the police believe their presence is likely to cause a breach of the peace because they may be attacked by demonstrators.

The Criminal Justice and Public Order Act 1994 created a new offence of intentional harassment; that is, using threatening, abusive, or insulting behaviour, *intending* to cause a person harassment, alarm, or distress. There is a defence that the accused's conduct was reasonable.

## Defamation

Reporters and photographers embarking on conduct that might be considered intrusive must be careful to ensure that the resulting story or picture does not convey a meaning defamatory of the person concerned (see chapters 18-20).

The divorced Duchess of Bedford received substantial damages from the *Daily Mail*, which reported falsely that she had been to a marriage bureau. The defamatory 'statement' was that she was lacking in friends and social resources.

A Colonel Allan, of the Royal Military Academy, accepted an apology and his legal costs in settlement of an action against the *Observer* magazine and *Express* newspapers for an advertisement for paint headlined 'Put a guard around your home'. A photograph showed Col Allan in full regimental dress and seated on a horse. The imputation was that he had behaved in an ungentlemanly way by allowing his picture to be used for advertising.

But in the absence of any defamatory meaning, the law of libel cannot help to protect privacy.

## Criminal libel

A journalist might be prosecuted for criminal libel if his revelations were so damning about an individual that, nominally, a breach of the peace might occur (see chapter 21).

But this remedy is available only if the story is defamatory and untrue and the journalist cannot show it is true and in the public interest.

## Malicious falsehood

In the case concerning the television actor Gorden Kaye (see above) the *Sunday Sport* planned to say in an article Kaye had agreed to be interviewed and photographed.

The Court of Appeal decided the article would amount to a malicious falsehood (see chapter 21) and made an order that until the matter came for trial the *Sport* should not publish anything that could convey to a reader that Kaye had voluntarily permitted the taking of photographs.

But the remedy is of very limited value. In this case the court was appalled by the conduct of *Sunday Sport*'s journalists and appeared to go to extraordinary lengths in an attempt to help Kaye.

## Breach of confidence

A journalist writing about a person's private life must be careful if he has received his information in confidence, either from the person himself or from someone who gained the information, directly or indirectly, from that person (see chapter 23).

In 1967 the Duchess of Argyll stopped the *People* newspaper from publishing her husband's intimate account of their marriage, which had ended. The courts said the Duke had an obligation of confidence towards her that resulted from their marriage. The judge said: 'No spouse or lover can exploit the verbal indiscretions of the double bed.'

'Lover' can include a lover of the same sex. In 1988 a woman was given leave to sue the *Daily Mail* for damages for a story about her love affair with another woman. The judge said: 'To most people the details of their sex lives are high on the list of those matters which they regard as confidential.'

Thus matters of privacy can sometimes lead to injunctions for breach of confidence. But journalists need to understand the difference between the two concepts. Privacy is concerned with the nature of the information whereas confidence is concerned with the way in which the information was obtained.

When in 1994 Camelot, organiser of the National Lottery, was attempting to prevent the media from publishing the name of a winner (see above) it sought an injunction for breach of confidence. But there was no evidence that the press, which had learnt the name, had done so as the result of any disclosure by a person with an obligation of confidence.

In 1994 also the Princess of Wales used the law of confidence to reach a settlement with a photographer who had used a concealed camera to photograph her exercising in a gymnasium. She successfully sued also the Mirror Group Newspapers, which had published the photographs. The publication was widely criticised as being a gross breach of confidence, but it is far from clear what the outcome would have been had the matter gone to court.

## Copyright

If the journalist is using copyright letters, other documents, or photographs snatched from a family album he must be alert to the possibility of an action for infringement of copyright (see chapter 29).

## Court reporting restrictions

This book has explained the restrictions under which journalists work when reporting court proceedings, and the protection given to juveniles and the victims of sexual assaults, among others (see in particular chapters 5, 6, 8, and 9).

Contravention of these restrictions normally leads to prosecution before a criminal court.

However, the person who believes he has been injured by such a contravention may be able to sue. In 1994 a rape victim won £10,000 damages from a local freesheet that gave sufficient details about her to enable her to be identified. In so doing, the paper was liable for the tort of breach of statutory duty.

## Wireless Telegraphy Act 1949

The Act prohibits the use without authority of wireless apparatus with intent to obtain information about the contents of any message, and prohibits the disclosure of any such information. The Act has been used against journalists listening in systematically to police radio messages. It is probably ineffective against journalists casually scanning the airwaves.

## Interception of Communications Act 1985

The Act prohibits unauthorised interception of public, postal, and telecommunications systems. It covers the situation where wires are tapped between the private property they serve and the premises of the telecommunications operator. In the case where a journalist tapped the phone of the actress Antonia de Sancha to record telephone conversations between her and David Mellor, a government minister, he used a telephone extension leading from de Sancha's flat to the garden. The 1985 Act did not apply because no tap was put on the line between the private property and the operator and in any case the tap was 'authorised' because de Sancha's landlord had given the journalist permission.

## Data Protection Act

A journalist using personal information gleaned from data stored in his computer lays himself open to a claim for compensation if the person concerned suffers damage as a result of the unauthorised disclosure of data. Under the Criminal Justice and Public Order Act 1994, the journalist is guilty of a criminal offence if he knowingly procures a disclosure of the data or if he sells or offers to sell the data (see next chapter).

## Proposals for new laws

The judge in the Gorden Kaye case was only one among a number of voices calling for greater protection of privacy. In 1989 Margaret Thatcher, the

Prime Minister, invited Sir David Calcutt QC to set up a committee and 'in the light of recent public concern about intrusions into the private lives of individuals by certain sectors of the press' to recommend how to give greater protection to individual privacy.

The committee reported in 1990 and its recommendations were amended by Sir David in a Review in 1992. The following year an all-party National Heritage Select Committee reported and the Government issued a Consultation Paper. (The references to all four papers are given in the Book List.)

A number of leading judges spoke individually of the need for privacy legislation. They included Lord Bingham, whose comments in the Gorden Kaye case are quoted above and who in 1996, by then Lord Chief Justice, said that if Parliament did not legislate to introduce a right to privacy, then judges might develop the common law in that direction.

New criminal offences recommended by the Calcutt Committee were:

1    entering or remaining on private property without the consent of the lawful occupant, with intent to obtain personal information with a view to its publication;

2    (a)  placing a surveillance device on private property without the consent of the lawful occupant, with intent to obtain personal information with a view to its publication;

    (b)  using a surveillance device (whether on private property or elsewhere) in relation to an individual who is on private property, without the consent of the individual to such use, with intent to obtain personal information about that individual with a view to its publication;

3    taking a photograph, or recording the voice, of an individual who is on private property, without his consent to the taking or recording, with a view to its publication and with intent that the individual shall be identifiable.

Calcutt recommended that a person 'having a sufficient interest' should be able to apply for an injunction against the publication of any material obtained by means of any of the offences. If the material had been published, the person would be able to get damages or an account of profits.

The report also recommended any criminal court should have the power to make an order prohibiting the identification of any person against whom an offence was alleged to have been committed.

## Questions

1    What difficulties confront the person attempting to sue for trespass someone who has intruded upon his privacy?

2  A wealthy villain has been telephoned twice by an investigative reporter. What legal action can he take against him?

3  Suppose the criminal offences proposed by the Calcutt Committee become law. What effect will they have on the work of journalists?

# 32 Data Protection Act

As stated in the last chapter, there is no general right of privacy in English law, but there is a right of privacy for the vast amount of information held about people on computer. This is provided by the Data Protection Act 1984.

The Act made it an offence for a data holder (see below) to disclose data to someone he knew was not entitled to receive it.

The Act aims to ensure that people handling personal data comply with eight Data Protection Principles, which are included in the Act.

They are:

1   The information to be contained in personal data shall be obtained, and personal data shall be processed, fairly and lawfully.
2   Personal data shall be held only for one or more specified and lawful purposes.
3   Personal data held for any purpose or purposes shall not be used or disclosed in any manner incompatible with that purpose or those purposes.
4   Personal data held for any purpose or purposes shall be adequate, relevant, and not excessive in relation to that purpose or those purposes.
5   Personal data shall be accurate and, where necessary, kept up to date.
6   Personal data held for any purpose or purposes shall not be kept for longer than is necessary for that purpose of those purposes.
7   An individual shall be entitled, at reasonable intervals and without undue delay or expense, to be informed by any data user whether he holds personal data of which that individual is the subject; and to access to any such data held by a data user; and, where appropriate, to have such data corrected or erased.

8    Appropriate security measures shall be taken against unauthorised access to, or alteration, disclosure, or destruction of, personal data and against accidental loss or destruction of personal data.

The Act requires those who process personal data on computer which relates to living individuals to register with the Data Protection Registrar, who has the duty to ensure that the principles are observed. 'Data users' include magistrates courts, the police, and local authorities and also all newspapers that keep personal data about people on computer.

A data user who wishes to pass information to a third party, such as the press, must include such disclosures on its registration form under the Act. On the registration form the organisation has to tick a box that says: 'Disclosure of data to providers of publicly available information, including press and media'.

The Home Office advised all magistrates courts to register (see chapter 12), but four years after the Act took effect newspapers were still having difficulties. In 1989 magistrates at Colchester and Southend said they were unable to release lists of defendants' names and ages and the charges because the information was now on computer.

The local newspapers had to call on the Home Secretary, the Lord Chancellor, and the local MPs before the courts agreed to comply with the Home Office advice.

In another area, a court clerk who had registered correctly under the Act refused to give information over the telephone on the ground that he could not be certain he was speaking to a genuine reporter and not an impostor.

It is true that, as stated above, the 1984 Act says it is an offence to disclose data to someone not listed, but the disclosure must be made 'knowingly or recklessly'. It seems extremely unlikely that if the clerk is told the journalist's identity and has no reason to doubt his good faith he will commit an offence by disclosure.

However, the extent to which registration enables a data user legally to disclose information to the press is open to question.

In 1989 police in the Isle of Man, whose data protection law is based on the British Act, began to refuse to issue personal details of accident victims held on police computers. Without such information journalists were unable even to obtain a condition report from a hospital.

The change followed pressure from the Isle of Man Registrar, who believed that while the police were entitled to release information they had received on a statutory basis, they could not release information given to them voluntarily in circumstances where the person involved was not aware that information would be given to the press. To do so would be to contravene the first Data Protection Principle, concerned with obtaining and processing information fairly.

The police later resumed their former practice but the Registrar takes the view that if he were to receive a complaint from, for example, someone who believed his privacy had been infringed by being named as an accident victim, he would have to investigate the complaint and, if necessary, take action against the data user (the police).

On this understanding of the law, it is possible to argue that, where the mayor is driving with his teenage secretary in the early hours and they are involved in an accident, the police can lawfully pass on the identity of the driver, who has given information under the provisions of the Road Traffic Act 1972, but not of the secretary.

But suppose the police release information, even when they have received it on a statutory basis, for a purpose of which the informant was not aware? Does that contravene the fairness principle?

In the United Kingdom the Registrar reported in her 1996 report that she was considering a complaint from a motorist, Ms X, who was involved in a minor accident. She reported the matter to the police, as required by law, and was asked to give a statement which included such details as her address, her age, and description of her vehicle.

She said she understood that these details were provided to the police to enable them to investigate the accident and she was given no indication that the information would have any wider circulation than was necessary for that purpose. Later several local newspapers carried the story and gave her personal details. The Registrar reported that she was currently investigating the case.

Irrespective of the above, the police have exemption under the Act allowing disclosure of data where failure to make the disclosure would be likely to prejudice the prevention or detection of crime or apprehension or prosecution of offenders.

People have the right to find out whether an organisation, including a newspaper or broadcasting station, holds information about them and if so what it is. They make an access request, and the item must be supplied within 40 days of the request. They can have it corrected if it is wrong and claim compensation if they have suffered damage.

Some journalists working in electronic newsrooms see the Act as an impediment to investigative journalism. In an article David Boulton, head of news and current affairs at Granada Television, posed the situation where a powerful villain was under investigation by a computerised news team. The villain suspected former associates had informed against him, and their information was stored on time-coded tape in the electronic news centre. He demanded access.

The information supplied to the reporters has not yet been checked. Some of it is clearly libellous. Truth and untruth, copper-bottomed fact and malicious fantasy are intermixed, not yet sorted and separated in the complex editorial process it must all undergo before any of it is broadcast ... There's an injunction, a gagging writ...

As a result, journalists working with computers are advised not to commit to their computer files anything they would not wish to be made public. These facts must continue to be recorded in the reporter's notebook.

Similarly, computerised newspaper libraries should contain only information that has been published and is therefore a matter of public record. Unpublished information, such as obituaries written in advance of the subject's death, should be retained on paper.

The Act preserves the confidentiality of journalists' sources by stipulating that a data user does not have to comply with an access request if he cannot do so without disclosing information relating to another individual who can be identified by that information.

A person who suffers damage as a result of inaccurate data is entitled to compensation from the organisation holding the data on computer. It is a defence to prove that the organisation took reasonable care to ensure the accuracy of the data at the material time.

A person is also entitled to compensation if he suffers damage as a result of the unauthorised disclosure of data.

The requirement to register affects managements principally, but it may be that the journalist is affected too. If a newspaper allows an investigative journalist to maintain computer files to which he or she alone has access, it may be that the management or the journalist is responsible for registering. The best solution in this case is for the contract to define which party controls the use of the data.

The Act includes wide powers of entry and inspection which may be exercised by the Registrar for the detection of offences.

Although, as stated, the Act made it an offence for a data holder to disclose data to someone he knew was not entitled to receive it, no specific criminal offence was committed by people obtaining such information.

In 1992 the *Sun* newspaper was able to reveal, without infringing the Act, that the Chancellor of the Exchequer at that time, Norman Lamont, had exceeded his Access card limit 21 times, information held on computer which could have been obtained only by improper disclosure.

But the Criminal Justice and Public Order Act 1994 created three new offences that might affect the work of journalists. They were: procuring the disclosure of data covered by the 1984 Act, knowing or believing this to contravene the Act; selling the data; or offering to sell the data or information extracted from it.

In 1995 the UK adopted the European Community Directive on Data Protection, which will require changes to be made in the law. The object of the Directive is to ensure that member states protect the 'fundamental rights and freedoms of natural persons, and in particular their right to privacy with respect to the processing of personal data'.

States may provide derogations (exemptions) from the provisions of the law for the processing of personal data carried out solely for journalistic purposes but only if they are necessary to reconcile the right to privacy with 'the rules governing freedom of expression'. These 'rules' include Article 10 of the European Convention on Human Rights (see chapter 1). As this edition of *McNae* went to press, a consultation process was continuing to decide how the Directive should be given effect in UK law.

## Questions

1   How may the Data Protection Act present difficulties for the reporter attempting to obtain information?
2   The *Downtown Gazette* has prepared in advance an obituary for Mr Big, a citizen with an eventful past, and has the 'obit' stored on its computer. What dangers or difficulties does this hold for the *Gazette*?
3   What criminal offence or offences can be committed by a freelance journalist who obtains personal data stored on computer?

# 33 The broadcast journalist

Broadcast journalists encounter the same legal minefield in presenting news and features as their contemporaries in print. For example, Channel 3 (formerly Tyne-Tees) Television was fined £10,000 in 1997 for the inclusion in a news broadcast of a few words which might have inadvertently led to the identification of an alleged victim of indecent assault (see chapter 8).

Additionally, there are some restrictions which are peculiar to broadcasting.

Commercial television is tightly controlled in general by the Broadcasting Act 1990 which, among other things, lays down that the Independent Television Commission (ITC) shall do all it can to ensure that nothing is included in programmes which offends against good taste or decency, or is likely to encourage or incite crime, or to lead to disorder, or be offensive to public feeling. The Act also stipulates that news is presented with accuracy and impartiality and that impartiality is preserved in matters of political or industrial controversy or current public policy. A code giving guidance in these matters has been prepared by the ITC. Both the ITC and the Radio Authority have power to force a company to broadcast an apology, to impose fines, or even to revoke a licence to broadcast. In 1994 the ITC fined Granada Television £500,000 for breaches of its programme and sponsorship codes.

BBC output is similarly controlled through the licence agreement which is part of its charter. The Home Secretary also has power to order that any item should not be broadcast either by the BBC or by the commercial companies.

## Libel

The Broadcasting Act 1990 re-asserts that for the purposes of defamation, publication by broadcast is to be treated as libel rather than slander.

It is sometimes assumed that a broadcast defamatory statement is less likely to lead to an action because of the fleeting nature of the message. A person who claims that he has been defamed may, however, in the legal process of discovery, seek a court order requiring a recording of the broadcast to be made available to his lawyers.

## Defamatory matter

A broadcast item may be construed as defamatory because of the combined effect of the spoken word and of film chosen to illustrate the topic, even when the film is shown for no more than a few seconds. This danger in 'wallpapering' arises where the voice-over is derogatory of a class of people and the film shows a recognisable face or someone's premises or car.

A Metropolitan Police detective was in 1983 awarded £20,000 against Granada Television for defamation arising in this way. During a documentary about police corruption, the voice-over said 'Some CID men take bribes' at the same time as film was shown depicting the plaintiff leaving West End Central Police station.

The problem for the broadcaster in finding suitable film for items criticising a class of people may be solved by the use of staff or actors, while making it clear in the broadcast that the film is a television reconstruction.

In another action, the choice of background music for a television programme led to an out-of-court settlement with payment of damages to a holiday company. The item about self-catering holidays included film which depicted the size of the rooms provided for the use of holidaymakers. As the film was shown, the theme from the Colditz series was used.

## Identification

Broadcasts have often led to defamation actions because of the failure of the reporter or presenter adequately to identify a company or individual referred to, or portrayed in film, in a derogatory manner, with the result that innocent namesakes have claimed that reasonable people would understand the words to refer to them.

In 1973, the BBC was ordered to pay £15,000 damages to Mr Christopher Floris, the Queen's confectioner, and his company, the House of Floris. A television investigative programme on public health hazards included film of conditions in the premises of another company which was referred to simply as Floris. The plaintiffs claimed that viewers would think the item referred to the House of Floris.

## Live broadcasts

Another hazard for radio and television is the broadcast of live discussions. In an unguarded moment, an invited guest or telephone caller may utter remarks which are clearly defamatory of an individual or company. Thus, not only may the person who utters the words be sued, but also the broadcast company which has published them. Many defamation actions have been brought in this way. In some cases the offending remarks have been made by leading politicians. Some commercial radio stations have an eight-second 'panic' button allowing the presenter to cut out offending words after they have been used but before they are transmitted.

Ideally, in items where there is potential for defamatory remarks being made, people should not be interviewed live nor calls taken directly on the air. If the words are spoken, the presenter should immediately dissociate himself and the station from the defamatory statement and should apologise without repeating the defamatory statement.

Section 1 of the Defamation Act 1996 provides a limited defence where the broadcaster of a live programme has no effective control over the maker of the defamatory statement. The Act requires that the broadcaster took all reasonable care and did not know and had no reason to believe that what he did caused or contributed to the publication of the statement. It says that in assessing whether this requirement is fulfilled regard shall be paid to the nature or circumstances of the broadcast and the previous conduct of the broadcaster.

How much use this defence will be is unlikely to become clearer until it is tested in defamation actions before the courts. However, in establishing that it took all reasonable care the broadcaster may benefit if it can show that it had a system for reducing the risk of such defamatory statements being broadcast. (See also chapter 19, publication.)

## Qualified privilege

The Broadcasting Act 1990 provides for the qualified privilege, which under section 7 of the Defamation Act 1952 protects certain fair and accurate reports published without malice in a newspaper (see chapter 20), to be extended to similar broadcast reports, subject to the publication if requested of a reasonable letter or statement by way of explanation or contradiction.

The absolute privilege for fair, accurate, and contemporaneous reports of court proceedings and the qualified privilege for fair and accurate reports published without malice of certain other occasions, set out in the Defamation Act 1996 and expected to come into force in 1997, applies to all forms of publication including broadcasting. (See chapter 20, privilege.)

*Gatley on Libel and Slander* suggests that where a person complains of a defamatory statement broadcast as part of a report protected by qualified privilege, the broadcasting station should, if requested to broadcast a reasonable letter or statement under the requirements of the Defamation Act, do so as part of the same programme or service.

## Contempt of court

Broadcasting runs all the same risks as newspapers and, additionally, judges have sometimes expressed concern that television broadcasts might bring some undesirable influence to bear on the proceedings, which might amount to contempt. However, in 1994 ITN was found not guilty of contempt in respect of an item in the early evening news which referred to the previous conviction of a man accused of terrorist offences. Lord Justice Leggatt said he was not persuaded that viewers would have retained the information for the nine months between the broadcast and the trial. He said a newspaper article would have been more likely to have been remembered than the broadcast since even a casual reader had the opportunity of reading a passage twice, an opportunity denied to the casual television viewer. (See chapter 17, the ITN case.)

In court reporting, judges desire the jury to reach its verdict on the basis of what is said in court and not on other interpretations of what might have happened at the scene of a crime, although there is no objection to straight reporting of the proceedings.

A judge at the Old Bailey in 1983 said it was folly for Independent Television's News at Ten to have broadcast a reconstruction, using actors in a street scene, of events related in evidence during the day's proceedings at a trial before a jury. 'Here was someone who was not there at the time and is not a witness trying to show all the world what he thinks may have happened,' he said. He was concerned not so much with the words as the pictures that accompanied the words and added that he had reflected on whether he ought to have initiated proceedings for contempt.

Four years later the Lord Chief Justice granted an injunction to restrain Channel 4 from broadcasting a re-enactment of the Birmingham pub bombing appeal while the proceedings were still in progress, even though there was of course no jury involved in the appellate proceedings. He said the portraying of witnesses was of particular significance as it was pretending to be the real thing and was subtly inviting the viewer to make what he would think was his own comment on actual events. Such a representation would not directly affect the judgment of the court but it would or might affect the public view of the judgment of the court.

The Court of Appeal in 1991 criticised the filming of interviews with three people who were to be witnesses in a drugs trial. After an approach by a television company to customs and excise, they were interviewed as though they were giving their evidence at the trial. The item was broadcast after the end of the trial. Lord Justice Watkins said leading prosecution counsel had been wrong when he advised that customs and excise could properly co-operate in the filming. Lord Justice Watkins said the defence had not been told that three important witnesses had rehearsed their testimony before a television camera. If the defence had known, they would have cross-examined the witnesses as to any difference between their filmed evidence and the evidence they gave at the trial.

Like newspapers, television is at risk in using a photograph of an accused person where identification may be an issue at the trial because a witness's evidence could be affected.

The BBC was held to be in contempt and was admonished in the High Court in Glasgow in 1992 for screening film of a man accused of murder being led into court for his trial from a police van. The judge said the man was clearly identifiable from the film. 'The publication of a photograph, a film, or an artist's likeness of an accused during a trial poses a potential risk to justice,' he said.

In 1985, a Metropolitan magistrate referred to the Director of Public Prosecutions (although no action was subsequently taken) an Independent Television News report of committal proceedings involving six men and women on terrorist charges. The report included an artist's impression of the court scene, drawn away from the court. The suggestion was that the artist's drawing of two accuseds' faces was so accurate that it would prejudice their subsequent trial, where identification might be an issue.

In 1990, Central Television, the BBC, and Signal Radio successfully appealed against an order made by a judge at Stafford Crown Court under section 4 of the Contempt of Court Act 1981 that there should be no broadcast reports of a trial while the jury was spending a night at an hotel prior to returning its verdict. The crown court judge had said when making the order that he did not want the jury to be deprived of television or radio but the Lord Chief Justice said in the Court of Appeal that the judge was wrong to make the order. He very much doubted whether any restrictions were necessary on what the jury read or saw in newspapers or by way of television in the circumstances of the case.

## Copyright in broadcasting

The basic principle that the author (creator) is the owner of a copyright work is carried into broadcasting. For the purposes of ownership of a broadcast, the author is defined as the person transmitting the programme, if he has any responsibility for its content, *and* the person providing the programme, who, with the person transmitting, makes the arrangements necessary for the broadcast. The effect of this is that the copyright in a programme is owned jointly by the broadcasting authority transmitting it and the company providing it.

Separate copyrights, owned by different authors, may exist in the underlying literary, dramatic, or musical works incorporated in the broadcast, eg the script.

Copyright is not infringed by the incidental inclusion of a work in a television programme, eg a background shot of a painting in a documentary, or the loudspeaker music heard behind the commentator's voice during the interval at a football match.

Use in a broadcast of brief excerpts of a copyright work, eg film, can sometimes be defended as fair dealing for the purposes of reporting current events or of criticism or review. Use of the excerpts for criticism or review must be accompanied by sufficient acknowledgment. (See chapter 29, Fair dealing.)

The moral rights provided by the Copyright, Designs and Patents Act 1988 apply to some broadcasting. The right to be identified as author or director applies, except to employees and to those reporting current events. The right, where it exists, has to be asserted by the author, however. The moral right not to have the work subjected to derogatory treatment does apply to employees if they are or have been publicly identified in the work, except where it is made for reporting current events. Derogatory treatment is defined as treatment amounting to distortion or mutilation, or otherwise prejudicial to the honour or reputation of the author or director. The right not to have a work falsely attributed to a person applies to broadcasting as does the right of a person who has commissioned a photograph or film for private and domestic purposes not to have it made available to the public. (See also chapter 29, Copyright.)

## Privacy

Broadcast journalists who infringe privacy are in a different position from print journalists in that they are thereby contravening a code which can be enforced by sanction.

The Broadcasting Act 1990 imposed upon the Broadcasting Complaints Commission (BCC) the job of considering and adjudicating upon complaints of unwarranted infringement of privacy in broadcast programmes. The Act did not define privacy.

In 1992 the BCC considered two complaints against Granada Television and found against the company. As a result, under the Act, Granada was required to publish the finding. Granada appealed to the High Court.

Granada had included in a programme 'How safe are our children?' a photograph of a child who had been raped and murdered two years previously. The company had not warned the parents before the broadcast. In the other programme, 'The allergy business', Granada had included a picture of a woman who had died three years previously aged 21. Again Granada had not warned the parents.

Granada argued that the photographs could not be an infringement of privacy because they were in the public domain and also that they did not relate to the people who complained but to their daughters.

But the court rejected Granada's argument, saying that the fact that a matter had once been in the public domain could not prevent its resurrection, possibly many years later, from being an infringement of privacy. And it would be an unacceptably narrow interpretation of the meaning of privacy and contrary to commonsense to confine it to matters concerning the individual complainant, and not as extending to his family.

## Covering election campaigns

Radio, television, cable or satellite programmes about a constituency or electoral area in which a candidate takes part are restricted by the Representation of the People Act 1983.

From the time that an election is deemed to be pending until nominations close no such programme can be broadcast.

Elections are deemed to be pending :

- *Parliamentary elections.* When Parliament is dissolved or at any earlier time when the Queen's intention to dissolve Parliament is announced, or at a by-election when the writ is issued or any earlier date on which a certificate of vacancy is notified in the London Gazette.
- *European elections.* Five weeks before polling day.
- *Local government elections.* Five weeks before polling day, or, in the case of by-elections, from the date of publication of the notice of the election.

Once nominations have closed such a programme is still barred unless the candidate gives his permission. The effect of this is that a candidate may lay down conditions for the item to be broadcast such as the deletion of some part on which he has second thoughts or the inclusion of particular matter.

Even if a candidate does take part and gives his or her consent, all the other candidates must give consent to the item being broadcast. Thus, one candidate can prevent an item being broadcast even if all the others who have taken part give consent. A candidate might on principle refuse to share a studio with an extremist or fringe candidate, or might not wish to appear in the same programme as an opponent more able to put forward his case. In by-elections where there may be many fringe candidates, it is almost impossible to secure the consent of them all. The Act often has the effect that only national politicians are heard in a programme about a constituency and viewers or listeners are deprived of the opportunity to judge the candidates for themselves.

The Act does not control items in which only broadcasters rather than candidates take part. Nor does it cover items where a candidate is, for example, canvassing and speaking only to an elector rather than to camera. Lord Denning, Master of the Rolls, said in the Court of Appeal in 1983 that control is exercisable only if the candidate has taken an active part in the programme. Candid camera shots of their canvassing did not require their consent because they were then the object of the film rather than participants in it (*Marshall v BBC* [1979] 3 All ER 8).

It also does not control broadcasts where a candidate takes part but which are not about his constituency, as where a leading politician is speaking in some other part of the country.

In 1994, the BBC was prevented by an interdict of the Court of Session in Edinburgh from broadcasting an interview with the Prime Minister, John Major, four days before the Scottish local elections on the grounds that it was a breach of the duty of impartiality set out in the annex to the BBC's licence agreement.

## Ban on voices of members of specified organisations

The ban imposed by the Home Secretary in October 1988, acting under powers vested in him by the Broadcasting Act 1981 and under the BBC's licence, was withdrawn in 1994 after the IRA had announced a ceasefire. The order banned the transmission on television (including cable and satellite) and radio of:

> Any words spoken, whether in the course of an interview or discussion or otherwise, by a person who appears or is heard on the programme in which the matter is broadcast where
> (a) the person speaking represents or purports to represent a specified organisation, or
> (b) the words support or solicit or invite support for such an organisation.

The specified organisations included the IRA, INLA, Sinn Fein, Republican Sinn Fein, and the UDA.

The ban did not apply where the words of a member of one of these organisations were read by a newscaster. Nor did it apply to words spoken in Parliament or in support of a candidate at a Parliamentary, local, or European election. It also did not apply where members of the organisation were speaking in some other capacity.

## Obscenity and racial hatred

Under the Broadcasting Act 1990, the Obscene Publications Act 1959 was extended to television and sound broadcasting in the same way as it applies to books and films (see chapter 21). No prosecution can take place without the consent of the Director of Public Prosecutions but a magistrate may, if satisfied that there are reasonable grounds for believing that an offence has been committed, authorise the police to require that a visual or sound recording of a programme be handed over.

A similar procedure is possible if it is suspected that an offence has been committed under the racial hatred section of the Public Order Act 1986 (see chapter 25).

## Questions

1   How can a broadcast be defamatory because of the combined effect of words and film? Give an example.
2   What are the dangers in the law of defamation when a broadcast mentions a complaint about a company but does not give the company's full title?
3   What risks does a broadcasting organisation face under defamation law in transmitting live unscripted programmes?
4   Explain how the defence of qualified privilege against an action for defamation is extended to certain broadcast reports.
5   Why do judges object to television reconstructions of evidence at a trial being broadcast before the trial is over?
6   How does the Representation of the People Act control television programmes in a constituency at election time?
7   How does the Defamation Act 1996 help broadcasters involved in live broadcasts?

# Glossary

**Absolute discharge**   A decision of the court to impose no penalty and no conditions, even though the defendant has been convicted.

**Age of criminality**   The age above which a child may be accused of a criminal offence and brought before a court (ten years).

**Arbitration**   The procedure by which civil cases, generally involving claims for less than £3,000, are heard in a less formal manner than in other courts. Arbitration generally takes place in private.

**Arrestable offence**   An offence for which an arrest may be made without a warrant.

**Assault**   In legal language, assault is a hostile act that causes another person to fear an attack. Battery is the actual application of force.

**Attachment, writ of**   An order to bring a person before court to answer an accusation of contempt.

**Bail**   The system by which a person awaiting trial, or appeal, may be freed pending the hearing.

**Bill of indictment**   An order made by a High Court judge, compelling a person to stand trial at crown court. A rare procedure, used to cut out the usual committal for trial by the magistrates, or to overcome a decision by the magistrates that there is no case to answer.

**Case law**   The system by which reports of previous cases and the judges' interpretation of the common law can be used as a precedent where the legally material facts are similar.

**Case stated**   Appeal by case stated is a procedure by which the magistrates court, or the crown court sitting as an appeal court, may be asked to state the grounds on which it reached its decision. By this procedure either prosecution or defence can appeal on a point of law to the Queen's Bench Divisional Court.

**Child**   A person below 14.

**Circuit judges**   Unlike High Court judges, circuit judges do not go on circuit. The name is a historical relic.

**Committed for sentence**   Tried at magistrates court and sent by them to crown court for sentence because magistrates' powers of punishment are insufficient. (There are no reporting restrictions on committals for sentence.)

**Committal for trial**   Sent from the magistrates court, either in custody or on bail, to be tried at crown court before a jury.

**Common law**   Law based on the custom of the realm and the decisions of the judges through the centuries rather than an Act of Parliament.

**Concurrent sentences**   Two or more sentences of imprisonment imposed for different offences; the longest one is the sentence actually served.

**Conditional discharge**   Decision of the court to impose no penalty even though a conviction has been recorded against the defendant, provided the defendant commits no further offence during a stipulated period.

**Consecutive sentence**   To follow one after the other, rather than concurrently.

**Coroner**   A solicitor, barrister, or doctor appointed by the Crown to conduct inquests in his area.

**Corporation**   Only individuals and corporations can sue in libel. A corporate body is one that has rights and duties distinct from those of the people who form it. An incorporated company is a corporation formed for the purpose of carrying on a business.

**Counsel**    Barrister (singular or plural), not solicitor.

**Decree nisi**    A provisional decree of divorce, usually made absolute six weeks later, thus allowing the parties to remarry.

**District judge**    An official of the county court who also adjudicates in the smaller cases, presides at public examinations in bankruptcy, and deals with cases under the informal arbitration procedure.

**Drink driving**    Not drunk driving, in heads and intros.

**Excluded material**    Such material is exempt from compulsory disclosure under the Police and Criminal Evidence Act 1984. It includes journalistic material that a person holds in confidence and that consists of documents or records.

**Ex parte**    *Of the one part.* An ex parte injunction is one granted after hearing only one side in the case.

**Fair comment**    A defence to a libel action; the defendant does not have to show the words were fair. But he must show they were honest and published without malice.

**Family proceedings**    Civil proceedings before magistrates, dealing with separation orders, maintenance of spouse or children, adoption orders.

**Habeas corpus, writ of**    A writ issued by the Queen's Bench Divisional Court to secure the release of a person whom it declares to have been detained unlawfully by the police or other authorities.

**Hybrid offence**    One triable either way – summarily at magistrates court or before a jury at crown court. On a triable-either-way offence, a defendant has the right to opt for jury trial at crown court. But even if he chooses to be tried summarily at magistrates court, magistrates may overrule him by deciding on crown court trial.

**In camera**    Proceedings of the court that are heard in the absence of the public and the press (eg, Official Secrets Act cases).

**In chambers**    Used to describe the hearing of an application heard in private in the judge's room, where the judge declares he is now 'sitting in chambers'.

**Indictable offence**   One that may be tried on indictment before a judge and jury at crown court.

**Indictment**   A written statement of the charges that are put to the accused when he stands trial at crown court.

**Information**   A written statement alleging an offence that is laid before a magistrate who is then asked to issue a summons or a warrant for arrest.

**Interdict**   In Scottish law, an injunction.

**Journalistic material**   Material acquired or created for the purposes of journalism. Special protection is given to 'journalistic material' in the sections of the Police and Criminal Evidence Act 1984 that lay down the procedure whereby the police may search premises for evidence of serious arrestable offences.

**Judicial review**   Review by the Queen's Bench Divisional Court of decisions taken by a lower court, tribunal, public body, or public official.

**Juvenile**   A young person below the age of 18. Above this age the juvenile will be tried at an adult court for any type of offence.

**Justification**   The defence in libel actions that the words complained of were true. The word is misleading, because there is no requirement that the words were published justly or with good reason.

**Lords Justices**   Judges of the Court of Appeal. They are not members of the House of Lords.

**Lords of Appeal**   They are usually known as the Law Lords. They sit in the House of Lords, not in the Court of Appeal.

**Malice**   In law not only spite or ill will but also dishonest or improper motive. An allegation of malice can be used by the plaintiff in a libel action to deprive the defendant of the defences of fair comment or qualified privilege.

**Malicious falsehood**   A false statement that is not defamatory because it imputes no moral blame but is nevertheless actionable because it could cause the plaintiff financial loss.

**Mandamus**   An order made by the Queen's Bench Divisional Court directing a lower court or public body to perform some duty for which it is responsible.

**Plaintiff**   The person who takes action to enforce a claim in the civil court.

**Pleadings**   The set of documents that set forth the issues between the parties in a civil action. Anything not contained in the pleadings will not be adjudicated upon, unless the judge agrees applications to amend or extend them.

**Prima facie**   At first sight.

**Quango**   The term stands for quasi-autonomous non-governmental organisation and is conveniently and loosely used to describe non-elected public bodies that operate outside the civil service and that are funded by the taxpayer.

**Recorder**   An assistant judge of the crown court who is usually appointed to sit part-time (eg for a spell of a fortnight) over a period of two or three years. Solicitors and barristers are both eligible for appointment as a recorder.

**Robbery**   Theft by force, or by threat of force. The word is often used, wrongly, to describe simple theft.

**Small claims court**   The county court procedure by which the district judge, generally sitting in private, deals by arbitration with claims for less than £3,000.

**Spent conviction**   A conviction that is no longer recognised after the specified time (varying according to sentence) laid down by the Rehabilitation of Offenders Act. After this time, a newspaper referring to the conviction may not have available some of the normal defences in the law of libel.

**Statute law**   Law derived from Acts of Parliament and from statutory instruments (detailed regulations introduced by Ministers under powers given them by Parliament).

**Summary proceedings**   Cases tried by magistrates. At the end of such a trial, however, magistrates can, if they consider their powers of sentence insufficient, send the defendant for sentence at crown court.

**Summons**   An order issued by a magistrate to attend court at a stated time and date to answer a charge.

**Supreme Court**   The name given to the Court of Appeal, the High Court, and the crown court. It is not in fact the supreme court; the House of Lords is.

**Taxation of costs**   The examination of costs lawfully chargeable to the unsuccessful party in a legal action to ensure that they are not excessive.

**Tort**   A civil wrong for which monetary damages may be awarded – eg, defamation, negligence.

**TWOC**   (taking car without owner's consent). Court reporters must not confuse this with stealing a car – a more serious offence.

**Ward of court**   A minor (a person under the age of 18) brought under the care of the court by the Family Division of the High Court.

**Warrant for arrest**   An order issued by a magistrate to secure the arrest of a person suspected of a crime.

**Young person**   A person 14 years of age but below 18.

# Book list

## The courts

Stone's Justices' Manual *A T Draycott, Paul Carr, Tessa Szagun, and Jane Hall (Butterworths)*

## Children in the news

Review of Access to and Reporting of Family Proceedings *Consultation Paper. Lord Chancellor's Department 1993*

## Contempt of court

Borrie and Lowe: Law of Contempt *Nigel Lowe and Brenda Suffrin (Butterworths, Third Edition 1996)*
Contempt of Court *C J Miller (Oxford University Press, Second Edition 1989)*

## Defamation

Carter-Ruck on Libel and Slander *Peter Carter-Ruck, Judge Richard Walker, and Harvey N A Starte (Butterworths)*
Defamation *Colin Duncan and Brian Neill (Butterworths)*
Gatley on Libel and Slander *Philip Lewis (Sweet and Maxwell)*
Defamation: Law and Practice *Julie A Scott-Bayfield (FT Law and Tax 1996)*

## Copyright

Blackstone's Guide to the Copyright, Designs and Patents Act 1988 *Gerald Dworkin and Richard D Taylor (Blackstone Press)*

## Breach of confidence

Breach of Confidence *Francis Gurry (Clarendon Press)*

## Information from government

Freedom of Information *Patrick Birkinshaw (Weidenfeld & Nicolson)*
Open Government *White Paper 1993 Command 2290*

## Privacy

Report of the Committee on Privacy and Related Matters *(the Calcutt Committee) 1990 Command 1102*
Review of Press Self-Regulation *Sir David Calcutt QC 1993 Command 2135*
Privacy and Media Intrusion Volume 1 *National Heritage Committee 1993 HMSO 294-1*
Infringement of Privacy *Consultation Paper 1993. Lord Chancellor's Department*
Media Freedom and Media Regulation *Association of British Editors, Guild of Editors, International Press Institute 1994*

## Law for photographers

The Photographer and the Law *Don Cassell (BFP Books, new edition expected in 1997)*

## Scots law

Scots Law for Journalists *Bruce McKain, Alistair J Bonnington and George A Watt (W Green/Sweet and Maxwell)*

## Media law

The Law of Journalism *Catherine Courtney, David Newell and Santha Rasaiah (Butterworths)*
Media Law *Geoffrey Robertson and Andrew Nicol (Penguin)*
Law and the Media *Tom G Crone (Focal Press, Third Edition 1995)*

The newsletter *Media Lawyer* records changes in this area of the law, and where necessary draws attention to the need to amend copies of *McNae*. Its editor and honorary consultant are the editors of *McNae*.

# Index

In this index, cross-reference items set in small capital letters refer to chapter headings; others refer to main index items.

Lawyers using the index should note that it is intended mainly for use by journalists and many cases are noted under the name of the defendant newspaper or broadcast organisation rather than the plaintiff.